CW00485534

# REGINALD REYNOLDS AN]

*Cover Design by Ron Waddams.*

*Ethel and Reg in the early years of their marriage*

# Reg and Ethel

## Reginald Reynolds
(1905 - 1958)

his life and work
and his marriage to

## Ethel Mannin
(1900 - 1984)

by
Robert Huxter

Sessions Book Trust
York, England

ISBN 1 85072 109 2

*To my wife*
*SHIRL*
*whom Ethel called*
*'that smashing lady'*

Printed in 10 on 11 point Plantin Typeface
by William Sessions Limited
The Ebor Press, York, England

# Contents

# Illustrations

# Acknowledgements

FOR OVER TEN YEARS, I enjoyed a close friendship with Ethel Mannin who passed on to me a considerable portion of the Reginald Reynolds' archive. She hoped that one day I would write a book about Reg's life and thought.

Then, more recently, Edward H. Milligan – ex-librarian, Religious Society of Friends, London – encouraged me to do the same. This time I got down to the job in earnest. I have aimed, as far as possible, to tell the story in Reg's and Ethel's own words.

Invaluable help has been given by Jean Faulks, Ted Milligan, H. A. Farrand Radley, Tony Skelton, Richard A. Wright and Shirley Huxter.

For their kindness and support, I also thank Joan Rhodes, Quentin Crisp, Kenneth C. Barnes, Wendy Hiller and Ronald Gow, Malcolm Thomas, the late Ben Vincent, Stanley Keeble, Wolf Mendl, Ron Waddams, Cecil Evans, Hannah Taylor, Derek Barbanell, and the staff of Friends House Library, London.

The book would not have been possible without a loan from the Joseph Rowntree Charitable Trust, and grants from the Edith M. Ellis Trust and W. F. Southall Trust.

It is something to have wept as we have wept,
It is something to have done as we have done;
It is something to have watched, when all men slept,
And seen the stars which never see the sun;
It is something to have smelt the mystic rose,
Although it break and leave the thorny rods,
It is something to have hungered once as those
Must hunger who have ate the bread of gods.

*G. K. Chesterton*

# Introduction

*'If you think my goats are difficult, wait till*
*you see my sheep'* – God.

Reginald Reynolds

A TALL THIN MAN WITH FAIR HAIR, large brown eyes and strong aquiline features lights a cigarette in the twilight. He tucks the cigarette beneath his tongue, dives into the swimming pool, swims a length underwater, emerges, and walks towards his audience nonchalantly reproducing the cigarette and smoking it.

Reg Reynolds was proud of his Swimming Pool Trick. This was the flamboyant Reg, a charmer, an imaginative wit with an impish sense of fun, a lover of noisy pubs, gaudy clothes and bawdy humour. Little sign here of Reg the ascetical scholar, existing for weeks on Horlicks while doing intensive research, or of that turbulent life dedicated to the struggle for justice and freedom, the tireless world-traveller in the cause of peace, racial equality and international understanding.

1

Merciless in his exposure of political opportunism which made a mockery of the revolutionary Christianity he espoused, he championed the underdog in East and West. His caring was of a particularly personal kind, whether it was going out of his way to help a stranger in distress or offering to visit the Pacific in protest against atomic tests. His stepdaughter Jean Faulks, a retired hospital almoner, recalls: 'He was fantastically generous, often giving away things he needed because he considered another person needed them more.' He spent himself too extravagantly on others to be confined by conventional standards of behaviour, his hours of sleep so few that he used his alarm clock to tell him when to *go* to bed.

Fame, money, career held no interest for him. His poem *Ballad Against Fame* appeared in *The Adelphi* of June 1939:

> We will not now praise famous men
>   Nor talk of goats and sheep;
> If lambs are in the lion's den
>   They still have heads to keep,
> And swords, less mighty than the pen,
>   Like sickles, also reap.

> The fatal stroke on Siegfried fell
>   And on Achilles' heel;
> Goliath never lived to tell
>   How little pebbles feel;
> The cunning of Ahithophel
>   Struck deeper than his steel.

> At Roncesvalles brave Roland lies
>   And Arthur's days are done,
> The shaft that blinded Harold's eyes
>   Awaits the Conqueror's son,
> And they may tell me who are wise
>   Who lost and who have won.

> These were the means that shaped their ends
>   In tales that dead men tell
> Whose dialectic comprehends
>   The primrose path to Hell
> And those dear daggers of his friends
>   That flashed where Caesar fell.

> Then let us not praise famous men
>   But eulogise instead
> All Daniels in the lion's den
>   Who have not lost their head,
> For one live Daniel is worth ten
>   Inexorably dead.

He liked to say that there were three Reg Reynolds, all of them married to Ethel Mannin: the Quaker pacifist and anarchist, supporter of nationalist movements for self-determination, whose life touched many of the master themes of our times – resistance to war, the turmoil of Spain, Indian independence, emergent Africa, Hiroshima, the tragedy of the Palestinian Arabs, the plight of refugees; the historical serendipitist (picker-up of unconsidered trifles in odd byways) producing, with Rabelaisian high spirits, works on beards, beds and water-closets; and the writer of satiric verses, which brought him great acclaim, on current political affairs for the *New Statesman*, creator of 'Og, King of Bashan, Who had an iron bed, Four across the beams And nine by the head.'

As a young man, he was Gandhi's *Angad*, his messenger, entrusted by him to carry his historic letter of ultimatum to the British Raj at the height of the Civil Disobedience Campaign. Reg cared about India, said Quentin Crisp, 'to an extent that was difficult for ordinary mortals to share'. He was, in his own words, 'a fire-eating political fanatic', though incapable of combining seriousness with solemnity. His first book, *White Sahibs in India*, acknowledged as a political classic, was the first analysis of the history of the country so that the present could be understood in the light of the past. 'He would, laughingly, call himself a Gandhi man', wrote Ethel Mannin, 'explaining his vegetarianism or his dislike of possessions, but such was his humility that he would no more have dreamed of calling himself by a title he so revered than St Francis of Assisi would presume – so it is said of that humble and saintly man – to call himself a Christian'.

If Gandhi was the first profound influence in the spiritual development of Reg Reynolds, the second was certainly John Woolman, the 18th-century Quaker. Woolman could perhaps be described as a Gandhi man, since it was his belief that 'if all inhabitants lived according to sound wisdom, labouring to promote universal love and righteousness, and ceased from every inordinate desire after wealth, and from all customs which are tinctured with luxury, the way would be easy to live comfortably on honest employments'.

After the second world war, Reg's disillusionment with politics was complete. In September 1945, he wrote to his old schoolfriend, Philip Aynsley Smith, that the early Quakers 'let political tides wash over them and I begin to see why, and how right they were. Until a new humanity can be created, politics will be a cynical game – and sinister'.

Without ever severing his contacts with the Religious Society of Friends (Quakers), he lost patience with it, attacked it, and was viewed with suspicion and even dismay by the counterparts of those purse-mouthed Friends who cold-shouldered John Woolman two centuries ago. However,

3

it was the example of Woolman, more than anyone, that led to his return to the Quaker fold where he roused the complacent while stressing the dark places he had gone through in reaching his ultimate faith. On Reg's death in 1958 at the age of 53, Kenneth Barnes wrote that the Society of Friends 'has lost its most original mind and perhaps its most outstanding personality'. But Barnes also maintained that to think of Reg primarily as a Quaker would be to diminish his significance, to make the mistake he so vigorously condemned – of regarding religion as an end in itself rather than as a way to God and to Truth, a way that 'blisters the false with relentless light'.

He said to puritans, who frowned on sin:
'The publicans and harlots enter in
Before you into Heaven.' This Jesus must
Have seemed a very Devil to the Just.

I see the Wise Men seeking in Jerusalem
In Rome, Paris, and Berlin; in London and New York.
They search the stars for wisdom that is sealed
And yet to fools revealed.

I hear a voice crying beyond Bethlehem
The forgotten gospel, the spiritual birth,
The sentence against which we have appealed:
'*To those who have goodwill* – Peace upon Earth.'

Sadly the Rich Young Ruler turned away;
Now the disciples seek him out and say:
'Take not to heart those words. He never meant
That you should part with more than two per cent'.

The apostolic baskets, as before,
Are filled – though the five thousand feed no more;
To comfort Dives new disciples try
To force the camel through the needle's eye.

In precious ointment trafficking, we sell
Heaven for the unassembled parts of Hell;
And those whose merchandise Christ drove away
Scourge him from every temple where they pray.

But here in Albion (where God's house affords
Hope of promotion to the House of Lords)
Episcopal pronouncements vindicate
Vicarious murder, sedentary hate . . .
Truly the Church, before the Christ can reign
Must also perish and be born again.

(Extracts from *The Loadstone* by Reginald Reynolds)

One of Reg's friends, the entertainer Joan Rhodes, had no idea that he was a Quaker. There was no outward evidence of religion about him. You saw what he did and knew that it transcended facile labelling. To Ben Vincent, a Quaker friend, he epitomised 'the left-wing intellectual of our generation. He was a marvellous orator – had them rolling in the aisles. He was delightful to watch with hecklers, would often have them eating out of his hand by the end. He made fun of what he called the Harpo Marxists (they were always harping on their dogmas). He would devastate fascists, both black and red, with witty repartee that hurt no one. Shortly before he died, he said to me: "Oh Ben, I do hope there's a chance to do a bit of spell-binding in heaven." He was a sort of Bertie Wooster, if you can imagine a Wooster who was a radical revolutionary'.

'I wonder if you'll be able to read Reg's books', said Ethel Mannin to the present writer. 'I never could! He was always too erudite for uneducated me.' Nevertheless he garnered rave reviews from leading critics in Britain and America, especially for his best-known study, *Cleanliness and Godliness* – 'my loo book' – a learned romp about sanitation which preaches the necessity for the return of sewage to the soil instead of the wasteful Western method of disposal in the sea. He chuckled, on occasion, at the smartness in his published works, their references ranging from the Bible to Errol Flynn, his amusement so frank that it was quite without conceit.

Blending good sense with good nonsense, his verses for the *New Statesman* – from 1940-1958, he wrote 156 – show the mutations of his comic spirit, for here can be found bitter satire, irony, gallows-humour, ribaldry, whimsy, drollery and fantasy.

*Thoughts on the Twenty-Third Psalm*
'This weapon is our defence, our security, our staff and our rod.'
                    (*Daily Express* leader on the H-bomb).

> Some pious Christians may read with qualms
>     This breezy reference to your staff and rod –
> From my own recollection of the psalms
>     Hadn't the staff something to do with God?
> But since you parody the Twenty-Third
> I am content to take you at your word.
>
> 'The valley of the shadow' – that's the verse –
>     You 'fear no evil' when your bombs descend;
> Your love of quoting Scripture makes it worse
>     That you pervert it to so foul an end.
> Why must we have such sanctimonious slime
> To smear with humbug each audacious crime?

The thaumaturge had but his soul to sell –
   Mad politicians sell the whole creation;
Faustus raised Helen – *they* are raising Hell
   To plunge a planet in their own damnation.
Faust knew what he was doing – more or less –
*This* gruesome gambit is a clumsy guess.

Doomed men may yet take pride in how they die –
   What pride is ours in suicidal gambles?
And in what Gadarene, half-human sty
   Do ghouls proclaim this Gospel of the Shambles?
I, too, can twist a text – the Race of Man
About to die, salutes you . . . *Caliban.*


*Fashion Note*

'For the girl who bemoans her lack of curves there is a new-style padded
bra, with shaped half-cups of foam rubber.'    (*Evening Standard*)

   How happy were they born and reared
      Who needed not this rubber bust,
   Who were, in fact, what they appeared,
      With bosoms generous, but just;

   Who did not, like Miss Mac, inflame
      By figures contrary to fact,
   Employing artifice to frame
      The solid glory that they lacked;

   Nor, like some sleazy dames we know
      (The tawdry Muses of the *Fleet*),
   Distort the news with foam and show
      Only the contours of deceit;

   Whom no such bloated Ego drove
      To crimes and blunders overseas
   Till they had pawned the kitchen stove
      In desperate economies.

   So once Britannia, laced in bone,
      Controlled – like reasonable rent –
   Sat not on Sandys, but on her own
      Broad and substantial fundament.

            (from *New Statesman*)

Reg married Ethel Mannin when she was at the peak of her success as a prolific and provocative author. Their relationship was, inevitably, unorthodox. ('Conventional marriage, like family life, is one of my ideas of hell', she said). An enduring love-match, they hardly ever lived together, a fact which caused rumour and puzzlement for over 20 years. Up to her death in 1984, she kept his memory alive in print as it was in her heart and mind. ('I have 10 pictures of him in this room!'). She wrote of his 'unfaltering, to-the-grave's-edge love for me. He was so dear and close to one as to seem part of one's very self, one's alter-ego. He had a capacity for friendship which amounted to genius. He was always very gallant, unfailingly giving up his seat to women and girls in trains and buses, no matter how tired he might be. All over the world there are people who have taken new hope from him through the moral force of his example. I've been told there are now little African boys called Reginald Reynolds. Had he known that I am quite sure it would have brought tears to his eyes – 'Oh, bless their hearts', I can hear him say. There is a family in Tokyo where he is mourned as a son. There is a man in England who has been for years in prison but who counts his long sentence worthwhile, since but for it he would never have known the one true friendship of his life. He knows that he has lost his Best Friend. So do many people, myself not least.'

The story of Reg Reynolds is principally a love story. In King's Road, Chelsea, scruffs and aristocrats greeted him every few yards. He gave affection and he needed it. He was hurt by rejection and misunderstanding and in despairing moments turned for reassurance to Ethel and to his oldest friends. In spite of appearances, he could be diffident when unsure of his ground. Some found him awkward, impossible to browbeat. His sardonic streak could infuriate, his linguistic fireworks overwhelm. A few times, he was ponderous and pedantic in print, so claimed Ethel Mannin, the literary 'pro'.

Teacher, factory worker, salesman, General Secretary of the No More War Movement, letting agent, Civil Defence driver, partner in a socialist book centre, broadcaster, journalist, toy theatre dramatist, Field Secretary to the Friends Peace Committee – Reg could seem a strange and incomprehensible mixture, but, said William Blake, one of his heroes, 'without contraries there is no progression'. Scraping away at his old pipe, he wrote books on Gandhi and Woolman in his tiny room in Chelsea, he whose favourite author was Damon Runyon. Swinging his multi-coloured golfing umbrella, Reg the romantic presented, with regal grace, a little bunch of mimosa to a chorus girl. He loved to sing, dance, drink rough cider, watch horror films, lay bricks, cleave wood and, in fancy dress, to caper with a pantomime horse. A Merlin of the lecture halls, his appeal, especially to the young, was magnetic. The small boy who stole screws grew into the man who was imprisoned for riding a bicycle without a light. Considered a 'danger' because of his political activities, in his confrontations with authority he continued to be an *enfant terrible* to the end. On his death, he had £200 in a post office account which Ethel Mannin sent to the Peace Pledge Union, and a collection of battered books which she later sent to the present writer.

His gusto was all the more remarkable as he was dogged by ill-health. Time, he believed, was against him. Living on a shoe-string of nervous energy, shedding all illusions, acting as a catalyst, his watchwords were vision, imagination and idealism, the neglect of which had proved disastrous to so many other revolutionaries. He called his book on the quest for Gandhi, *To Live in Mankind* (Andre Deutsch, 1951), quoting on the title page a line from the Vachell Lindsay poem '*To live in mankind is more than to live in a name*'. At the end of the book, he quoted the most stirring lines from that poem:

A hundred white eagles have risen, the sons of your sons,
The zeal in their wings is a zeal that your dreaming began,
The valour that wore out your soul in the service of man.

These were the words he remembered when he heard of Gandhi's death, and it can be said of Reg Reynolds, too, that he lived in mankind and wore himself out in the service of man.

This book is a celebration not only of a life and of the people – and chiefly his adored Ethel – who helped to shape it, but also of a conduct of life which, though far from perfect, speaks volumes to a world in need of spiritual rebirth.

'Blessed are the confused', wrote Reg, 'for they *may* see the light. And beware of those who know all the answers, for they are always wrong.'

# CHAPTER I

# A Nasty Little Brat

LECTURING IN AMERICA, Reg said that he had heard more fundamental wisdom spoken in Quaker gatherings than anywhere else. He added that if even one tenth of that wisdom were applied in the lives of Quakers not only the Society of Friends but the whole world might be a very different place.

Quakerism, he told his audience, began as a protest against a dead letter religion. George Fox, the founder, posed the question, 'Christ saith this and the Apostles say this, but what canst *thou* say?' Fox 'invites you to put aside all your secondhand knowledge and give the Holy Spirit a chance to speak. There was nothing new in this. Jesus himself often taught by riddles and questions which only the pure in heart could answer – each question a challenge to conscience. Or he would use a conditional clause in such a way that each hearer must apply it to himself. (He could have said "Not one of you is without sin, therefore none of you should cast a stone". How feeble that sounds, compared with the searching irony of the original words!)'

Reg's poem, *Easter Song*, published in 1947 in *The Friend*, the British Quaker weekly journal, touched on this theme:

'But Mary (Magdalene) stood without at the sepulchre, weeping.'

> What is your heart saying, Mary,
> Here upon Easter Day?
> Is it for us you are praying, Mary,
> That we may learn to pray?
>
> We who slept in the garden, Mary,
> Kept not watch and guard;
> We have need of pardon, Mary,
> But the way is hard.

Show us a true beginning, Mary,
That we may enter in;
In our denial of sinning, Mary,
Greater was the sin.

If we were forgiven, Mary,
And our hearts forgave,
All the world were Heaven, Mary,
Hell, an empty grave . . .

'To affirm absolute standards', he wrote in his book *The Wisdom of John Woolman*, 'does not imply, of course, more than a partial understanding in ourselves, any more than belief in God implies complete comprehension of all that God is. The doctrine of the "inner light" is often taken to be an assertion of personal infallibility – setting up as many Popes as there are people, said an old friend of mine'. All that Quakers affirm in this doctrine of the inner light 'is the existence of absolute truth, and that its light shines within us – the Holy Spirit in man. But Friends are too conscious of their own imperfections to claim that they invariably hear, infallibly understand or faithfully follow on all occasions the guidance in which they believe. They recognise fallibility, therefore, not in the "light", but in themselves; it is our understanding, not truth itself, which is relative and finite. Only in that limited sense can we speak of applying absolute standards, recognising that our deepest intuitive conceptions (the "self-evident truths" upon which reason and aesthetic values depend, no less than religion and morality) are our nearest approach to reality'.

In his youth, when he was tearing the Society of Friends to tatters, comparing present day Quakers with those from the 'glorious past', his friend Horace Alexander admonished him: 'You read your Quaker history all wrong. The Society never was what you think it was. It was something from which very fine men and women sprang who did very fine work; but from John Woolman to Elizabeth Fry and since, you will find nearly always that they had to proceed almost alone, with very little backing from Friends and sometimes none. It was only later that we accepted them and took credit for what they had done'.

All societies, Reg came to acknowledge, lag behind inspired individuals, but inspired individuals can ultimately pull the society with them: 'Sometimes, when I have criticised Friends, people have said to me, "Then why do you remain a Quaker?" And I have a very simple answer. I say, the Society which was good enough for John Woolman ought to be good enough for me.'

Reg had inherited Quaker blood. With his two older sisters and two younger brothers, he was taught that true Christianity was not a static body of dogma but an organic growth, that the gospels were starting points, their application resting entirely between God and the individual, that the dynamic of religious experience was the light within, not an arbitrary authority without. The Quaker vision, he saw, was universal, not sectarian. In the depth of the silence there was a binding thread between people. Worship was a being searched, it was discovery, it was communion. 'You cannot silence a silent worship', he wrote, 'you cannot censor a good life, or break the peace of God in the hearts of men. If we have known the lighthouse of a living faith, if we have known the guidance of God, have we yet dared to think what miracles can yet be done by the guidance and power of God through the hands of men?'

☆     ☆     ☆

The Reynolds children owed to their father a solid radical upbringing. J. Bryant Reynolds's Liberal forbears had proceeded with Quakerly caution. The young Bryant, however, invested his capital in a market gardening business only to see it melt away on uncertain local outlets for his flowers and on such uneconomic novelties as a steam plough. At the time of Reg's birth, he was a commercial traveller based in Glastonbury. In her diary for 1906, his wife recorded that Reg was 10-weeks old and weighed 12½ pounds. After the weights of Reg's sisters, Dorothy and May, Bryant had inserted 'gross' but after his, he wrote with characteristic accuracy, 'net'.

Bryant's grandfather, James Clark, founded two businesses in Somerset, Clark's Shoes at Street and Clark, Son and Morland, makers of sheep-skin products, at Glastonbury. In 1832, the patriarch of the Morland family seriously injured his wrist, causing him to believe that his intended second wife might be saddled with 'an impotent man for her lord'. He need not have worried: with four children from his first marriage, he went on to sire a further five, one of whom, John Morland, married Mary Clark, daughter of James. Fanny, another daughter, married Arthur Reynolds but only after Arthur, a heavy drinker, had promised to sign the pledge. Duly reformed, he died young, leaving 10 children (one of them Bryant) over whom Fanny – Reg's grandmother – ruled tyrannically. She also presided over the Clark and Morland retail business at Bridport.

Reg's mother, a timid soul, was terrified of the formidable Morlands. His great-aunt, Mary Morland, brandished an ear trumpet, and wore a bonnet and voluminous rustling skirts. A chapter in his book *Beds* – on bedaboos (something to be feared or avoided, something not done in bed) – contained a story about Mary who once lost her denture and had the whole household ivory hunting. The teeth still missing, Mary remembered a crust

11

which she had unsuccessfully tried to masticate and then thrown to her dog. She argued that she might have inadvertently thrown the teeth as well as they were firmly embedded in the piece of food. The suspect beast was dosed with medicine but failed to deliver the elusive chompers. Months later, one of Reg's cousins, negligently running her hand down the opening between the seat and arm of a roomy chair, was sharply bitten. Mary had obviously mistaken the aperture for one of the many pockets in her skirt.

On Mary's first visit to the Glastonbury home of Bryant Reynolds and Florence, his bride, the old lady solemnly asked, 'Did thee make that cake?' 'Yes', said Florence, proudly. Mary examined another cake bought from a shop. 'Thank thee,' she said, 'then I'll have some of this.' Florence, Reg's mother, admired the stiff-backed Mary for daring to be her cussed self, but revenged herself on most of Bryant's folk by imagining that they were characters – and she knew exactly which – from *The Forsyte Saga*. When Mary's husband, venerable head of the Morland dynasty, celebrated his 90th birthday, a wag described the party as having all the pleasures of a funeral with none of the disadvantages. 'Longevity was such a strong point with my Somerset relatives', wrote Reg in his autobiography *My Life and Crimes*, 'that they spoke with something closely akin to moral condemnation of any member of the family who died before the age of 80'.

Bryant Reynolds advocated an idealistic socialism tempered with Quaker moderation. In 1910, at the age of 40, he promoted the cause of Free Trade, returning from a business trip to Germany with loaves of black bread. Standing on a cart, he broke up the loaves, as if to feed the 5,000, and hurled the pieces among the crowd. That, he told them, was the kind of bread people ate in a protectionist country.

Reg's mother, the daughter of a radical businessman, was never able to master the complexities of politics. She showed little interest in women's suffrage, which Bryant supported, and, the battle won, continued to vote as he advised. Only once did she vote without consulting him. She had plumped, she told him, for a Municipal Reformer. To her bewilderment, Bryant shook with laughter. He had always held forth so keenly about reform that she had been sure which side he would favour. It was gently pointed out to her that Municipal Reformers were disguised Conservatives.

Two years after Bryant died, Florence was 'a pathetic little grey-haired woman, reading the newspapers with a puzzled frown and a succession of naive queries. My mother was a woman of fine qualities but not until my father's death did I realise how utterly dependent she had been on him for such small understanding as she had of what happened outside our home'.

Florence and Bryant loved each other deeply. Reg appreciated and respected his mother but it was his father to whom he was most attached, the father who read Pepys and Hardy and Woolman, wrote papers on Tolstoy and Whittier, sang West Country songs, played the flute and performed conjuring tricks. Father and son shared a love of Bridport on the Dorset coast, where Bryant grew up and where he married Florence in the Friends Meeting House. It was at the Meeting House that one of his great-grandfathers, William Stephens, was married in 1788. Bryant's father had inherited Stephens' drapery business at Bridport, Bryant eventually running the branch at Beaminster for a spell. Here he fell in love with Florence who became a convinced Quaker, deriving solace and inspiration from the welcoming Society. At this time, Bryant was a strict teetotaller. Two of his great-uncles had been dedicated drinkers, not to mention his father, Arthur, until he was 'rescued' by the indomitable Fanny, but Aunt Mary (she of the false teeth) never ceased to disapprove of Arthur's serving alcohol to his friends.

Reg was proud of the fact that Bryant extended his kindness to German prisoners of war, and that the staff at the London office of Clark, Son and Morland looked on him, their manager, as a father. On his retirement from business, Bryant returned with Florence to Street, spending his last years, severely crippled, in planting trees. Like Reg, he always considered himself a Somerset man. Like Reg, too, he was once or twice mistaken for a tramp.

☆     ☆     ☆

Reg, at five years old, was living at Sanderstead in Surrey, then almost a country village. His sister Dorothy complained that she was ill; the doctor pronounced that she was suffering from Original Sin. Apart from great-uncle George who wore a skullcap, studied bees and fossils, grunted a lot and issued warnings, the family enjoyed the doctor's joke. However, the infant Reg was also heavily unamused. He had misheard Original Sin as Reginald's Sin and was perplexed as to what this sin could be, even though he was developing, as he admitted, into a nasty little brat.

He wondered if his sin was being so often in the right at the wrong moment, like the time he was misbehaving on a station platform. Placing him on a seat, his mother told him not to move 'until the train goes'. When the train drew in and the rest of the family climbed into a carriage, Reg sat immobile, like a self-righteous little statue. The distracted Florence shouted to the guard who held up the train while she ran and grabbed her impenitent charge. 'You told me', he protested, as she thrust him into the train, 'to stay till the train went.' ('You haven't changed', said Ethel Mannin to Reg.)

13

Deliberate efforts at being good proved of no avail either. His two sisters had hit on a simple way of getting free chocolate by putting one tiddlywink after another into the chocolate machine at Sanderstead station. 'What's happened to the tiddlywinks?' enquired Florence. The guilty duo – and Reg, who was in on the secret – pretended to search for them, then, dreaming up a new ploy, Dorothy and May persuaded the station master to unlock the machine, as they were intrigued, they said, to see inside. 'What are those pretty coloured things?' asked May, gazing shyly at the tiddlywinks. The station master said that *some* children were naughty – they tinkered with the machine. May, innocence personified, asked if she could have the coloured pennies. The station master, genial to the last, presented them to her, the girls telling Florence that the tiddlywinks had been found in their boxroom. Reg branded himself as an accomplice, devious as they. Had he not eaten the stolen chocolate and lied during the great tiddlywinks hunt? Conscience demanded that he own up, which he did, with the result that his wicked sisters refused to speak to him for a week.

Better, perhaps, to revert to a life of 'crime', and the opportunity soon came in the form of A Reprisal. In the 1910 election, the house next door was the local Tory headquarters, so Bryant the defiant plastered the Reynolds house with Liberal posters. This was a sore sight in such a Tory stronghold as Sanderstead, indeed, so bitter were the Right that the posters were torn down or defaced, at which the Reynolds children, risking their father's displeasure in the use of aggressive tactics, started to desecrate the numerous Tory posters on fences and gates.

Early political passions now faded, or rather, they were refocused for Reg was enamoured of his young kindergarten teacher. This paragon of femininity was Miss Gay and full of gaiety she was, that is, until she was arrested, charged, convicted, imprisoned and appeared at school no more. Miss Gay, banners flying, was a militant suffragette. Miss Gay, blood on the boil, had pushed incendiary matter through pillar boxes. Reg was unconcerned; after all, he neither wrote nor received letters and the ethics of sabotage were quite outside the interest of a smitten eight year old. In Miss Gay he saw only the romance of revolution, he saw her 'as a beautiful and gracious lady who suffered for her principles in an unequal battle, goodness and beauty pitted against wickedness, ugliness, brute force and bloody ignorance. Nobody, surely, has ever died on the barricades for dialectical materialism; but only a cad would refuse to die for Miss Gay'.

In the summer of 1914, the Reynolds family moved from Sanderstead to Croydon. During an air-raid, the two women supervising Reg and his younger brother (Bryant and Florence were away temporarily) decided, for safety, that they should all nestle together in a double-bed. Reg

14

remembered the feelings of indignity this caused far more than the bombs themselves. For three years, he was a pupil at a snobbish preparatory school. With the headmaster 'a confirmed sadist', the experience was dismal. He often got into scraps, on one occasion tripping a boy who then fell on top of him. Both contestants were devastated when Reg was found to have a broken collar-bone. The boy was flogged. His sense of injustice aroused, the 11-year-old Reg confronted the headmaster – couldn't he see that it was just the boy's bad luck that he'd inflicted the injury, and how was the boy to know that Reg had particularly brittle bones?

His 'criminal' activities were on the upswing. He had a new symbol of power, his screwdriver, and a new obsession, the collecting of screws. 'Joyous Garde', 'Cheng Tu', 'Waverley', 'Miome', 'Chez Nous' – the names on the local garden gates meant little to him but the metal plates on which these names were imprinted meant an unholy yearning. Each plate had four screws to hold it in place and each screw he had a wild desire to extract. As he explained in *My Life and Crimes*, 'One screw, that might have been overlooked without comment by anyone but a connoisseur, had the distinction of coming from a door-knocker. Its capture had involved reckless courage with such a pounding of the heart that only professional pride had prevented me from abandoning the enterprise before I had obtained the treasured booty. I knew, with an awful thrill of joy and terror in the knowledge, that this secret hobby was a form of STEALING. For me the descent to Avernus was not easy but hard as a martyr's path, heavy with responsibility, perilous and paved with sacrifices.' The day came 'when something like a minor crisis struck the screw-collecting industry. On every route, every eligible name-plate had yielded its toll of screws; short of removing the plates altogether or leaving them hanging from the corner by a single support, I could do no more'. Beautiful name-plates, unrifled treasures 'had to be passed without even an attempt on their smug virginity'. It was as near as he came to remorse, 'for this compulsion was the closest thing in my experience to what I was to identify later as a sense of duty. The compulsions of Satan are far more exacting than the easy standards of virtue, handed down from the time when Elisha gave his temporising counsel to the Syrian captain. Something had to be done in loyalty to that which demanded screws'.

That something was, inevitably, the removal of as many screws as possible from his parents' house. Punishment loomed but nothing could dent his resolve and in the next few days, the mesmerising mission was accomplished. Had wisdom prevailed, the screws in the smallest room would have been regarded as inviolable, for there the eye was bound to detect what was amiss. Sure enough, a dangling finger-plate was soon reported. Reg dashed to replace the missing screws, so clumsily that the finger-plate cracked. Trembling, he withdrew. Time was running out, other rooms were being examined, arrest was imminent. Then it was announced that the lavatory door was no longer screwless and there was this ugly crack . . . 'Like a cornered gangster I waited in my lair. There they found me. I knew that my conduct had been unforgivable, like the sin against the Holy Ghost.'

What astonished him was the family's mirth: 'It shocked me by its blasphemy, that anyone would find such things funny – that which was a religion to me and a crime to society.' How could his devilish heroism be laughed to scorn, his consecrated roguery be so flippantly dismissed? When the family recounted the story to their visitors – and it was a set-piece – Reg would hide in his bedroom to blot out the sacrilegious guffaws. *They* would have brought him close to tears. With adults treating his adventures as malarkey and not with the awful respect due to Sin, his whole universe of good and evil was shattered.

CHAPTER II

# Ike

BUT NOT FOR LONG. Aged 12, and for the next five years, he was a boarding scholar at the co-educational Friends School, Saffron Walden, Essex. It was an acceptable place for the misfit and oddity he considered himself to be. Though games were compulsory – that dreaded word – life at the school was 'more than tolerable'. As he never went to university he was, according to Farrand Radley, 'probably our best scholar-manqué. So his emotional loyalties remained with the school and the Old Scholars Association'. 'Unlike me', wrote Ethel Mannin, 'Reg believed in that myth called "education", and I have always remembered him observing once, when I was defending "free" schools and A. S. Neill's ideas, and declaring that all real education happened outside the schools, "There speaks the self-educated person". I've remembered it because I smarted a little under it. But I've never deviated from those ideas I had in the 1920s.'

Saffron Walden still thrives as the oldest Friends school in the United Kingdom. It evolved from a workhouse at Clerkenwell, started in 1702, where boys, the elderly, the sick and ex-prisoners cleaned, spun, wove, made shoes and repaired clothes. The purpose of the community was to provide an adequate standard of living for those who worked there rather than to profit the founders. The guiding hand behind the enterprise was that of the Quaker, John Bellers, who wrote: 'It is more charity to set a Man's broken leg so that he can go himself, than for ever to carry him.' In the last decades of the 18th century, the educational aspects of his workhouse assumed greater importance. The children were transferred to a new building in the Islington Road, then the workhouse grew into a Friends school, moving to Croydon and, in 1879, to Saffron Walden.

Reg, in his adolescence, symbolised youth's revolt against age, irreverence against decorum. Hiding both introspection and vulnerability, a thorn in the flesh of his schoolmasters, though he secretly admired and

17

loved many of them, he contrived to snub conformity and indulge eccentricity. He had the double distinction of being the cleverest boy in the school and of failing to be appointed a prefect, a cause for silent humiliation. He lapped up information outside the school syllabus, spurning set books and boasting that he could pass any examination by swotting for three weeks only. In his last year, he revenged himself on heavy snorers in the dormitory by telling the younger boys under his care that they must abide by two laws – they should dream silently and, in all other matters, they should not be found out. To stifle snoring, he chose four 'navvies', armed with pillows, who, on his instruction, stood two on either side of the bed where slept the offending grunter and wheezer. Each 'navvy', issued with a number, struck as Reg counted, while he 'lay in comfort like an Eastern Potentate whose casual tongue deals death from the cushions of the seraglio. I must have been a singularly unpleasant youth'.

Tony Skelton and Reg were 'new brats' together at Walden in May 1917, 'and our friendship commenced that first term. During most of those five years at school neither Reg nor I excelled at games but preferred to spend our half-days in long walks of 15 or more miles in the Essex countryside, and on one occasion, when the school went by train to Cambridge to see the Australian cricketers we too went to Cambridge and back – but on foot!' Roy Yardley remembered Reg entering a competition for the best short essay on the merits of Wincarnis wine, 'and he won the prize which was a half-bottle of the wine. I know this because he shared it round the class and we all had a sip and thought we were frightful dogs'. To Edna Byrne, he was 'always playing, never quite serious, always a slightly crazy companion with very individual flights of fancy'.

☆     ☆     ☆

Such fancies persisted. In 1956, he wrote for Pollock's Toy Theatre a one act play, *The Massacre of Penny Plain*, the first of a series of toy theatre plays published to celebrate the birth of Benjamin Pollock 100 years before. Pollock married a Miss Redington whose father ran a toy theatre shop in Hoxton Street. When old Mr Redington died, leaving his shop to his daughter, young Benjamin learned the craft of toy theatre making and publishing. The Juvenile Drama had begun in the days of the Regency but few new plays had been presented since the middle of the century and by the time that Pollock had mastered the trade it was already rather passé. Nevertheless he continued making toy theatres exactly as his father-in-law had taught him, reprinting the same plays on his lithographic press and colouring them by hand for sale at 'a penny plain and twopence coloured'

18

for each sheet. After years of struggle, Pollock and his quaint little shop became fashionable with artists, actors and writers and he died a man of fame. Thanks to him, the art of the traditional toy theatre survived. (In performing a Pollock's Toy Theatre play, the characters are cut out with a pair of scissors and the names of the characters written on the back of the appropriate sheet. The bases of the scenes are trimmed, resting flush with the floor of the stage; the scenes and wings are arranged and the characters placed in wire slides. Two people are required to manipulate the figures and the plays can be acted by one person changing voices or by several behind the scenes.)

The characters in Reg's play included Two-Gun O'Hooligan (a Bad Man), Simeon Sly (a Crook Lawyer), Sheriff Doublecross and Sam Straight (a Good Cowboy).

Says the Sheriff to O'Hooligan:
> I understand
> Thar's gold in them thar hills – grab
> All the land.
> Foreclose all mortgages and do your worst:
> Evict the lot – widows and orphans first!

Says Chief Tomahawk (an Indian Chief), firing his gun:
> Vengeance is ours, my Braves! The
> Paleface Baddies
> In the Bad Hunting Ground have
> Joined their Daddies!
> Let every Paleface hear and understand:
> Never again shall Bad Men steal our land!

Says Sam Straight:
> Two-gun Hooligan? What had he
> Been doin' to them? He's a Baddie?
> If Injuns gunned for him –
> darnation! –
> He must have given provocation.

The hectic plot reveals Sam and Molly (a Pretty Barmaid) tied to the railway track. Then an engine, 1870 style, appears with a lassoo around its high funnel, pulling up just before it reaches the star-crossed pair. Climbing out of the engine is Hercules Headlong (Guv'nor of the State) who says a deal will be made with the Sheriff.

Enter Chief Tomahawk on his horse.

Tomahawk: Guv'nor! The Bad men killed our squaws
> There is no good in Paleface laws.

19

Headlong: My honest Injun, noble Chief,
This news is sorrow, pain and grief.
We will avenge this horrid deed
When these two Goodies have been freed.

Sam captures the Sheriff:
I got him, Guv'nor, thanks to you,
Right from the train, with my lassoo;
And Lawyer Sly, I think, is dead –
An Injun shot him through the head.

Headlong: That's fine! Secure all Baddies –
bind 'em –
Bury your hatchets where you'll find 'em
When next you need 'em (contradict'ry
But an essential tip for vict'ry)
Just throw the corpses in a carriage –
I guess we finish with a marriage.
We'll find a parson, Sam, to state
That Molly here is Missis Straight.
I hope the Injuns will attend
The wedding of a Paleface friend.

Tomahawk: The massacre of Penny Plain
Still grieves us. But we've seen a train
And seen the Baddies beaten, too,
Thanks, Guvernor, to Sam and you;
And furthermore we understand
We shall regain our stolen land.
So other squaws we'll find, no doubt,
Or maybe we can do without.
But first we'll see how White Man's Law
Unites a White Brave and his squaw
And smoke the peace pipe with our friends
Who for our loss have made amends.

☆     ☆     ☆

At Saffron Walden, Eileen Clark felt repulsed by Reg's inky grubbiness
'but I could not help admiring something of the spirit which was apparent
even in his early teens. He loved to thrash things out and got very tired when
his friends (or enemies) would not argue logically. You have a rag-bag mind,
he once shouted at me. It needs sorting'. David Pearson heard him say that
Saffron Walden Quaker Meeting was a 'birthplace of atheism' and Edward

Bawden, later a well-known artist, recollected 'a lively boy with straw-coloured hair and dark eyes set in a long narrow face. As a kid in the lower fourth he would be jumping about, shouting provocative remarks, being chased and at the same time giving the chaser a good deal of "lip". At the time of a General Election, which must have taken place soon after the end of the first world war, the school held a mock election with masters standing as candidates for three parties. Labour won handsomely and how much those of us who voted Labour loathed the Tories was made manifest by the fierce arguments that broke out everywhere. Reynolds supported the Liberal cause and defended it well, but he gave the impression of being a one-man Liberal Party with ideas and a policy peculiar to himself.'

Reg also castigated the Tories during his school years, an activity he never stopped:

*Ballad of Babe Farmer*
The youngest canvasser at North Lewisham was the Tory candidate's grand-daughter, aged nine months. Her pram carried a poster which read: 'Vote for my grand-dad'.

> Born at the Carlton in Fifty six
> Raised on the speeches of Joynson-Hicks,
> Larned in her cradle them old-time tricks,
> Like Davy Crockett, she'd seen on the flicks.
> Baby . . . Baby Farmer,
> Queen of the Valentine fight!
>
> Digged how to rock 'n roll in her pram
> Canvassin' voters down in Lewis*ham*,
> Teached her Gran'pa in a bid fer slam,
> Fer facts an' figures she don't give a damn.
> Baby . . . Baby Farmer,
> Bawlin' with all her might!
>
> Labourites cool on the Suez mess,
> Gunned for Mac in their wicked red press,
> Tories didn't have a lot to say, I guess,
> Gotta have a Babe bawls louder'n the res'.
> Baby . . . Baby Farmer,
> Sarvin' them Injuns right!
>
> Doesn't hold with Cypriots or African blacks,
> Scorns to reply to them cowardly attacks,
> Figures a yell is the wisest of cracks,
> Keeps her politickin' on old party tracks.
> Baby . . . Baby Farmer,
> Holdin' her rattle tight!

Ain't so hep in financial affairs,
Leaves all that to the old Teddy Bears,
That chinless man, with the rest of the squares
An' the cats who dabble in stocks and shares.
Baby . . . Baby Farmer,
Queen of the Lewisham Fight!

*Brouhaha for a Carlton Club Quartette*

When Milton first was heard to state
   That God preferred His Englishmen
The Slave Trade was immaculate,
   For this was God's Commandment then:
'Trade, Britannia! Britannia, trade in Man!
Get some money, money, money where you can'.

Jehova (*circa* 1807)
   Said we must close such monstrous shops
And by a new Decree of Heaven
   Britons became Anointed Cops:
Hail, Britannia! Britannia, bash the knaves –
Britons never, never never trade in slaves.

The Lord then let us understand
   Some forms of theft he viewed with phlegm;
We must not take men from the land,
   But we could take the land from *them*:
Grab, Britannia! Britannia, rob the Wogs –
Britons ever, ever, ever are Top Dogs.

When we had seized the larger swag
   We looked in horror at the Wops,
Who went marauding with a flag
   In the Close Season – when it stops.
Shout Britannia! Britannia, bid them cease –
Britons never, never never break the peace.

Now (through Saint Anthony) the Lord
   Says that He's changed His mind once more –
With Russia we have firm accord:
   *A war no longer is a war.*
Read, Britannia! Read your Gutter Press –
Britain's in a bloody, bloody, *bloody* mess.

                  (from *New Statesman*)

One of Reg's 1918 outfits was a knickerbocker suit with a large patch resembling the ace of spades in the seat of his trousers. Philip Aynsley Smith recalled his 'rather high-pitched voice, with its rapid speech and unhesitating, precise enunciation, breaking when he was amused (which was often) into a distinctive, breathy laugh which rose almost into a cackle. It would be a profound mistake to suppose that because he was so patently different from his fellows there was anything remote about Reg. His cast of mind was predominantly intellectual but for all his gifts and his sensibilities he was no hot-house plant.

When he was 13 he had already achieved notoriety by lampooning the kindly but irascible George Morris in a parody of 'Young Lochinvar' which continued to be quoted around the school. What was more, he had had the temerity to send it through the post to his victim and out of foolhardiness, or possibly through downright carelessness, had not taken the trouble to disguise his handwriting. Thus, inevitably, he was brought to book. The very nickname, 'Ike', which he acquired in his later years at school, was in some way suggestive of a disreputable character.

I well remember when Senior Lit., where the customary offerings were plodding chronicles like *A Holiday in Devon*, was suddenly shocked into life by a contribution from Reg entitled *One-Eyed O'Leary of Dead Man's Gulch*, or *Devils of Columbia versus Britain's Best*. We sat on the old Lecture Hall benches and wriggled with excitement while we watched the faces of the staff assume that familiar 'we are not amused' expression, as they listened to this turgid extravaganza, with its mingled elements from sixpenny Westerns and empire builders' tales out of *Chums*. Of course he had done himself less than justice with this piece of nonsense, but the very solemnity of our literary gatherings was an invitation which he could not resist.

There was an occasion when we all attended a lecture on Temperance and were afterwards encouraged to submit essays on the subject for a competition. This was an opportunity for Reg to deliver himself of a magnificent diatribe in which the wickedness of alcoholic indulgence, startlingly portrayed, was roundly condemned in resounding Miltonic prose. The choicer passages were read to me as we sat in a corner of the Lecture Hall, where he had been writing: 'We must banish this unmitigated evil for ever from our midst,' Reg intoned. I had no idea what 'unmitigated' meant, but the polysyllable was impressive and my admiration boundless. To Reg it was all great fun, an intellectual exercise, and, I need hardly add, he was awarded the prize. As for me, the phrase stuck; from that day to this there has been no evil that, in my mind, has not been 'unmitigated'.

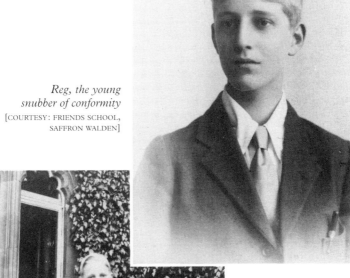

*Reg, the young snubber of conformity*
[COURTESY: FRIENDS SCHOOL, SAFFRON WALDEN]

*Reg aged about 15 outside the front porch at Friends School, Saffron Walden*
[COURTESY: TONY SKELTON]

*Ethel was 'Mary' to Reg. This photograph is inscribed 'To my sweet Mary'*

There was a term when Reg returned to school enthralled by the discovery of Malory's *Morte d'Arthur*. The Arthurian legend exercised a particular fascination for him because of its association with his ancestral town of Glastonbury, and for many months afterwards his imagination seemed continually to be playing upon the mythical golden age of chivalry. Of course it is nothing new for schoolboys to affect medievalisms in speech and writing, especially when they want to be funny, but in the case of Reg it seemed to arise from a deeper feeling. It was probably at this period of his school life that his form was required to set one of Aesop's fables in ballad form. The ballad chosen was that of the Lion and the Mouse. Reg's poem was of course couched in medieval English and, for good measure, the simple tale was given a sardonic twist quite characteristic of Reg. The mouse, bidden to a feast to celebrate the lion's escape, found himself by an unfortunate accident not *at* the table but *on* it, and the poem ended:

> 'He made a lordlie dysshe,
> And in ye lyon's revelrie
> He passed for grillèd fysshe.'

Out of the climate of those years in which he grew up at Walden – a climate which was in part his own creation – sprang that intense and abiding affection for the school which he carried wherever he went. It was one of the most constant elements in his life, enduring through personal sorrows, doubts, struggles and occasional despair. Walden is a recurring theme in letters which he wrote to me over more than 30 years; anticipating reunions, deploring separations, wherever he was in the world, he turned towards Walden in spirit as the devout Jew turns towards Jerusalem. It was his Holy City, embodying that which he loved most in life. I do not believe he could really hate any individual. What he hated was attitudes, concepts, and these he fought ferociously when he deemed them to be wrong. 'How I hate X!' (a member of the staff) he once wrote just after he had left school, but it was clear that it was not, in fact, X whom he hated but what he believed X stood for. There were those at school who thought him disruptive and irresponsible, but it must be remembered that there is a tendency on the part of authority, particularly in schools, to equate responsibility with compliance. Compliant Reg could never be. Two things stood in the way. In the first place, he had the critical, analytical mind of the reformer, for whom institutions, ideas, movements are the servants, not the masters of humanity and are acceptable only to the extent that they fulfil this supreme function. Secondly, he was an artist, which meant that he must, to a significant degree, be an individualist, even at times a solitary, for in the last resort the creative processes are something peculiarly and intensely personal. Thence stemmed the unorthodoxies in Reg which shocked or dismayed the susceptible.'

Throughout his boyhood, the man who influenced him most was the Saffron Walden history master, Stanley King-Beer. A militant pacifist, Stanley spent some years of the first world war in prison, from which he burst into the school, enthusing the boys with tales of great deeds, inducing garden birds to enter his house and rehearsing a hilarious mock opera with his colleagues.

Reg listened avidly to his prison experiences. The prison doctor had tried to belittle him for being anti-war, anti-capitalist, anti-meat, anti-vivesection, anti-everything. Yes, said Stanley, he *was* anti-everything that was rotten. 'You're just a crank', accused the doctor. 'May I remind you that a crank is a thing which makes revolutions', replied Stanley.

Reg worshipped him, this Romantic Revolutionary (shades of Miss Gay) in his coat of corded velvet, looking like a poet and often talking like one. At mealtimes, Stanley would boom down the table, 'Does anyone want any more corpse?' Reg took the hint and suddenly announced that he had become a vegetarian. 'Your parents have to state at the beginning of the term if you're to receive vegetarian food', he was told. 'You can't decide to be a "veggie" in mid-term and on your own initiative.' Oppressive, that. He was and he had. Logic. Reginald's Sin. Very well then, he would reject all meat and accept no substitute. After authority had corresponded with his parents, authority capitulated and Reg guessed that it was Stanley who had negotiated the surrender. Such was Stanley's impact, but the deepest lesson he learned from him was on the insanity of war.

### Ballade for Ancestral Voices

Sir George Thompson, nuclear physicist and Master of Corpus Christi, is reported in the *Manchester Guardian* as saying to the International Press Conference at Vienna that 'What our age needs is not so much permanent peace, which is unattainable and perhaps not even wholly desirable, but sanity in its wars.'

> As Hitler said, (who wants a better guide?)
> Perpetual peace is not a healthy state;
> There is a golden mean for homicide
> In bombs that kill but not obliterate.
> Our modest duty is to re-create
> The world of Genghis Khan and Tamburlaine,
> Or Alexander, who was called the Great
> Because his wars were gentle and humane.

War for War's sake – all sane on either side;
Slaughter's the aim, not to discriminate.
Toss for the choice of weapons: have you tried
Napalm, Sir George? It's a *heroic* fate!
Or, with a club, could you not emulate
The cannibal (so eminently sane)
Who served his prisoner upon a plate,
Because his wars were gentle and humane?

If the United Nations would provide
Some place for bashing people on the pate
Then Nature's Pruning Hook could be applied
With more precision. One might speculate
In pools and private bets, then calmly wait
The close of play (reading the number slain)
And good Sir George's name commemorate
Because his wars were gentle and humane.

### ENVOI

Master of Corpus Christi, on the date
When something hits you – harder than your brain –
I hope that there will be a record 'gate'
Because your wars were gentle and humane.

(Unpublished satire)

*Dear, Dear Brigadier*

The *Manchester Guardian* has apologised to the Member for Worthing for reporting him as saying that the fun had gone out of war. He only said that the fun had gone out of the Army.

Dear Brig. Prior-Palmer,
We hope you feel calmer –
Hon. Member for Worthing,
We know you said northing
So utterly barmy,
But referred to the Army.

In your Brigadier boyhood
And tin-soldier toyhood
Armies were playthings
In red coats and gay things
And soldiers were gluttons
For bull and brass buttons.

28

(That's buttons for dressing,
Not push-button pressing –
They placed no reliance
On gimcracks and science,
And phrases like FALL OUT
Were just things to call out.)
In short, they were gayer
Than the troops of today are.

These drawbacks admitted,
The man is half-witted
Who credits the rumour
That shortage of humour
Is characteristic
Of the nuclear ballistic.
So hushaby, honey,
War's still very funny –
We *do* beg your pardyon,

Ed. Manchester Guardian.

(from New Statesman)

☆    ☆    ☆

Saffron Walden was his Eden and, as Ethel Mannin remarked, he positively pelted there for reunions. In the late 1920s, he wrote a poetical account of the Old Scholars Association Christmas Party:

When Tony Skelton first suggested that
I should discourse per medium of my hat
(Like Mauger) on the subject of the Party,
The tone of my reply was scarcely hearty.
However. . . . Last December 29,
Diverse Old Bottles, bursting with new wine,
Assembled, strange amusement to pursue
In Quakerism's latest G.H.Q.

The evening opened (I confess with shame)
With 'Bigamy' – a most outrageous game.
'Musical spoons', which followed, it is feared,
Suggested food, which manna-like appeared.
The buns devoured, our babel hushed to hear
Queer folk discoursing upon topics queer.
First Arnold Green discussed our Modern Girls:

29

On Thorns (forgive the mixture) fell his pearls.
Bedford Lemere's strong plea indignant waxed
That men untangled* should remain untaxed.
In the cucumber Howard Diamond's mind
Sought the banana's missing link to find.
Then Kenneth Whitlow's peroration showed
The reason why the Chicken crossed the Road,
And last Paul Mauger's erudite address
(Made thro' his hat) was a complete success.
While some now cleared the tables, others tried
In Limericks their betters to deride,
And while the Judges, with censorious eye,
Impartial judgment to their wit apply,
Two noble souls (whose names† won't fit my metre)
Sang like the lark – less shrill, that is, but sweeter.
The crowd then ceased to wave their arms and shout,
While Mr Rowntree read the Limericks out.
Maud Tyler (primus) chose with craft and care
A weighty theme – no less than B. Lemere.
The rest, with various inspiration fired,
Assailed such persons as their wit inspired:
One, with scurrility as cruel as funny,
Abused the character and 'dial' of 'Bunny'.
A slanderous bard, self-styled 'X.Y.Z,'
Sang of the hairs of our illustrious Head –
A galaxy of doubtful wit, in short,
Which you will find (I'm told) in the Report.
Now, prone on hassocks, racing down the hall,
The bristly sex essay the Australian crawl;
Which done, our sisters, chasing egg with fan,
Display a subtle skill unknown to man.
The evening then concluded (in a line)
With dancing, lemonade, and Auld Lang Syne –
A real old Christmas Party, to my mind,
Which leaves an Annual Soiree far behind.
The invitations, which informed us all
That ambulances were in easy call,
Proved unessential, for I hear that none
Were so far gone as not to go alone.

From each experience I always strive
Some general proposition to derive,

30

Some weighty aphorism that affords
An epigrammatist a use for words;
Methinks the following sententious verse
Is not so bad that it might be worse:
'School-days departed, Youth still grows apace,
The boys in Wisdom and the girls in Grace.'

* Men untangled: Batchelors, in the vulgar usage.
† Two noble souls: Eva Diamond and Irene Mauger.

☆    ☆    ☆

The history of the school was of endless fascination to him. Alluding to bed-bugs in his book *Beds*, he told of a certain Christopher Fox whose remedy was considered almost miraculous. A minute from the Committee of Ye Workhouse of the People called Quakers for 1722 read:

> The Steward is ordered to give a copy of the following certificate to Christopher Fox.
>
> *Christopher Fox in Hollywell Lane Shoreditch Undertakes to Destroy Buggs.*
>
> These are to certify that in the year 1721 we agreed with him to destroy the aforesaid vermin in 4 Rooms Containing 49 beds all which was performed with a Liquid so inofencive that the Beds were made use of the same Night and were so Effectually performed that notwithstanding the Beds Walls Ceiling etc. were Exceeding full yet upon diligent observation now the Weather grows warm have not found above three Live Buggs, and any who pleases to Come to the House may see the Beds and have further Satisfaction.
>
> Signed by their Order 28:3:1722
> Richd Hutton
> Steward.

In November 1722 there was a memorandum of an 'agreement between Richard Hutton Steward and Christopher Fox by Order of the Committee that the said Christopher Fox shall keep and Preserve Friends Workhouse all and every part of the Said House and Beds Standing or hereafter may Stand there in Clear and Free from Buggs and in consideration hereof the said Richard Hutton shall duely pay the said Christopher Fox Thirty Shillings per year.' It was not recorded how long the periodic debugging continued but it looked as if the bugs had the upper hand – by 1756, the beds were again full of vermin.

To mark the school's 250th anniversary, Reg wrote an historical pageant, *The Gateway of the Past*. Shortly before, he had a special maroon corduroy jacket made, which he wore with his grandfather's stock, for the school's Whit dance. In 1951, he addressed the Annual General Meeting of the Old Scholars Association:

'When, a year ago, I became President of this Association, I was so touched by the honour that the responsibilities at first escaped my notice. I looked forward to a gay interlude in my drab life, during which – like the king – I could do no wrong. My error, as I soon discovered, was rooted in inexperience. I had known so little of responsibility that I had preserved a child-like innocence. (Every child knows that when you are grown up you can stay up as late as you like and eat Gorgonzola.) Indeed, I am probably the first of your Presidents who was never a prefect while at school – or at *least* a member of the school staff.

Of these responsibilities – as distinct, so to speak, from the Gorgonzola – many have found the Presidential Swan Song the most exacting. Swans have no training in this department. . . . But there be geese who have cackled all their lives and I belong *dans cette galère* – that is to say, in that gaggle. Who would have imagined that such a goose would be hard put to it on an occasion like the present? My Roman ancestors, who saved the Capitol, must turn on their spits.

It was only after long thought, as I sat nursing a cold in the head, three weeks ago, surrounded by a bleak wilderness of Victorian boarding houses known as Llandrindod Wells, that something occurred to me: I had enjoyed, thought I, exceptional opportunities in the past year. They were opportunities such as few O.S. Presidents could have had before me. It had been my privilege to live in the school of 1951, sharing to some extent its life, becoming increasingly friendly with the staff and scholars of today. And all the time I had been able to view them as part of an historical procession which began at Ye Friends Workhouse in 1702.

The School Tower, where I lived as a pampered guest, has always had double associations for my generation – associations equally formidable. It was, for those who shared with me those vintage years, the abode of John Edward Walker, whose shrewd understanding of human nature in general and *Homo Juvenis Waldeniensis* in particular may have been due to the excellent acoustics of the adjoining boys' bedroom, known as the Pit. Indeed, I learned quite a lot myself without any specialised training. The other association with the Tower, in my days, was that somewhere up there – I believe in a room now occupied by unsuspecting members of the domestic staff – was a kind of Condemned Cell. It was the room, or shall I say the rumoured room, where one might spend one's last night at Walden if leaving precipitately.

In my Ivory Tower I could therefore combine both these experiences, being, in my own imagination, at one moment a stately Headmaster with a fine white beard and at the next a doomed culprit. It was a fitting *mise en scène* for the drama which unfolded from those leather bound volumes, carried into the drawing room for my use by willing minions. For *Homo Juvenis Waldeniensis* still relishes any excuse to be doing something not on the time-table. Seated in a comfortable chair or lying (as Jennie Ellinor once discovered me, to my intense embarrassment) at full length on the hearth-rug, I could indulge in long, long flash-backs of Waldens before Walden was. Even the Presidential stomach, perhaps because I was lying on it, failed to warn me of time's flight – a few meagre hours into the future, while I travelled a million times more swiftly than the clock, anything up to a quarter of a millenium, and widdershins, at that. The dinner gong would take me by surprise, when I heard it at all. Sometimes, indeed, my first warning was a curious rumbling like distant thunder which would shoot my mind back from Clerkenwell or Islington to Saffron Walden 30 years ago or more. It was the great surge of chairs in the dining hall, a familiar and venerable noise, quite unimpaired by efforts to minimise its effects on the foundations. Long live the deafening roar of the Domes of Silence!

Within a minute I would be there, part of the present once more. And so time passed between the remote past of the old volumes, the nearer past of personal memory, evoked by a familiar sound or smell (the stinks laboratory, the swimming bath or the boys' wash-room) and then this sudden precipitation into the year 1951. . . .

It is from this medley of reading, recollection and present experience that my thoughts for this occasion are drawn – by-products of the happiest hours I have ever spent in research and writing, as the past unrolled and the Walden Scrap-Book gradually took shape. One of the fragments which found a place in this jig-saw puzzle was the first recorded letter of an Old Scholar. It was written in 1717 to Richard Hutton, Ye Steward of Ye Friends Workhouse; and Richard was so touched that he copied ye letter in to Ye Complaint Book, which sounds odd. Of course it was not really a Complaint Book – it had no title and was probably just a sort of commonplace book; but the commonplaces of the Steward's life were mostly of such a nature that it came to be known as Richard Hutton's Complaint Book. But it did contain other things, such as instructions for brewing ale.

This letter was one of the few other entries which do not justify the title of complaints. 'Kind Steward', wrote this Old Scholar (he had evidently but recently left the institution), 'These are to acquaint thee that I am safe arrived.' And so on. It ends: 'My love to thee and to thy wife also all the Friends of the Committee' (how many of you ever send your love to the

School Committee?) 'and to my master, that taught me to write. My love to the Ancient Friends and all the children of the Workhouse, which were my schoolfellows, and I should be very glad to hear of any of their welfare.'

My last visit to Walden in the course of this interesting job was at the end of the Summer Term; and I combined it with another pleasurable duty, that of presiding over the Leavers' Party. It was difficult to think of words suitable for such an occasion and it was not until later that David Bolam, whose researches have been so much more thorough than my own, drew my attention to the way leavers were admonished at Clerkenwell. This admonition took the form of a printed pamphlet, published in 1778, and is full of good advice which I neglected to offer the leavers in 1951. For example:

> Be careful never to enter an alehouse, unless sent there by thy master or mistress on business. (The business is not specified, which is a pity.) Nor drink to excess on any occasion: drunkenness is a most dangerous vice, unfits a man for business (note the insistence once more on this subject), is reproachful to society, and has led many to commit the most atrocious crimes.

One thing that interested me in our records was the international character of the school apparently throughout the 250 years of its history. From the time when Scipio came to Clerkenwell we seem to have been quite an international centre. Most of you must have heard me talk of Scipio one time or another, but for the benefit of those who have never heard of him, here is the first record of the young man. It is in the minutes of Peel Monthly Meeting, 27th of 6th month (which was August in those days) 1718:

> George Wingfield haveing a Black Boy named Scipio fallen under his care and being desirous he should have a Christian Education and requested of us that he may be admitted into friends workhouse and he will pay the Expenses thereof to which this meeting consents and desires John Russell to acquaint the Committee thereof.

I have tried to parse this sentence, but without any success. The marginal reference consists of two words: 'Black Boy'. Friends in those days made history so casually that you have to read twice to make quite sure you aren't imagining something.

Croydon records are positively cosmopolitan. There was Frederick Gröne, the German boy, who seems to have been at the school roughly from 1862-1867 – later an active member of the Society of Friends . . . and in 1866, *The Echo*, a Croydon magazine, refers to an old scholar, one Philip W. Lemprière who had returned to his home in Jersey and been imprisoned at St Helier as a conscientious objector to military service. A Jersey paper gave a very favourable account of Lemprière, and he appears to have been released after 48 hours. Joseph Radley, a Croydon master who had a long and excellent influence on the school, made this case the subject of a French essay competition for what was called the 'Przyiemski Prize'. Here was another strange foreign name which soon led me on one of my wild goose chases.

Colonel Przyiemski, I found, was one of the Polish revolutionaries of that period, an exile whose exciting adventures had taken him as far as Turkey. But he had ended up in Tottenham. Here he taught at Grove House School and lived, as he tells us, 'in a narrow little room, the abode of poverty, a few books my sole companions'. When the mistresses at Croydon expressed a very creditable wish to learn French, it was Przyiemski who was engaged for the purpose of teaching them. But what exactly the Przyiemski Prize was I still don't know.

The Polish colonel died a member of the Society of Friends. But Croydon School must surely have been greatly daring when they engaged him in 1857 – the very year in which his revolutionary reminiscences had appeared, under the title, *Sketches of the Polish Mind*. It was reviewed in *The Friend* quite favourably, but with the comment that the book 'breathed something of the spirit of war'. Eight years previously another Polish revolutionary had married one of the Croydon mistresses – a shocking thing in those days, for it involved the young woman's disownment (by the Society of Friends) and led to packets of trouble in the future.

The internationalism of Croydon was generally on a less sensational level. Clarice Benezet was there in the 1840s – surely one of that Huguenot family of which Anthony Benezet, pioneer crusader against slavery in America, was the most celebrated member. And in 1863 there left Croydon a young Frenchman, Théophile Toussaty, who must have been one of the first objectors to military service in France. Unwilling to make a martyr of him, the French authorities exempted him on account of 'a little roughness of speech', whatever that may mean.

In my own schooldays there were not, so far as I can remember, any Negroes, Poles, Germans or Frenchmen about the place. But we cultivated a good international spirit, which I shall always associate with the name of Stanley King-Beer. I can still, I think, trace his gentle influence on 'the men who were boys when I was a boy' – in a broad, liberal outlook, not in the party sense of the word but in its true and original meaning. And when I was living in my Ivory Tower my descents into the present from the treasures of the past revealed to me a continuation and development of that good tradition. Indeed, I wish you could all have enjoyed the privilege which was once mine of hearing Sunday Evening Meeting taken by senior boys and girls who had attended Junior Yearly Meeting at Friends House, London. It struck me as a courageous innovation which showed confidence in the capacity of *Homo Juvenis Waldeniensis* to think for himself – or herself. And they *do* think. Parents can take my word for it. The process which began when Joseph Radley and others encouraged and stimulated the intellectual and aesthetic life of young Croydon Scholars is still finding its way to fulfilment; and the future possibilities seem all the more exciting when one has traced their roots in the past.'

☆    ☆    ☆

Reg had often discussed enabling a boy or girl, just leaving school, or a young Old Scholar, to give a limited period of service abroad. The idea came to fruition after his death in the form of the Reg Reynolds Memorial Award Scheme. Mindful of all that the school had lost in him and as a memorial to all that he stood for, the scheme ensured that young people maintained his concern for the deprived corners of the world. Fare money was provided but recipients had to earn their keep in such countries as Gambia, Madagascar, Lebanon, Botswana, India, China, Zimbabwe and Britain. Ethel Mannin was one of the first to contribute funds; between 1960 and 1984, 26 awards were made, totalling just under £4,000.

The award in 1973 went to an older man, the late Will Warren, towards his social and reconciliatory work in Northern Ireland. In thanking the Old Scholars Association, Will said:

I am fortunate in being trusted by many groups of people in Northern Ireland and this means that I can play a role of bridgebuilder. My contacts with gunmen of both sides have led me to realise that they are as honest and devoted to their cause as any pacifist and far more committed. It is true that they have little regard for the lives and property of those they consider their enemies, but they are equally thoughtless of their own lives, safety and comfort in order to gain their objective, and there is possibly a lesson in this last part which many of us pacifists could learn to our benefit.

There was something Woolmanesque about Will Warren. He, and frequently his wife, Nellie, lived in Derry where he made clear his pacifist beliefs and sought to understand what drove seemingly ordinary people to maim and murder. Members of the Royal Ulster Constabulary, the Protestant Church, the Provisional IRA and the Ulster Defence Association all agreed that, without Will's restraining presence, Derry would have seen considerably more bloodshed. As Alan and Julie Longman wrote: 'Like Reg, he was a fighter for the truth, fearless when the rest of us were frightened'.

Will, who once said, 'The Quaker Meeting for Worship is the only effective training in non-violence that I have ever found', always carried this declaration in his pocket in Northern Ireland:

I am a Christian Pacifist who has come of his own free will to Ulster, in the full knowledge that the situation is a violent one, and may involve his death.

Should this prove to be the case I want it to be clearly understood that I accept full responsibility and that no one else should be blamed. In particular I am convinced that no search for, or punishment of, my killers should be made.

I am persuaded that non-violence is the way out of our troubles, and this necessitates non-retaliation and non-punishment of people who inflict hurt upon me. It may be that if the authorities take no violent action against the users of violence both sides will be enabled to come together peaceably to discuss what practical steps can be taken to avoid further bloodshed. However, if punishment is inflicted it will only embitter the situation and make the efforts of peacemaking even more difficult.

Will was a classmate of Reg's at Saffron Walden, a school that has nurtured its fair crop of 'originals'. As far as Reg is concerned, the value of the school – the open-handedness, the teacher-saint Stanley King-Beer, the warm companionship – was inestimable. Here was hatched the fervent crusader, the gentlemanly rebel, the loyal friend ('Friendship is meat and drink to me.') Here, his wings were sometimes clipped but his imaginative talent was unexcelled by any of his Walden contemporaries.

# CHAPTER III

# Uncle Laurence

STARRY EYED AND NEARLY 17, he left Saffron Walden clutching his parodies of Chesterton and Belloc. He fell violently in love, pouring out reams of inferior romantic verses; immortal flowers of poesy they were not. Girls were one pleasure, tobacco another.

*Hic Jacet*

The London Cremation Company has advised its shareholders not to accept an offer by the Amalgamated Tobacco Corporation to buy the Golders Green Crematorium. The Directors consider that 'a company formed to deal with tobacco is unsuitable to run a crematorium'.

> I measure my grub in roentgens now,
>   And the cream I get from Devon
> Can show you how a humble cow
>   Has a bigger pull than Bevan;
> *He* can create a Welfare State
>   But *hers* is the key to Heaven –
> For that is the use of her Strontium juice
>   And Cesium one-three-seven.
>
> So if I should die before the Fall
>   From a dose of Polonium
> To a Conway Hall Memorial
>   I'd like my friends to come;
> You mustn't smoke at the Ethical Oak
>   So it *would* be rather rum
> To light your pipes in the solemn slypes
>   Of the Crematorium.

But if I die like a pig in a poke
   For God, Mac, Queen and flag,
It isn't a joke that my holy smoke
   Should be confused with shag;
After the crash the nasty ash
   Of stogie, pipe or fag
Shall never mix, this side the Styx
   With the Cobalt hunter's bag.

Can radio-active dust discern
   The ruins of Golders Green?
Then, when I burn, my funeral urn
   (If you rumble what I mean)
Will keep my ash from lesser trash,
   So write what I have been:
The sort of bloke who liked to smoke –
   But kept his ashes clean.

(from *New Statesman*)

With the aim of drilling an over-teeming mind, he attended lectures on international politics at Woodbrooke, the Quaker college in Birmingham. The lecturer was Horace Alexander whose verve and dry humour Reg prized. Intending to stay for a single term, further studies in medieval and modern English history so enthralled him that he was still at Woodbrooke two years later, having failed to qualify for an external degree from London University. The stumbling-block was Latin, which he had always disliked, though the lore of medieval Latin writers became not only a hobby but a passion.

Nineteen years old and, naturally, the Continent beckoned. For one term, he found an unpaid job, with free board and lodgings, as a *répétiteur* at a school in Savenay, a small town between Nantes and St Nazaire. Brief conversational classes with his unwashed and unfragrant pupils allowed him plenty of time to improve his French and brush up his Latin. Some of the Bretons, almost his age, were already equipped, he suspected, with mistresses. 'Never', he wrote, 'was such a guileless Daniel thrown to such merciless lions.' Sticklers for discipline, the *professeurs* paid scant regard to the boys as individuals, grudged all that margin necessary for healthy relationships.

Reg, escaping the oppressive atmosphere, swam for hours in a nearby lake. Baked by the summer heat, his downtrodden students would gleefully join him but their taste of freedom soon turned sour. Acting on complaints from local anglers, the *directeur* of the school deemed the lake out of bounds. Reg he could not forbid; neither would the boys be curbed, a trait Reg encouraged. Before he left Savenay, they gratefully presented him with a photograph of them all disobediently yet undeniably up to their waists in water, and a sketch drawn by one of the boys of the grim *directeur*, the title of which was 'Scrooge'.

His next job, lasting 18 months, was as an assistant prep schoolmaster in an Anglicised pocket of South Wales. Cocooned against the political ferment outside – this was 1926, the year of the General Strike – the principal of the school interpreted, over breakfast, the views of the Tory press. Reg would bite his tongue and dream of holidays. Holidays meant his home territory of Somerset and it was here that he first met Laurence Housman, his 'Uncle Laurence' as he called him affectionately and slightly tongue-in-cheek.

The 60 year old Housman lived with his sister Clemence in Street, and was a neighbour of many of Reg's Clark cousins. 'Somerset is as near to heaven as I am ever likely to get', he said. He had chosen the town for its rural seclusion and Quakerly milieu. Staying there previously with his friend Roger Clark, Laurence asked him if he could find him a house, then 'that will do', he decided, as they passed one on the road. 'Well', said Clark, 'if you don't mind waiting for it for 10 years or so, you can have it. But cousin Joseph lives there, and he's only 86.' In the event, Laurence's house, 'Longmeadow', was built on part of a large field he purchased from the Clarks in 1923.

The irrepressible Laurence, son of a solicitor and younger brother of the poet A. E. Housman, was educated as a day-boy at Bromsgrove School where the headmaster goaded the boarders into denigrating their poorer brethren. As his mother lay dying, she said to Clemence, four years his senior, 'Take care of little Laurence. His legs are weak and he will need you'. Laurence trained as an artist and worked as an illustrator and critic, but his heart was set on authorship. Clemence was their father's unofficial head clerk, expert at penetrating the mysteries of income tax. She went on to earn a modest living from wood-engraving and in 1890, her novel *The Were-Wolf*, illustrated by Laurence, was published; on reading this gruesome story, her brother Alfred wrote to her, 'Capital, capital, capital!' Unlike the emotionally fractured Alfred, Laurence, especially in the company of friends, threw caution to the winds; he once posed for a photograph naked, sitting in a tree. He edited a selection of the writings of William Blake and in 1895, his first book of poems, *Green Arras*, appeared.

Clemence followed with her novel *The Unknown Sea*, a haunting tale of self-sacrifice; suffering for the sins of others was a subject that fascinated her. Laurence's novel *A Modern Antaeus* (1902) included a portrait of Clemence under the name of Marcia. Marcia/Clemence felt too strong for her sex; what a prison it was to be capable and not be permitted to use your gifts; threading needles and darning stockings was a waste; if a man wanted to break out, he could, but not a woman!

In 1909, Clemence was a banner maker for the Women's Social and Political Union. When Mrs Pankhurst and her delegation handed in a petition to Parliament and were arrested, and crowds of women tried to storm the doors, the voice of Laurence was heard in the Central Lobby – 'The women of England are clamouring to be admitted!' Alfred was worried about Clemence's stand as a tax-resister. He suggested she read H. G. Wells' *Ann Veronica* and be warned that that unruly heroine was sent to prison as a militant suffragette. Clemence ignored the warning. She refused to pay house duty on her rented cottage and stocked it with other people's furniture so that the bailiffs were unable to seize it. However, in 1911, she was arrested, sentenced and imprisoned in Holloway, the *Evening Standard* showing a photograph of Clemence and Laurence outside the prison gates.

During the first world war, Laurence was the secretary of a home for Belgian refugees in Ealing. Atrocity stories abounded and a rumour arose that the Germans had cut off the hands of one of the children under his care. A newspaper reporter investigated, was satisfied that the grisly tale was nonsense, but claimed in his printed report that he had actually seen the mutilated child. Laurence's protest to the editor went for nothing. The 'Peace lost at Versailles' turned Laurence into a pacifist. He wrote the first of his *Little Plays of St Francis* –'in the serene sanity of St Francis I found such blessed escape from a world gone mad'.

Reg was familiar with the *Little Plays*; they had been performed on Sunday evenings at Woodbrooke. Now, friends with the celebrated playwright, his literary life had reached a crest. Now, he could discuss his scribblings with a fellow brother of the Muses. Plain bad was Laurence's verdict on one of his poems. On another, which Reg read aloud, 'Well, of course, when you read it *with your sympathetic voice. . . .*' For compensation, a further poem delighted him, and he asked Clemence who might have written it. 'Alfred', she said. From Clemence that was praise indeed.

Reg had the deepest reverence for the handsome Clemence. Of a fastidious and retiring nature, she was skilled in embroidery and an exquisite cook. Before she returned to the Anglican worship of her

41

upbringing, she was an attender at Street Quaker Meeting, mainly when Laurence was absent. Her characteristically whimsical reason was that she really couldn't stomach hearing him pronounce words in Meeting differently from the way he pronounced them in ordinary conversation. Reg's love of the *Morte d'Arthur* led him to read Clemence's complex saga, *The Life of Sir Aglovale de Galis*. At 21, he was bowled over by it. His eyes waxed dim from studying it – 'the most amazing book I have ever read'. Written at white heat in the early hours, drinking whisky to get her through the night, Clemence's message was that Arthurian honour was a fake – Arthur indulged in incest and Lancelot was adulterous and these broken laws were the laws of God. The book was a commercial failure and Clemence wrote no more apart from, at the age of 92, working on a new chapter for a new edition.

Reg had no compunction in telling Laurence that Clemence was a better writer than he was, better even than Alfred, *A Shropshire Lad* notwithstanding. Laurence agreed. Reg vowed there and then that if he was ever in a position to promote her works among a wider public, nothing would please him more. His best attempt to do her justice was his article 'The Third Housman', published in *English* (1955), the quarterly journal of the English Association.

At the bottom of the Housmans' garden was Laurence's wooden study, known as the Elbow Room or as the Sin Against the Holy Ghost. Here he was oblivious to the noise of Clemence's vacuum cleaner which he christened Pentecost – it filled the house with a mighty rushing wind. Outside the Elbow Room, over afternoon tea, the young Reg would revel in Laurence's intellectual glamour. He wrote years later that he was 'the kindliest critic and best friend a man could wish for. At the age of 90, he could still laugh like a schoolboy. He brought laughter into religion, religion into politics'. Laurence searched hard for a religion in which he could feel at home. The established churches' approval of war was the final straw between himself and any form of orthodox Christianity. The Quakers spoke most to his condition, in them was 'a sort of spiritual liberty lacking in the Church of England and in Rome'. He came to believe that people truly follow the will of God if they bear the fruits of the Spirit: love, joy, gentleness, peace, long-suffering, mercy and endurance. One of his Roman Catholic friends, very devout but surprisingly blasé on worldly matters (over the moral laxity of a relative in India, she was quite sure that 'our Lady would make allowances for the climate') nevertheless had a block about the Jews. Said Laurence: 'My dear, I do wish you would sometimes remember that Christ himself was a Jew'. Said she, undeflected, 'Only on his Mother's side!'

Such stories Reg would relish, and when Laurence reminisced about the great literary figures of the past, he would listen spellbound. There was Oscar Wilde, for instance. Wilde had praised a story of Laurence's in the *Universal Review* which resulted in a warm acquaintanceship, Wilde assuring him that 'your soul has beautiful curves and colours'. After Wilde's disgrace and his exile to France, Laurence met with George Bernard Shaw and Frank Harris in London's Café Royal. They instructed him to discover Wilde's whereabouts in Paris and to pay his rent, a mission he fulfilled on several occasions. Wilde told him that if anyone asked, he was to say that Wilde was beginning to write again but 'in my heart – that chamber of dead echoes – I know that I never shall'. Laurence rated Wilde 'incomparably the most accomplished talker I have ever met. What I admired most was the quiet uncomplaining courage with which he accepted an ostracism against which, in his lifetime, there could be no appeal'.

☆     ☆     ☆

Hitching himself to the star of Laurence Housman was Reg's most rewarding experience since Stanley King-Beer. He made himself useful, too. When Laurence asked him to join the cast for the Glastonbury Festival, the rollicking life of an actor suddenly seemed an exciting prospect. The Festival was Laurence's baby though he worked in conjunction with the founder, the composer Rutland Boughton. The players were mainly amateurs, strengthened by a few professionals. Gwen Ffrangon Davies had performed at the Festival in a previous year, and a continuing feature was the inclusion of dramatic readings by distinguished authors. One year, John Drinkwater was to read his play on Oliver Cromwell but he had brought the wrong manuscript. Nothing daunted, he read instead his narrative poem 'The Old Mill', a new version of the story of Paolo and Francesca in which the old mill is struck by lightning, falls and buries the lovers in its ruins. As the reading finished and the applause died down, an aged clergyman rose solemnly from his seat: 'In the name of Jesus Christ, I protest against this glorification of fornication and adultery.' Drinkwater froze: 'Who is in charge of this meeting?' Rutland Boughton ran up to the platform, urging Drinkwater to respond to the challenge. Said Drinkwater to the audience: 'I don't think this is the proper place and occasion for a debate on morals. . . . Whatever else may be thought about their story, I think most of you will agree that those two unhappy lovers were to be pitied. But you will notice that in my story there was one important character which had *no* pity for them, and that was' – looking straight at the clergyman – 'The Old Mill!' Loud applause, and off.

43

Reg played a number of small parts at Glastonbury with the soon-to-be-famous Frederick Woodhouse, Vivienne Bennett and Maurice Evans. Acting was fun but off-stage camaraderie was better. He lodged with his cousin, Roger Clark, rehearsing on the verandah of his house in Street where the company would gather for meals, to wash up and to sing folk songs. This was the Festival's last year. Some of the actors went on tour in the autumn, and at Christmas, appeared in London in a modern dress production of Laurence's *Bethlehem*, which had once been refused a license because it dared to depict the Holy Family. The play, with Herod as a toff and Salome as a vamp, was a flop, and the Festival company disbanded.

Reg was at a loose end. The thought of plodding along as a schoolmaster in another murky outpost was anathema, besides, he longed to stay in Glastonbury. Glastonbury stimulated his imagination by the richness of its legend and history and the nostalgic smell of its peat fires. 'I believe that one's memory for scents', he wrote in *My Life and Crimes*, 'is something that begins at an earlier point than other memories and is more tenacious. In my case this memory is older than anything in my conscious mind and it stirs me yet more deeply than the smell of ships and harbours, of rain after drought or mouldering autumn leaves, of farmyards or tarred wooden huts or even the polish used on my grandmother's floorboards.'

He was in luck. His father arranged a job for him with the family firm of Clark, Son and Morland, in a factory near the vanished fulling mill of the Abbots of Glastonbury. From the cottage he shared with the factory's caretaker, he could watch the Tor wreathed in silver mists, like an island in the sky – Malory's holy city of Sarras. The four hills – Wyrral, Tor, Chalice and Edmund's – were his El Dorado, but work in the factory kept his feet on the ground. He started by putting in eight and a half hours a day trimming sheepskin rugs, shears in one hand, metal comb in the other. His colleagues were convivial enough, expecting that, as Bryant's son, he was aiming for the managerial heights, 'though God knows there was no fear of that'. After learning about the classification of skins, he became a less than competent assistant to the assistant of a departmental head. One of his regular duties was to send back faulty workmanship to the benches. His popularity was not increased; if the thunderous looks of the women on piece-work were intended to mortify him, it was all too obvious that they had succeeded. A spark of comfort was offered by Harry, the future managing director of the business, who made no attempt to hide his own shortcomings. Harry would waver between Catholicism and atheism, sometimes in the middle of an argument. He was hoping for a son so that he could call him Julian Apostate Stokes, but the Lord, reigning absolute, destined him to four daughters only.

Pursuing the grail of Experience, Reg took to the road as chauffeur to the firm's ageing representative, and that was when he wrecked the company Armstrong. Certain that a driver in a side-road was giving him right of way, he accelerated just as the smaller car nosed forward, shooting it into a ditch. Reg was accused of being a danger to the public. The case came up at Cheltenham where the other driver's honesty was found to be shaky. Vaunting above truth his desire to collect insurance money, he tried to incriminate Reg for speeding. His downfall was in granting far too short a period of time between first seeing the Armstrong and the ultimate crash, and his evidence was discredited. In Glastonbury, Reg was greeted by cousin Amy Morland: 'I'm so glad to see you, Weginald, we all thought you'd be sent to pwison'. The elderly representative probably wished that he had. Immured within the disciplines of his profession, he had complained about Reg's uncommercial behaviour and, not least, about his flashy clothes.

Reg and Ben Vincent boasted that they were the first young men, other than labourers, to wear corduroy trousers. 'We decided one day', said Ben, 'that they were so sensible, we went round trying to find a tailor who would make us some. The Quaker tailor, John Gosse, laughed at us and we had quite a job to find one who didn't, and at last we were measured up and then the tailor asked us about straps below the knees! He explained that everyone who wore cords had these to prevent the rats running up the legs, but we had them made the normal size for gentleman's wear. In a surprisingly short time, considerable numbers of young bourgeois were going about in cords, and then we went over to cord jackets. Very posh.' After Ben had organised a peace exhibition, Reg wrote a poem for him, which began:

> About Ben Vincent, may his tribe increase,
> Awoke one night from a sweet dream of PEACE
> And saw, cross-legged, upon the bedroom floor
> An angel writing in a book of WAR.
> 'What writest thou?' asked Ben with some effrontery.
> 'The names of them as loves their king and country.'
> 'Then put me down', said quickly comrade Ben,
> 'As one who only loves his fellow men.'

Reg himself, while not embracing the whole human race at this point, undoubtedly loved the Housmans who provided him with a retreat from Clark, Son and Morland. He was also susceptible to feminine allurements, falling prey to artful girls with whom he formed imprudent connections. His heart was broken by more than one *chère adorable*, in fact, he was emotionally bleeding to death and self-respect was rapidly waning. It was

45

now the spring of 1929 and, to save further embarrassment, he expressed his willingness to resign from the firm. The sales manager, his sympathetic feelings overpowering his discretion, magnanimously suggested sending him to the London office where he could continue to work until he made other plans. He gratefully accepted. Weary of footling his life away and seeking relief from the pangs of despised love, he was ready for 'something really preposterous'.

And it happened that very spring. His Woodbrooke tutor, Horace Alexander, turned up one weekend and lightened his darkness. Horace was an old India Hand and had written his first book on the country, *Indian Ferment*. Reg walked with him on Street Hill, part of the long ridge south-west of the Vale of Avalon. He confided that he was disastrous in business and in love, his judgement was enfeebled, his hold on life was slack and to carry on as he was would be to fare worse. Horace listened, nodded, and then said suddenly, 'Why don't you go to India?' He might as well have said Hell or Timbuktu. 'Where should I go in India?' 'To Gandhi's ashram.' 'What do you mean – you can't just go to a place like that.' 'But that's just what you can do.' 'And what happens then?' 'Oh, you leave that to Gandhi. He'll find a use for you all right if you could fit into the life there. And I think you would. Go, and leave the future to work itself out.'

So there it was – present griefs diverted at a stroke; a unique opportunity, a chance in a million, and just in the nick of time. The only problem was money. In the London office, after visiting customers in the City, he sat with his father for a heart-to-heart. Bryant had insisted on Reg having shares in the business, even transferring some of his own; Reg was to pay him at a fixed rate of interest and, in due course, to repay the precise value of the shares at the time of transfer. The value of Clark, Son and Morland Ordinaries had risen appreciably, Bryant told him, 'and you are richer by £200. The money is yours, not mine, but,' he added gravely, 'had the shares fallen, I should have expected you to pay me the same sum'. Reg knew, of course, that Bryant expected no such thing.

He was on air. He got himself engaged to Richenda Payne, an attractive young woman of good Quaker stock. He spent a holiday in the Norwegian mountains with Horace Alexander and other old Woodbrooke friends. He had the windfall of £200 and, on his return from Norway, a letter of invitation, received through Horace Alexander. The letter was signed 'M. K. Gandhi'.

# CHAPTER IV

# English Youth in Indian Revolt

'THE EAST BEGINS WHERE MEN WEAR THEIR SHIRTS outside their trousers', he was told. As his ship docked at Port Said, there was no doubt that the East was where he was. Roused by a bewitching mixture of romance, politics, escapism and curiosity, the 24 year old Reg was on his way to the ashram of Mahatma Gandhi at Sabarmati near the town of Ahmedabad, a night's journey to the north of Bombay. He was already studying Indian economic and social history – which he was to continue for another seven years – and he was determined to make amends, so far as one person could do so, for all the degradation that Indians had suffered at the hands of the British.

Within an hour of his arrival, a CID man was keeping tabs on him. Europeans were extremely rare in Indian ashrams but at Sabarmati there was also Mirabehn (Madeleine Slade), daughter of a British admiral, who was now like a daughter to Gandhi and who often fell ill when separated from him. The ashram, Reg found, was half farm, half monastery. He was captivated by its primitive simplicity, that in the very centre of India's political life he was able to slip thousands of years behind the 20th century. 'I think', he wrote in a journal letter of October 1929, 'that it is perhaps the Mahatma's secret – he works his reforms by appealing to the reactionary who is so strong in every one of us'. The interminable chanting of prayers he could never fully appreciate nor did he welcome over-earnest questions concerning God or Civilisation.

Gandhi was away on a speaking tour. He wrote to Reg on coarse handmade paper, giving advice about health and nutrition, asking him 'to get the meaning of the verses and hymns at prayer time', and to correspond with him regularly, stating freely his impressions. Without Gandhi, Reg felt that he was looking at Hamlet minus the Prince of Denmark. A hundred times a day he heard mention of 'Bapu' (Dad), 'Mahatmaji' or 'Gandhiji';

any argument could be clinched by quoting him. He knew that Gandhi claimed neither holiness nor a striving to be holy yet some of his rather bogus followers insisted on raising him to the level of sainthood; their deportment reminded Reg of Parson Gorick's words, 'Gravity is a mysterious carriage of the body to conceal a defect of the mind'. A few months earlier, Gandhi had experimented in existing on unfired food. Like many other people who try to live more healthily, he became ill, as did most of his imitators. 'One, however, seemed to thrive on the treatment', wrote Reg, 'and is still sticking to it. But if you talk to this man you will find that nothing is farther from his mind than health – or so he says. To him the whole affair is a kind of mortification of the flesh and his object is the "realisation" of God through the suppression of the natural man. He was most contemptuous of my suggestion that God was at least as much "realised" by those who accepted life as by those who rejected it. It seemed to me that any gilt left on *his* gingerbread disappeared when I heard him engaged in a loud and angry argument in which he was maintaining that as he ate no cooked food he ought not to have put in the hour's work for the kitchen that everyone is supposed to give'. Another man had fasted for 55 days but during his delirium would cheat and solicit food, adding, 'Don't let Mahatmaji know'. Reg had a craving for coffee and nicotine which was fair enough, he reckoned, as he was not a holy man and his plain living had little to do with high thinking.

At the ashram, he rose at 4 am, hurrying to the prayer ground with a hurricane lamp. Between 5 am and 6 am he bathed, dressed and cleaned his room, a square stone cell with two shelves, two cupboards and a rough bedstead. Before breakfast, he helped to cut up vegetables, then, at 7 am, worked outdoors for three and a half hours, hacking at the compacted earth. The communal midday meal at 10.50 am consisted of rice, unleavened bread, boiled vegetables and pulses, after which he learned ginning, carding, spinning and weaving at the technical school, breaking for lessons in Sanskrit and Hindustani or a lecture on the Khadi (or Khaddar) movement, the effort to build up the hand-spun and hand-woven cotton industry as a decentralised village craft. At 4.30 pm, he swam in the river with the children and at 5.40 pm, ate an evening meal, followed by Hindi study, another prayer session and finally, bedtime at 8 pm. The regimen was rugged and his sprightly nature was ignited, but his companions were liable to be dour. He was soon to discover, to his delight, that Gandhi was quite otherwise. Verrier Elwin, champion of the Indian jungle people, and a friend of Reg's, once visited Gandhi with a high-caste Indian lady. She was disinclined to offer Elwin hospitality in her home for reasons of caste which she would not own up to. She said instead that she had no spare room.

Gandhi, seeing through her, suggested the verandah. 'But what about his bath?' asked the lady. 'He doesn't bath', said Gandhi, enjoying himself. 'And the toilet – – – ?' 'Oh, Verrier sublimates everything', was Bapu's rejoinder.

The ashram community was roughly divided into four categories. Firstly, there were the members of the ashram including its permanent staff who had taken vows of celibacy and poverty. Secondly came the students, mostly young men from every class who were taught the whole science of spinning and weaving, from the construction of machines to the economics of the Khadi movement. They then worked in centres in their own districts, supplying cotton to the spinners and yarn to the weavers, the products being sold again without a middleman's profits. The immediate object of the movement was to relieve poverty and unemployment. Indians believed that Britain held India primarily for the good of Britain's own trade. The British government, which was opposed to the movement, had fostered the industry of Britain and especially the cloth trade of Lancashire at the expense of India. The Indian politicians argued that by destroying British commercial interests in India they would destroy her political interests, and Khadi was part of a general boycott of foreign goods which would hit Britain hardest. It was Gandhi's wish that everyone should spin, if only for half an hour a day, and by this plan he hoped to unite all classes and castes through a common cause and a common occupation. Thirdly, there were the children at Gandhi's model school. One of his charges against the British government was that its system of education was an attempt to Anglicise the nation; English language and literature had ousted Hindi and Sanskrit and the teaching of history was political propaganda. Fourthly, there were the guests, such as Reg, who worked and ate with the members and students and accepted the discipline of the ashram.

A leading personality among the guests was the politician Shitla Sahai. Reg recorded one of his adventures: 'A few years ago, a small gang of terrorists held up a train in the Central Provinces and made off with some bullion after shooting one of the passengers who refused to obey their orders. In the course of time, arrests were made, and among the arrested was Shitla. He was kept three months in prison without trial and only released in the end as a result of repeated protests from influential friends. During this time, the treatment he received was worse than anything I have heard of in the treatment of criminals or political prisoners, though he was supposed to be awaiting trial. At one time he was kept in solitary confinement under disgusting conditions and repeatedly urged to confess his crime. He was half-starved and brutally treated. When he was at last released, he naturally wished to stand his trial so as to vindicate himself, but instead of being released on bail he was released under a Public Safety Act by which the government delay proceedings when the 'Public Interest' is endangered, withholding power to re-arrest at any time on the old charge. Another man I know who was here was released after some trumped-up charge under the same act – it is very convenient, and enables the government to arrest these men at any moment. In Bengal, men have been lying in prison for years without trial'.

☆    ☆    ☆

Gandhi now returned to Sabarmati. Reg was making a carpet in the weaving shed when somebody behind him laughed. He turned around and Gandhi said, 'Well, stranger'. Reg confessed: 'I was quite prepared for the lack of "distinction" in the old man's face. I was *not* prepared for anything quite so typical of the minister's gallery in one of our own Friends Meetings. Such a dear old man, with his bald pate and spectacles, beaky nose and birdlike lips, with his benign but somewhat toothless smile, I have seen perched at the head of many a silent gathering, and when he spoke there was the same mixture of sense and sobriety and shrewd but economical humour. But of that other thing that gives him power over people and draws them like a magnet from all parts of the country just to look at him, I could see no trace. It cannot be his intellect, for though his common sense is acute he is anything but a genius. I suspect it is the simplest and rarest of things – his absolute sincerity'. It did not surprise him that 'Bapu plunged immediately into a catechism regarding my health and constitution, coupled with a homily on dietetics. His mind switches rapidly from big schemes to small details. At Sabarmati, his time was divided between affairs of political importance, the management of the ashram, guests, and his spinning wheel'. Reg called him old, though he was only 60. 'He shows the vitality of a young man in his untiring industry, but he always looks at least 70 and is waited on hand and foot like an aged invalid – it is all a strange mixture. On Wednesday, Bapu gave me half an hour to talk over my plans. I thought we should be by ourselves, but there were four other people in the room and several more crowding round the open doors in a way that would be considered disgustingly bad manners in England. It was known that this half an hour had been allotted to me, so everyone else kept silence – I "had the floor". But to leave us alone would never have occurred to them; they stood round to listen to the conversation. If this is a fair example of the way the East treats a Mahatma, I no longer wonder at the way Jesus was continually escaping up a mountain or into a boat.'

Reg saw that Gandhi had none of 'the coy, evasive, mincing puritanism of the last hundred years'. He also noticed that he never put on an act. When he was arrested in 1930, the government surrounded him with armed police and he was given a few minutes to do or say anything he chose, a splendid opportunity for the grand gesture. His only comment was: 'Thank you very much; I think I'll clean my teeth'. His attention to detail, while under extreme pressure of work, was outstanding. He sent a note to Reg expressing his anxiety that two American guests visiting the ashram 'should have the necessary creature comforts supplied to them so long as it is in our power to do so'.

Travelling with the Gandhi menage to Wardha ashram in the Central Provinces, Reg witnessed the full extent of the people's adoration of their hero. Gandhi would speak to them on the curse of untouchability, the need for Hindu-Moslem brotherhood, the Khadi movement, women's rights, and, encompassing all, his dedication to non-violence. Recalling his time with Bapu, Reg wrote: 'I find myself impatient of those pygmy minds which have so often employed themselves in finding flaws and inconsistencies in his life. With Bapu I soon realised that nothing he did was unobserved. Can we wonder if we find imperfection when every momentary weakness or forgetfulness is faithfully placed upon record? Yet before the searchlight of history, this man stood unafraid, asking no mercy, exposing every weakness in himself to pitiless publicity. Not only so – for, in addition to the truth, he had to face a truly phenomenal barrage of misquotation and plain downright lying. There can scarcely have been another man living who could have stood up to all this and survived the ridicule of mankind. Even in 1929, when the rest of us could not imagine such a thing to be possible, Gandhiji knew the real danger towards which he was heading. An attempt was made by terrorists to blow up the Viceroy's train. Bapu said, 'I shall be the next one'. Then he added: 'Congress use me as their tool, and I am a willing tool; but the day will come when I shall say "no" and our ways will part. I have told them this and they all know it'.

At Nagpur, Reg lectured to 800 students, then addressed the people of Wardha on the causes of Western domination, its suicidal nature and the imminent collapse of Occidental civilisation unless it mended its ways. Next, he told an audience at Hinganghat what a lot of scallywags they were to shout 'Mahatma Gandhiji' when so few of them lifted a finger to help him or even wore Khaddar. As always, he marvelled at Indian 'kindness especially as political feeling against British rule was nearing its peak.

En route for Delhi, Gandhi invited the crowds to abandon their caps of foreign cloth and throw them into his carriage, and a bonfire was made of them at Itarsi station. He and three other leaders, including Motilal Nehru, father of Jawaharlal, had an interview at Delhi with the Viceroy, Lord Irwin, in a final attempt to reach agreement before Congress met on Christmas Day. Congress was adamant that if India was refused Dominion status, it would rally for independence. Lord Irwin imagined that minor adjustments to the constitution, not affecting its vested interests and overriding powers, would pass for the requested status, but the Congress leaders shook their heads. As a whole, the Labour government considered impudent the demand for such a status; Winston Churchill, for the Opposition, even objected to the Viceroy so much as negotiating with Gandhi.

Forward to Lahore, where Reg was a member of Gandhi's camp at the historic meeting of Congress. Volunteers policed the tents with military officiousness, one of them pointing to the achievements of Mussolini and the Fascists as a good example. 'Inkalab Zindabad' (Long Live Revolution) was the most popular cry, thanks to the government which had imprisoned several students for shouting it in the streets. Jawaharlal Nehru was elected President of the Congress. He, his father and Gandhi were nettled by a group of Bengalis and a 'right-wing' faction wanting further compromises with the government, but the Gandhi-Nehru combination won the day. At midnight, 1st January, 1930, the resolution for independence was carried, the national flag was hoisted, and the crowd sang the seditious 'Bande Mataram', an anthem that had provoked imprisonments and thrashings by the police.

☆       ☆       ☆

Reg toured on his own for a couple of months. He was appalled by the petty tyranny of the Indian administrative class in their dealings with their fellow countrymen, and the ferociousness with which they hated all who were true to the ideals they had themselves betrayed. In the United Provinces, half-starved villagers would make way for the English sahib, salaaming very low; time and again he would hear of the foul treatment meted out to them by both British and Indian officials. At Mailani, a memorial to Lala Lajpat Rai was unveiled. He, one of the last great moderate leaders, had been murdered by the police while trying to quieten a mob, the police resenting such encroachments on their privileges. As Reg's Indian friends remarked, if the boot had been on the other foot, and a British officer had received a death blow from the mob, the news would have been in every British newspaper. In few of the Christian missionaries he encountered did he see any sign of the unstinting devotion that characterised the Hindu leaders. The Christians had luxurious houses, wore expensive clothes and ate elaborate meals. When he told an American missionary that he had come from Lahore, she, reclining among the cushions on her couch, said loftily, 'That's where all those nationalist people met, wasn't it? I expect they'd like to bomb me'. Reg understood why Bapu always advised the missionaries to live in a hut with the peasants.

In a Sitapur courtroom Reg, at the invitation of the magistrate, Sucha Singh, attended the preliminary proceedings against a woman for alleged infanticide. 'In the middle of the proceedings, an English officer walked in, and going straight up to Sucha, began to talk to him about the fresh gun license he wanted for a new gun. Sucha referred him to the District Commissioner – he said he could issue new licenses. This would take a few days which didn't suit the officer. He wanted the gun now; couldn't some special arrangement be made on his behalf? This went on for about 10 minutes. Outside the court, I exploded with holy wrath, and asked Sucha why he didn't order the man out. Sucha smiled and shrugged his shoulders. "As a matter of fact", he said, "I really ought to have got up and offered him a chair". I thought he was jesting, but have since heard of two cases in which Indian magistrates have got into trouble for similar "offences". What is one to make of a regime in which an officer's gun license takes precedence over the majesty of the law and can hold up a whole court in the hearing of a capital charge?'

A pleasanter experience was spending two weeks in the North Kheri forests with M. D. Chaturnedi (nicknamed Chats) who became Inspector-General of Forests for the whole of India. Reg explored the jungle with him, on foot and on an elephant. (Ethel Mannin repeated the exercise nearly 20 years later.) After visiting Lucknow, he set off for Chapra, crossing the River Sarya on a crocodile hunt. Spanning the river was a railway bridge built on piles. When first constructed, the bridge had caused drastic changes in the course of the river which had swept away an entire village. Since this was not an isolated case, Reg began to realise that damage done to bridges and embankments was due to promoters' and investors' insensitiveness to the demands of nature, resulting in immediate profit for the few and disaster for the many.

Another important lesson was learned as he was driving with three forestry experts along a grassy track on the borders of India and Nepal. The forest on the Nepalese side was largely clear of undergrowth but on the Indian side, tangles of moist weeds were choking up every available space. In a journal letter to Quakers, dated 30th January, 1930, he wrote: 'Most significant of all was the size of the trees. The Indian ones were all big and there was the usual absence of saplings. On the Nepalese side were trees of all sizes, and the contrast was startling. The wet, thick weed is acid and chokes the seedlings. The burnt and sun-dried mould on the other side of the frontier is alkaline, and seedlings thrive on it. In Nepal they have no Forestry Department. Every 10 years or so, they wake up with a bump and say "By gum, it's time we cut down some more trees", and by this easy, inefficient way of doing things they keep a regular source of revenue with the minimum expense, while the forest cooperates with natural regeneration.

What irony! British Efficiency, with the best intentions in the world, has been spending Indian money by the thousand – in ruining Indian forests! And now the Wise Men go to Nepal to learn inefficiency, and take photos of real trees growing under natural conditions, to show their colleagues in highly technical magazines! To me it is a parable of British Rule. Just as the experts from Europe, obsessed by their pines and resinous trees, applied the fatal fire-protection methods to the sal forests of India, so our complicated and expensive legal system has destroyed the village panchayat.'

An alien education was wrecking Indian culture. British commercialism was ravaging the delicate mechanism of successful village industries. Irrigation systems were silted up and useless. 'For the most part', stormed Reg, 'it is just an unpardonable waste, or worse, of the revenues of a starving country. After this, you may call me, if you like, an extremist. Personally I cannot see the object in understating a case for the pleasure of being called "moderate". I know Friends always like to see Truth in a bathing costume, because it's so shocking the other way, but I'm resolved to show them the real thing or nothing.'

At Santiniketan, he was introduced to Rabindranath Tagore who pointed to the perils of industrial civilisation and the futility of seeking escape in an artificial simplicity. He criticised the impiety of asceticism and spoke up for fulness of life, Reg wishing that some of his philosophy would pervade the citadels of Hinduism. On his arrival in Calcutta, he met J. H. Whitley, ex-Speaker of the House of Commons and leader of the Whitley Commission which was investigating labour conditions in India. Whitley told him about the few surviving panchayats (ancient village councils, also responsible for education) he had visited, giving him a clearer conception of a decentralised society. When he returned to England, Reg embodied his feelings on local self-government, with special reference to the history of the panchayats, in an article for *The Spectator*, finding that the bulk of the article was quoted in a vast footnote to a memorandum on Native Administration by the Governor of Tanganyika! The Governor believed that the same principles applied to the problems of Africa, that there, as in India, the idea of a local organisation which 'is always viewed as a representative body, and not as a body possessing inherent authority', was all too common.

Throughout his travels, Reg was continually attempting to sum up what he really thought of Gandhi, which, he conceded, was an act of 'sheer impertinence', but he hoped that the impression made by the Mahatma on a young Englishman, who was by no means uncritical, might possibly be of interest. He wrote that Gandhi 'is one of the few people I have ever met who understands that true toleration does not mean vacuity or sitting on the fence. His opinions are strong, and with some, notably those on sex and other sociological questions, I personally cannot agree. I look on him as I would a great Catholic saint, admiring wholeheartedly his character and spiritual power, whilst judging his views with complete detachment'. However, contrasting strangely with his 'complete detachment', he was soon writing: 'I see him, a pathetic and tragic figure, drawn by circumstances over which he has no control into a position from which there is no turning back. Other people's stupidity has produced the crisis, and the country looks to him to see it through. No one dreads this struggle more than he does; but he feels it has been forced upon the country and knows he is the only man who can hope for success, however dim the hope. No one will ever know what agony this decision has cost him. I no longer wonder at the devotion of the blind masses. Rather am I one of them'.

He wrote several articles, including one for *Political Quarterly*, explaining the nature of the coming conflict through the eyes of Congress, and then he posted a letter to Gandhi, asking if he could be of any immediate help. Gandhi replied: 'The real thing is likely to begin not before March. The ashram is your home to come to whenever you like'. The 'real thing' meant the Civil Disobedience Campaign. It was time to return to Sabarmati.

☆　　　☆　　　☆

Reg was perturbed on two counts. He anticipated the probability that, as a 'seditious' Englishman, the police and military would single him out for victimisation, and he was frustrated that he could do so little to correct the distortions being printed in the British newspapers. On the one hand, they were saying that Gandhi was a cipher, on the other, that he was the sole cause of 'disaffection'; Congress was said to represent only 'an infinitesimal minority', yet its decisions at Lahore won front-page coverage.

Gandhi told Reg that he had a job for him, if he was willing. He was writing a letter begging the British government, through Lord Irwin, to think again. As it gave a time limit, it became famous as 'Gandhi's Ultimatum', though it was couched in the most courteous terms, beginning with 'Dear Friend', and assuring the Viceroy that his object was 'no less than to convert the British people through non-violence. . . . I do not seek to harm your people. I want to serve them even as I want to serve my own'. 'This letter,' he ended, 'is not in any way intended as a threat, but is a simple and sacred duty peremptory on a civil register. Therefore I am having it specially delivered by a young English friend who believes in the Indian cause and is a full believer in non-violence and whom Providence seems to have sent to me, as it were, for the very purpose.' The letter, signed 'Your sincere friend, M. K. Gandhi', was dated Satyagraha Ashram, Sabarmati, 2nd March, 1930. Gandhi took pains to ascertain that Reg was in total agreement with the contents of the letter, the taking of which was symbolic of the fact that the struggle was not simply between the Indians and the British. Gandhi from India was using Reynolds from England as his courier. Indian and Englishman were as one. Let it be broadcast to the world.

Reg studied the contents minutely. 'Though I hold British rule in India to be a curse', wrote Gandhi, 'I do not, therefore, consider Englishmen in general to be worse than any other people . . . I have the privilege of claiming many Englishmen as dearest friends. Indeed, much that I have learnt of the evil of British rule is due to the writings of frank and courageous Englishmen.' He held that 'conversion of a nation that has, consciously or unconsciously, preyed upon another, far more numerous, far more ancient and no less cultured than itself, is worth any amount of risk'.

Gandhi enquired if he had any criticisms of the document. Reg said that he endorsed it wholeheartedly apart from one minor point. 'Well?' asked Bapu. 'There's a comma missing – here.' Bapu looked, nodded, and wrote in the comma, the comma that represented, Reg felt, 'the extent of my contribution to Indian history'.

The mission itself was a formal affair. Reg had been briefed to answer questions concerning the terms on which Gandhi would suspend the launching of Civil Disobedience. He arrived at the Viceregal Lodge in Delhi, wearing khaddar shorts and a Gandhi cap, and after an hour and a half, handed the letter to Lord Irwin's Private Secretary. The young English courier now hit the headlines. He was notorious. He was Mystery Man incarnate. Many fictitious interviews were printed, British reporters going out of their way to hold him up to ridicule tinged with malice. The *Bristol Evening News* obtained the simple facts from his sister Dorothy, but seemed surprised that he was indeed a real person: 'The *Evening News* is able to state that "Reg Reynolds", who conveyed to the Viceroy of India the "ultimatum" with regard to civil disobedience, and whose identity has in some quarters been a mystery, is none other than a member of a well-known Somerset family – a Quaker not yet 25 years old. Reginald Reynolds – the name is actually not assumed – was born at Glastonbury, and is a great-grandson of the late Mr James Clark, one of the founders of the firm of C. and J. Clark, shoe manufacturers of Street'. The *Daily Express* ran the story, 'Manicure Set in Stone Cell. English Youth in Indian Revolt', claiming erroneously and sarcastically, that he was manicuring his fingernails as the reporter approached him. His fiancée, Richenda Payne, said the *Daily News*, had no idea when he would return to England and his mother revealed to the same paper that she was very worried about his exploits.

Reg was unprepared for the torrent of publicity. He welcomed it as a boost to his morale after long years of drifting. He also acknowledged that he had done nothing to merit the adulation of the Indian crowds, which was soon to be his.

☆  ☆  ☆

The people of Sabarmati prepared for the 'Salt March' but Reg, to his great disappointment, was asked to stay behind and assist in producing Gandhi's weekly journal, *Young India*. The ashram was invaded by huge crowds and countless reporters, press photographers and film cameramen. On 11th March, 10,000 were gathered; the next day, an even larger number formed, Reg helping to clear a path for them as they trekked towards the sea. Gone with Bapu were most of his best friends, leaving him lonely and with an almost unbearable sense of anti-climax. He filled the time by working on *Young India*, studying, writing for the press, sweeping up and amusing the children. Ever an object of curiosity, he was belaboured by endless questions such as 'Do you prefer Eastern or Western civilisation?' When he said, 'Western – decidedly', he then had the wearisome task of reassuring his crestfallen Indian interrogators that his preference in no way diminished his veneration for Gandhi or his impassioned belief that India should be independent.

'You I hold to be a gift from God for the advancement of the work', wrote Gandhi to Reg. A few weeks later, though, he was writing in a different vein. The *Bombay Chronicle* had published an offensive article on Bapu and Reg, in a fury, had shot off a reply to the paper. 'I did not like your writing', admonished Gandhi. 'It is not *ahimsa* (non-violence). When you have a good cause, never descend to personalities. What I want to emphasise is not merely bad manners. It is the underlying violence that worries me.' Bapu recommended that Reg apologise to the writer of the article but only if he perceived the necessity of doing so. Reg, still seething, was not sure if he did. Then, on reflection, and swallowing his pride, he acquiesced, stressing that he was sending his letter at Gandhi's request so that the Bombay writer who had flung such vitriol would appreciate the Mahatma's magnanimity. 'That is what I might have expected from Gandhi', was the chastened writer's response. Thus, thanks to Bapu, were two hotheads becalmed.

Gandhi and the Salt Marchers were aiming for the Gujerat coast where salt fields were left by crystallisation after the subsiding of floods. The illegal collection of the salt began on 6th April, and that morning Reg, as one of 7,000 people at a meeting near Ahmedabad, read an extract from the Magnificat. The 'salt satyaraha' spread to all parts of India and selected leaders were arrested. Reg – now something of a legend – was asked to investigate reports of police brutality at Dholera, a small coastal town. Close by, he saw the salt deposits which, on government orders, had been spoiled by mixing them with earth. Some of the law breakers, clutching their salt, were caught, but on this occasion – unlike many others – the police behaved with restraint, a fact Reg noted in an article for *Young India*. Early in May, the military authorities at Peshawar conducted a massacre. The bravery shown by unarmed peasants under fire was enheartening, as was the refusal of a Hindu regiment to mow down their Moslem fellow-countrymen.

Although Gandhi wanted him to take over the editorship of *Young India*, Reg's health was deteriorating and he was far from keen. Besides, he felt that the right place to be was back in England, counteracting the propaganda of the press and the Labour government. In the local jail, he bade farewell to some of his dearest friends. Then came news from Dholera that 30,000 people had defied the salt laws on one day and that women had been savagely beaten with lathis and rifles. Horrors galore were on the increase. Sickened by the viciousness of officialdom and its equivocating minions, there was not a shadow of doubt in Reg's mind: the British must be told the truth about what was happening in their name, and straight from the horse's mouth. He left Sabarmati on 25th May, the ashramites making the sacred mark on his forehead and garlanding him with yarn spun by Bapu on his march. Would he speak to them, they asked. No – he was too full up for that. Words stuck in his throat. If he had tried to express his gratitude to them, he would have broken down. They stood in the road as the tonga rattled him round the first bend. They were singing 'Bande Mataram'. The anthem rang in his ears as he struggled to regain his composure.

He wrote his last journal letter: 'I certainly came out here with a strong belief in the right of every nation to self-determination. But at the same time I then fully believed that Britain was probably governing India to India's material advantage, even though I considered that a principle greater than that of material advantage was being violated. I believed in British justice, I believed that the national movement (though right in principle) was not yet really a popular movement, and I believed in the good faith of the Labour government. In all these things I have ceased to believe; and if today I say that I believe India to be badly governed, if I say that "British justice" in India is a farce, that the masses are opposed to our rule, and that the Labour government has shown a despicable lack of courage, no one can say that I fitted the facts to pre-conceived theories. All these statements represent changes of mind in a mind that does not change easily. They are based on what I saw and heard, and in the case of the Labour government the conviction was forced upon me against the strongest feelings of party loyalty. It was a bitter and cruel disillusionment'.

☆     ☆     ☆

His adventures in India were not quite over. He was joining a group of Congress volunteers on their way to Dharasana, a prime trouble spot, before moving on to Bombay. The night train they had boarded suddenly screeched to a halt and the police swooped down on his companions. No laws had been broken, so why the furore? The volunteers demanded to see a warrant. The spokesman for the police turned purple. 'Warrant?' he shouted. 'What are you talking about? I'm the DSP.' More officials rushed into the carriage and hurled the volunteers on to the platform; Reg they left alone, satisfied that he was heading for Bombay. The volunteers were rounded up as an 'illegal assembly' in spite of the fact that the law was only empowered to arrest people if they refused to disperse.

Reg jumped out of the train and asked the DSP if it was true that he was arresting the occupants of the carriage as an illegal assembly. It was. 'Then you will have to arrest me, too', said Reg. 'Very well, then, I will!' The volunteers cheered, and the DSP thought again, barking: 'Are you going to Dharasana?' Reg replied that where he was going had nothing to do with the question. 'Did you get into this carriage by accident then?' 'I don't generally get into a carriage by accident.' A higher ranking officer intervened: 'Mr Reynolds can go', he announced. Reg was fit to burst: 'It's the biggest damned farce I've seen!' 'What!' shrieked the DSP. 'Who are you calling a damned farce?' 'I'm not calling anybody anything. I'm only saying that this business is a damnable farce!' The police led away his companions and he returned to the carriage, muttering 'So much for trying to get myself arrested!' (Authority was stricter with some: an American missionary was expelled from India for giving Reg a night's lodging and inviting his friends to meet him.)

Crowds were thronging every station to greet the volunteers and Reg patiently explained what had befallen them. He had not been able to obtain a ticket at the start of the journey, and before he could find his money to pay the train inspector, an Indian stranger who was sharing his carriage paid the fare for him. He resented as an insult Reg's attempt to repay him, saying that it was the least he could do to show his appreciation of a friend of his country.

The day he arrived in Bombay, the police had fired on a party of Moslems. Congress workers and high-caste Hindus cared for the wounded and for a number of passive resisters sent from Dharasana, whom the police had injured. The following day, he spoke to 15,000 Moslem nationalists and was persuaded by an American film crew to record a 'message' for the camera.

Gandhi, in prison at Poona, had asked to see him, but when he reached there, the prison superintendent forbade the meeting. Reg found out later that Gandhi, as a protest against this mean and arbitrary ruling, had told the superintendent that his 'allowed' visitors should also be turned away. For 48 hours, Reg fasted in a stone cell at the Christa Seva Sangha, one of the few Christian (High Anglican) ashrams. Then he relaxed in Madras, and at Madura, was rescued from pressmen by a small band of missionaries who, like Reg, wore Khaddar. One of them, a Scot, the police attacked with lathis on account of his hand-spun clothing. They drenched him with green water and arrested him on fabricated charges only to drop the prosecution for lack of incriminating evidence.

Reg was now homeward bound, crossing the seas between India and Ceylon. At Talainannar Pier, Customs scrutinised his books, papers and private letters, and removed his passport which, he was told, he could recover at the CID office in Colombo. Here, he was besieged by hero-worshipping immigrant Indians who insisted that he address a public meeting on the political situation in India. In vain did he plead the state of his health and the fact that a speech on this subject would be considered seditious by the government, surely leading to his arrest, an arrest he could now do without as his passage to Tilbury was firmly booked. Remonstrate as he might, the speech was delivered. 'My visit to Ceylon had been rumoured for some days,' he wrote. 'My host told me that the political apathy of the island was disgraceful and that he relied on me to make a stir. I hope he is satisfied with the stir I created. There were more flags and garlands and cheering crowds and everything I have come to hate.' How near he was to arrest was established on the *Orsova* by a British police officer. It was the booked passage that had saved him; if the authorities had interfered with his travelling arrangements, they would have handed him more publicity and a possible martyrdom. En voyage, he settled down to writing articles and planning an Indian freedom campaign on his own home ground.

# CHAPTER V

# The Political Firebrand

*Ballad of Love and Revolution*

As I set out for – where was it? – by proud St Pancras' Station
My mind was in a ferment with a froth of speculation;
I couldn't find the platform and I nearly missed the train
For I surely lost my luggage when I lost my heart again.

I thought the railway carriage was a coach to Gretna Green –
The waiter murmured 'Coffee?' and I answered 'Hippocrene'.
And when the fat inspector came my business to demand
Said I: 'I follow Flecker on the road to Samarkand'.

My solemn fellow-passengers looked curiously on
As I breathed upon the window-pane and wrote these words thereon:
'Love is the railway of our lives whose lines fulfil their function
Without the least necessity for changing at the junction.'

The people stared at me in awe, then one by one they rose
And slunk along the corridor these matters to disclose;
And when those men in bowler hats had left my fancy free
I said, 'They have abandoned hope who have abandoned me!'

The cord of many penalties I've always itched to pull
I severed with my pocket-knife because my heart was full,
And when the guard came blustering round to ask me what I meant
I said a sign and symbol was the whole of my intent –

I said: 'Oh paunched and pompous one, I did this thing to show
That it were better we should stop than we should go so slow
And life is severed at a stroke, but joins in knots of steel
*And Love is stronger than the State, and breaks the common weal.*

61

And all these foolish passengers, so haughty and so proud,
They understood not, for their heads are bloody, but unbowed –
For them the tumbrils roll afar, for them the Red Dawn breaks,
But first, O man, this little bird within my heart awakes,
*Yea, Love, O foolish passengers, in my own heart awakes.*

(unpublished poem)

Until freedom for India was achieved, it remained Reg's principal concern. His gruelling campaign was laden with obstacles, and embarking on love affairs with ladies of accommodating inclinations did nothing to lessen the rigour. Richenda Payne had jilted him. She married the Quaker Peter Scott, and developed an interest in medieval economic history and contemporary religious thought, ending her days as one of the Society of Friends' most formidable lights, sharp-witted and self-mocking.

In the autumn of 1930, Reg and a few of his friends founded a small organisation in aid of 'The Cause'. He lobbied MPs, lectured, wrote pamphlets, sat on two committees concerned with Indian affairs, and polished the ire of retired military men and former members of the Indian Civil Service by debating with them in the correspondence columns of newspapers and journals. His opportunities were limited 'because repression in India was being carried out by a Labour government which defended its policies with Tory arguments. I attacked the Labour government with more ferocity than I should have considered necessary in dealing with Conservatives, because it added to the crime of imperialism the nauseating vice of hypocrisy, exploiting sentimental clichés about the working class to win votes at home and ignoring the most elementary rights of its Indian and colonial subjects'.

Unwilling to join the Independent Labour Party as it was still affiliated to the Labour Party, he nevertheless published his articles in the ILP's weekly *New Leader* and its monthly *Socialist Review*. He also addressed ILP branch meetings and the less orthodox Labour gatherings in addition to independent groups sponsored by religious bodies. He was bitterly disappointed that Indian freedom was not a cause that, in 1930, the majority of Quakers wholeheartedly endorsed. They were, according to him, 'tinged to the last with fatal timidity. I had hoped to undertake my crusade through the Society, feeling confident of Quaker support because of the essential affinity between the professions of the Society and the practices of Gandhi, who represented – in my eyes – the fulfilment of a philosophy of life and conduct which the Quakers had failed, on the whole, to carry to its logical conclusion. While the Quaker support, which I had tried to invoke, was not available, the ILP support (with regard to which I was at first very doubtful) was forced on me. For at least 10 years this affected my life, because it forced me to think in terms of political groups and parties where I would sooner have approached the Indian and other problems on a different level'.

As an antidote to the Society's rejection, he treasured his correspondence with Romain Rolland, extracts from which were published in Rolland's journals. Rolland had written to him with warmth and kindness, confirming Reg's conviction 'as to the personal value of any struggle for freedom – the value of those who participate in it. Reflected glory is only ridiculous when we mistake it for our own; for to live and work with greater and better people than oneself is (to my mind) a legitimate source of happiness and even of pride – the pride of having been accepted into their company'.

To Gandhi he wrote seldom, only if he felt justified in taking up his time. But when, to his amazement, he heard of the signing of the 'Gandhi-Irwin Pact' and the suspension of Civil Disobedience; when, to his distress, he heard that Gandhi was to travel to the Round Table Conference, he who had stood out for 'a Square Table Conference, where we know where we are' – such a conference as would have resulted from the execution of his original terms in 1929 – that Bapu should now agree to attend the conference on any other terms, was too much to bear. Reg wrote to him as soon as negotiations were reopened with the government; as one of the few promoters of the Congress case in Britain, he wanted to know just what it was up to. Gandhi thanked him for his 'long, frank and emphatic letter', said that he completely disagreed with his opinions, and asked him to remember 'that Satyagraha is a method of carrying conviction and of converting by an appeal to reason and to the sympathetic chord in human beings. It relies upon the ultimate good in every human being'. Fine, but this was no explanation, Reg thought, for the change of policy. Gandhi encouraged him to criticise further – 'if this does not satisfy you, do by all means strive with me. You are entitled to do so' – signing off with words of praise for the way in which he was presenting the Indian case in Britain.

He took up the challenge. Part of his second long letter was published in *Young India* together with Gandhi's reply. Gandhi believed in publicising views in conflict with his own, even those of a 25 year old whose support or opposition could have made no difference to him. 'Don't therefore desert or give me up', he wrote from Sabarmati, and then, Reg having confided in him about his private life which had temporarily gone awry, 'But I am more concerned with your personal references than with your spirited attack. If you are not at peace with yourself there, will you not come here? You know that the ashram is your second home.' The letter moved Reg deeply and when he went to India for the second time in 1949, he had the feeling of keeping an appointment.

Lecturing in public was becoming second nature to him. Discarding notes, he spoke straight from the heart, sometimes swaying the mood of the audience with all the ardour of a political firebrand. At other times, he was not so fortunate. In an economically deprived area, following his usual practice of only using facts that could be substantiated, he painted a picture of Indian gloom and despondency. He lifted the lid on repressions, killings, and the lawless 'ordinances' placing life, liberty and property at the mercy of a few individuals, the cocks of the dunghill. His outburst was met with a frozen silence, after which a troubled old man rose from his seat: 'I just don't believe such things are done by any government of which George Lansbury is a member'. As the audience applauded, Reg knew that the old man was speaking for millions of decent English people bamboozled by the wiles of the powerful. So as not to augment their almost tangible incredulity, Reg forbore to tell his listeners that Lansbury was in full possession of the information he had given them and that he had defaulted as a pacifist, a weakness he later, and with some courage, admitted.

☆　　☆　　☆

From the minute he set foot in Britain again, Reg was regarded as a seditious character, and he soon perfected the art of spotting detectives. Leaving his parents' house at Coulsdon for the railway station, he noticed two tall men conspicuously loitering at the bottom of the road. 'Treat policemen nicely,' he remembered Gandhi saying. (A certain police inspector always approached Gandhi direct instead of lurking behind a tree. 'Don't you know', said the inspector's angry superintendent, 'that everyone who comes into contact with that man goes over to his side?') Acting on Gandhian principles, therefore, but eager for fun, Reg waited until the last minute before boarding the London train. The two tall men dashed into a neighbouring carriage while Reg stepped back on to the platform, his pursuers leaping from the train as it started to move. Later, he saw one of the men on the underground: 'you *are* rather obvious, aren't you?' The detective mumbled that he was only doing his duty. 'That's all right', grinned Reg, 'now just take out your notebook. I'll give you a list of all the places I intend to visit and how long I'll be at each place.' Word got around that the odd young boffin was amenable and harmless, to the extent that new detectives came up to him and introduced themselves. A high point of absurdity was reached when Reg had a two-hour appointment with Labour

64

MPs at the House of Commons. As the two hours stretched into three, he excused himself to reassure his friends from Scotland Yard that he had not tried to escape. After this incident, questions were asked. What was the Labour Home Secretary afraid of? Reynolds had been *invited* to the House of Commons, so for what purpose was he being watched, and watched by police under the orders of the Labour government? What could be more ridiculous? The situation was right out of comic opera, especially as Reg was enjoying the most courteous relationship with the forces of law and order.

The relationship paid off handsomely. Gandhi was due to arrive for the Round Table Conference. Realising that weighty officials were planning to monopolise him, Reg was determined that he should not be overlooked, that he should be on the quay when the ship docked at Folkestone. To this end, he appealed to Scotland Yard. No matter, they said, that he lacked a quayside pass, the burly Sergeant Evans would meet him there and answer any challenge from the Folkestone police.

'I want to see Gandhi before anyone else sees him', said Reg to the officer-in-charge as the ship dropped anchor. Said the officer: 'There's a big list of people who want to see him. The best I can do is put your name down on the list, then I'll show it to Gandhi, and *he'll* decide which people he sees and in what order'. That was good enough for Reg. Surely Bapu would forsake velvet acquaintance for a homespun friend, a loyal comrade. 'Reginald Reynolds first', came the call. Of course! On fortune's cap he was the very button! He ran up the gangway and greeted his mentor.

And that was not the last of Sergeant Evans: he was among those assigned to 'guard' the Mahatma during his stay in London. The Round Table Conference had ended in deadlock but Sir Samuel Hoare, the Secretary of State for India, was moved to ask his intransigent foe if there was anything he could do for him before he left for home and another term of imprisonment. Yes, there was; Bapu would like Sergeant Evans and another favoured 'guard' to accompany him as far as Italy. The request was granted, and the two detectives each received a watch from Gandhi for their trouble. Twenty years on, and Sergeant Evans popped up again. A Quaker friend of Reg's was conversing on a train with an elderly stranger who displayed a surprising knowledge of Gandhi and of Reg Reynolds. 'I don't mind telling you', said the tough Welsh ex-cop, 'when I heard of Gandhi's death I sat down and cried like a child.' Reg phoned him up for a session of reminiscence. He was particularly tickled to learn how Mirabehn (Madeleine Slade), at Oxford, had pleaded with the Sergeant in a posture of ashes and mourning. She had committed the crime of forgetting Bapu's goat's milk – what could he do to help? He promised to contact the Chief

Constable of the County, no less, with the result that the Flying Squad, on motorbikes, were despatched north, south, east and west in an attempt to find somewhere that stocked the blessed potion. After his last journey with Gandhi, Evans had returned to Scotland Yard. 'Well, Evans, I suppose you're glad *that's* over!' said his chief. 'No, sir', was the doleful reply. 'I'm not. I feel like a mother that's lost her child.'

Reg was desolate as Gandhi's train pulled out of London. This was the last time he would see him. From the table of the conference, Bapu had written to him that the economic concessions he had offered should not be attributed to lack of firmness, as Reg had accused, but to sympathy for the British people whose economic problems he had taken to heart. Three more letters, full of affection and gratitude, were sent from Yeravda Jail – 'You do not know how glad we all are when we hear from you'. Reg was humbled and embarrassed. His efforts for The Cause were puny, he believed, yet he knew that Gandhi was incapable of flattery.

Absorption in Leftist politics – 'I could see Trotskyists at some distance to my right' – meant that he gradually drifted away from Gandhian philosophy. 'Why don't you tell me something about yourself?' asked Gandhi in a postcard in 1935. Reg was reticent, preferring not to discuss his hardening political line. However, in 1938, for personal reasons, he risked Bapu's disappointment by divulging his deepest feelings. 'My heart goes out to you', Bapu wrote back. 'What does it matter that on some things we don't see eye to eye? The fact that you are a seeker of truth is enough to sustain the bond between us.' The letter was addressed to 'Angada', a name Reg had acquired in India. Angada, residing in Ceylon, was a white ape employed by the gods when opening hostilities against the powers of darkness.

By the end of the war, Reg had returned to a more positive pacifism and was ready, in 1945, to relearn 'from the greatest man of our time what he could teach me about the sources of spiritual vision, of human understanding, of tolerance and charity'. Few could follow Gandhi all the way. 'Many people could have expressed themselves more clearly but nobody could have offered a clearer testimony in terms of life. The great thing that one came in the end to appreciate about Mohandas Gandhi was that what a man is and does matters so much more than what he says. Most of us can talk better than we live; but Gandhiji, who said many fine and memorable things, overshadowed his own words. If they were sometimes hard to understand, his life was a beacon set upon a hill; its meaning could not be mistaken.'

☆　　☆　　☆

Six months after his return from India – where he had worked for his keep and nearly always travelled third class – Reg's money had dwindled alarmingly. 'Here's a cheque', said a bountiful relative from Street. 'You're doing useful things but you can't live on air.'

Weakened by headaches and insomnia, his health was seriously threatened. Nervous strain and relentless controversy were producing rising blood pressure. To avert a total breakdown, he searched for a job in the country. He longed for rural pursuits and manual labour, and landed up in The Colony, 'a school for criminals', a farm-training centre for men and boys, many sent by probation officers, from the Poor Law institutions.

With the title of 'Brother', he was put in charge of a squad of youths, supervising their surly endeavours at felling, quarrying, fencing and roadmaking. The Colony was Dickensian – icy cubicles of bedrooms, incontinent bladders, inadequate food, uncontrollable tempers, and floggings by the 'Christian' superintendent. Reg did his best to draw out the boys' finer qualities. If they refused to buckle down, 'You can do what you like', he would say, 'but if my squad won't pull their weight it shows I'm no good as a so-called Brother. In that case, I get the sack. I'll be sorry to say goodbye to you, but there are better jobs to be had than this one. I wonder who you'll get. Somebody like Darky, perhaps (whom they all hated). Oh, well, just please yourselves', a ploy which usually worked.

One inmate, a particularly disruptive influence, challenged him to a fight. 'I'm not going to fight you', said the agitated Brother, trying to bring his eyebrows back into neutral, 'but if you don't go down those stairs I'll take you down. It's up to you.' The boy stood still. Reg gripped him and jostled with him. They tripped down the steep steps and rolled over each other, the boy squealing with pain. As Reg released him, the boy nursed his bruises. 'I'm sorry about your arm. If you'd stopped struggling, you wouldn't be hurt. But if you've not had enough I'll take you down another flight.' To his enormous relief, the boy submitted and skulked off to his dormitory. For a would-be disciple of Gandhi, the whole episode was a shameful memory. But it had its ironical side, for from then on, he was saved from a similar situation. He was now hailed as a near wrencher-off of limbs and when he was approached about his prowess at wrestling, an art of which he was innocent, he would shrug and smile enigmatically. His health improved, he concluded his six months at The Colony with a spate of haymaking, harvesting and threshing, and he left a hero, rescuing one of the boys from drowning in a treacherous current.

☆     ☆     ☆

67

Dinah Stock was a lecturer and local organiser of the Workers Educational Association. She was also the assistant editor of the *Socialist Review*, working from a tottering office in Bloomsbury where burning coals from the hearth would roll down the sloping floorboards. Reg came to write his political articles here, and was introduced to a ripe assortment of poets and rebels in the secondhand bookshop of the red-bearded Charlie Lahr.

In the winter months, Dinah arranged for him to teach at the WEA evening sessions in Sussex, which would give him enough to live on and a little to spare for tobacco. Based at Lewes, and riding to his classes on a pushbike, he gained a host of new friends whose homes were always open to the lecturing nomad. There was a disabled ex-ironfounder with a bottomless lust for knowledge, there was a dentist who disliked being paid for his services, there were people who loved the arts 'without pretentiousness or the ghastly self-consciousness of "culture"'. And there was the Reverend James Whittle and Betty, his wife, of the Peacehaven vicarage.

Whittle stories were among Reg's favourites. Jimmie, a frequent pub crawler and handy with his fists, was urged by his Bishop to serve as an army chaplain during the first world war, Jimmie emerging from the slaughter a convinced, if bellicose, pacifist. In Africa, he stood for a mayoralty, and his rival, resorting to bribery, hissed through his teeth: 'Do you want a new wing for your bloody church?' 'Not', said Jimmie, 'if you're bloody well paying for it'. 'Then do you want your bloody church burnt down?' Both the church and the Whittles' house were subjected to an arson attack, Jimmie won the election, and his rival became his trusted churchwarden. In Newfoundland, where he was chaplain to a lumber camp, he heard that a couple of prostitutes were on their way to entertain the men. 'I made a rapid calculation. Two into 2,000. There would be hell let loose.' The ladies of expendable virtue he decided to disorientate, and boarded their train when it rumbled into the nearest station, the pockets of his overcoat bulging with bottles of the strongest liquor. By the time the boozy sirens had awoken from their stupor, Jimmie had long since departed and the duped Delilahs were 200 miles past their destination. As the vicar of All Saints, Peckham, Jimmie visited Reg at Bart's Hospital in 1940. One afternoon he entered the ward the worse for wear. 'In God's name, Jimmie', said Reg, 'what on earth have you been up to?' 'Is it so obvious?' 'Smelt you from the door.' 'Reg, I've been drinking with the whole Australian army'. Years before, an Australian army sergeant had stolen some of Jimmie's belongings. Jimmie and Betty had taken him in hand, even inviting him to live with them. Now, the grateful culprit, stumbling by chance upon his old redeemer, insisted on celebrating their reunion. The snag was, he was accompanied by 14 of his mates. It required of Jimmie small perception to discern that each hearty soldier would proffer him a drink, and he, too much of a gentleman to raise a scruple and murder joy, and so as not to rupture the unique occasion, had willingly surrendered to insobriety.

In the years ahead, Reg shared his Whittle stories with Ethel Mannin who used some of the material in her novel *Lucifer and the Child* (1944): her Reverend Charles Drew is Jimmie to the life. The novel concerns Jenny Flower, a child from the London slums. At Lammastime, she meets a Dark Stranger with horns on his head but finds him in no way frightening. Jenny never weeps, and don't they say that a *witch* has no tears? Was she 'possessed'? Was the Dark Stranger Lucifer? Is everything which appears supernatural open to natural explanation?

The daughter of the Reverend Charles Drew (Jimmie Whittle) befriends young Jenny and protects her. The Drew/Whittle vicarage resembles a circus in a state of uproar. Charles/Jimmie, a little steamroller of a man, given over to righteous anger and booming rhetoric, is a voice in the wilderness, appealing to the few with what he calls 'spiritual vertebrae', the few who may survive the Gadarene descent. Contemptuous of 'nice' parsons, money-grubbers, kow-towers and yes-men, he doesn't care a jot what people think of him. Weddings and christenings make him cry, funerals sometimes make him laugh. His children adore him and he loves them so much that it incenses him to contemplate the matter. He says his kids haven't a brain between them but he's proud of them to the point of apoplexy.

For the WEA, Reg lectured once a week at Heath Common, Storrington, and it was here that he started making notes for a book with the tentative title of *Ajax, or the Future of Water Closets*; when he came to write *Cleanliness and Godliness* a decade later, he was glad that those grubby scraps of paper had been hoarded. With the termination of the WEA classes, he stayed on at Storrington, monitoring events in India, writing political journalism, dancing at all-night parties and bathing in the moonlight. Heath Common attracted a galaxy of fantastic personalities such as the 'King of Poland' to whom Reg and his cronies gave their support. His 'Highness' had been prosecuted for 'publishing' obscene literature when in fact he had only shown it to a printer who, unluckily for him, turned out to be a Baptist. Freed from prison, the 'King' went to live next door to the vicarage at Thakeham where he would taunt the vicar by setting up an altar to Apollo and by practising pagan rites. There was fun to be had from the 'King' but Reg soon wearied of his snobbery and his regal pretensions.

☆     ☆     ☆

Too inflammatory for Quaker taste and a nuisance to the politicians, Reg was also frowned on by most of the pacifist organisations, including the No More War Movement (NMWM). The members of the NMWM, formed in 1921 as a direct successor to the No-Conscription Fellowship, were committed to anti-capitalism as well as to anti-militarism. They refused to participate in any warlike activity 'whether by bearing arms, making or handling munitions, voluntarily subscribing to war loans, or using my labour for the purpose of setting others free for war service'. They pledged to 'strive for the removal of all causes of war and to work for the establishment of a new social order based on cooperation for the common good'. The Movement's attitude to Gandhi Reg found contemptible though for some members at least the Mahatma's methods of non-violence, which had produced specific changes for the better in a world that a grasping commercialism was threatening to engulf, were a shining symbol of the right way forward.

The organising secretary of the NMWM was Walter Ayles, a Labour MP who, according to Reg, was exploiting the Movement, shaping it to bolster up official Labour policy. Reg no longer paid subscriptions to the Movement but he read its publications. In one of them, he noticed that a new General Secretary was being sought. With little hope, and almost as a lark, the 27 year old outsider applied for the post. He suggested, in his application, that he could save the cowardly and treacherous NMWM or smash it in the attempt. He enclosed a cutting from *Young India* in which Gandhi had praised him warmly, and a testimonial from Laurence Housman who wrote that Reg had influenced him more than he had influenced Reg, especially with regard to India. At the same time, Laurence sent him a private letter telling him that he was arrogant, intransigent, cantankerous and altogether a pain in the neck, but he was very fond of him anyway. Shortly afterwards, Laurence wrote to Canon (Dick) Sheppard about him: 'That poor lamb does give himself a hard time of it by his bitter judgements on people who disagree with him. Me he forgives each time; so I guess I'm good for him, just for that reason. But his greatest good comes from his love and reverence for Gandhi and Father (Verrier) Elwin; he allows them to have mistaken notions without imputing it to them for unrighteousness and betrayal of a sacred cause. But talk to him about Ramsay (MacDonald), Hoare or even Irwin, and you need patience and charity to put up with him'.

Reg was not to know that, in the depths of the economic depression, the NMWM was undergoing what was probably the most unsavoury internal wrangling in the history of the British peace movement. There was the Walter Ayles faction who believed that war might be abolished through the

70

services of institutions like the League of Nations, and there was Wilfred Wellock and his band of revolutionaries who saw that unless inequitable social structures at home and violent imperialist programmes abroad were totally transformed, wars would inevitably rage. Again and again, Joseph Southall would move a resolution urging all MPs who voted for war credits to resign from the Movement and each time Ayles and his followers would accuse him of 'heresy-hunting'. Ayles and Lucy Cox, as the Movement's organisers, were both paid a salary and when Ayles lost his parliamentary seat in the 1931 election, he was suspected of 'serenading' important donors for his own benefit and to the detriment of the cause he was employed to promote. Then a fire broke out in the house of a member entrusted with documents relating to the Movement's financial affairs. Had it been started deliberately? For a pacifist society, this was irony run riot, this was the ultimate sickener. Ayles and Cox resigned and were replaced, as an interim measure, by Muriel Nichol, daughter of an ILP MP and Ben Parkin, a young taciturn schoolmaster with Marxist leanings.

Reg's application was well-timed. The Movement was riven, in no mood for soft soap. 'The war against war is also the war against hunger and oppression', was his view, and 'War had to be tackled at its roots and our first task concerned oppression and ways of ending it – by means other than bloodshed – which pointed directly at Gandhi.'

In August 1932, he accepted an invitation to attend the World Anti-War Congress at Amsterdam. The NMWM had sent Ben Parkin as their representative and it was Ben who, returning from Holland, determined that Reg should be interviewed for the vacant position. In the Movement's office in Doughty Street, Reg sat facing the chairman, Wilfred Wellock. The committee members, ranged down a long table, gazed at the stubborn young beanpole, mindful of his reputation for flamboyance and frivolity. Reg, ever courteous, but militant, continued his criticism of the Movement's past policies. Half of the committee thought him A Good Thing, half were dubious. Wellock appealed to the office secretary – 'You see how it is, Mabel. This committee can't make up its mind between two applicants. One is a safe man. The other, Reg Reynolds, well. . . . Whichever we choose, *you* will have to work with him. I think your views at this point would be helpful'. The dark-haired Mabel Eyles was decisive. That evening, Reg received a telephone call. He had won out over 250 contestants. The job was his. The committee, recoiling from the hazards of careerism and bourgeois pacifism, had voted for idealism, zeal, dedication – and controversy.

# CHAPTER VI

# Comrade, O Comrade!

WITHIN A FEW DAYS, Reg was at his desk in Doughty Street, taking the Movement down the revolutionary socialist road. What was the non-violent answer to military might? How to reconcile pacifism with stemming the rise of the Fascists? How to get pacifists into the thick of the struggle? How to push for the Gandhian tactics that some British pacifists found too aggressive? Were socialism and pacifism becoming incompatible?

As these and other dilemmas hammered at his brain, the most urgent task before him was to rescue the Movement financially. Appointed at £300 a year to succeed Ayles and Cox, both of whom had earned more, he recommended that his salary be cut in half, and £150 was indeed all that he lived on. As a personal saving, he rented one of the office rooms, installing a camp bed so that he could work through the night or recover after a strenuous speaking tour.

His friends – West End layabouts, journalists, actors – he would meet at Cheffie's Restaurant. Cheffie, tall, middle-aged, Romany-looking, called all her customers by their Christian names or, more expressively, 'Hulloh, you little bastard, where've you been all this time?' Her generosity was legendary; down-and-outs were fed at her expense. When Reg confessed his poverty and assured her that he would pay for his meals in a couple of days, she followed him into the street – 'Is it true, Reg, that you really haven't *any* money at all?' 'Just about enough for a bus fare.' 'You'd better take this', she said, shoving a ten shilling note into his hand, 'You may want food somewhere else and you can't rely on tick where you aren't known.'

Cheffie was a true blue Tory with a belief in keeping foreigners in their place but Reg loved her and for years visited her regularly. Anyone in trouble with the law would be certain of her help. She had provided an alibi for a young tearaway, and, on behalf of some regular – or rather, irregular – customers, she had secretly burned their incriminating documents while

72

the CID searched her premises. During the war, after bomb raids, she would don her tin hat and 'collect' frightened people from the street, plying them with food and drink. Then one night, her restaurant was blown to smithereens and Cheffie the brave, the lawless, the coarse-grained comforter, Cheffie the 'gypsy' was no more.

☆   ☆   ☆

Disgusted by the Communists' manipulation of the Amsterdam Congress and forced to endure their personal libels and slanders, Reg nevertheless cooperated with them – uneasily – as they were obviously sincere in their hatred of imperialism. Besides, he had now joined the Independent Labour Party, which had split from the official Labour Party, and formed a volatile working relationship with the Third International. Some members of the NMWM were still trying to nail the Movement to the mast of the old Labour Party, others wanted politics to be swept under the carpet. Reg's radical policies had led to a serious loss of membership but at least the Movement was living within its means and allowing him to plead for Indian independence and colonial freedom. Laurence Housman's private letter struck home. 'Yes, Laurence is right', he told himself. 'I must watch it, cool down. For a man who believes in loving his enemies, I'm quarrelling with a hell of a lot of my friends.' He was in danger of sinking beneath his workload – the levering of public opinion; helping to organise public meetings, demonstrations, educational forums and summer schools; lecturing and arguing till he was hoarse; writing and distributing lengthy bulletins on topics of the day, such as 'The Truth About the Palestine Riots' in which he compared the debates reported in *Hansard* with politicians' 'offstage' remarks.

Assailed as he was by the very people with whom he was collaborating, those who remember him at this time all agree that he maintained an inspiring personal integrity, an incorruptibility which, far from bringing him to a more 'moderate' standpoint, drove him further to the Left. He tussled with the Left's favourite stalwarts. Bertrand Russell – a subscriber to his news-sheet *Indian Events* – appeared to damn Gandhi outright because he was 'religious'. Put off, when he met him, by Russell's intellectual snobbery and his boyish desire to shock, he fared no better, at first, with C. E. M. Joad. Joad, he felt, was diabolically brilliant at the cost of truth. He said to him, after a conference at which they had clashed: 'Were you by any chance educated at one of the seminaries of the Society of Jesus?' 'No, why do you athk?' lisped Joad. 'You seem to have an unusual mastery of the art of casuistry.' 'Well, I thtudied logic at Oxford, and that'th more or leth the thame thing.' 'You're so damned clever', Reg railed, 'and now you have the satisfaction of having confused and bewildered people less smart than yourself.' 'My dear man', reasoned Joad, with the sweetest of smiles, 'I wath only tothing up the ball for your *ecthellent* batting.' Wrote Reg: 'He defeated me every time that way. His compliments may have been insincere, but the difference in our years and status made them gracious; and his good temper under provocation always made me feel that, however wrong-headed he was, he was the better man. It would have been so easy to treat me as an ill-mannered cub, but he met me always on the level, with compliments and courtesy. He lived what he preached better than I did.' Reg's poor opinion of himself was consolidated when, turning up at Hyde Park Corner for the arrival of the Hunger Marchers, he vaulted over a railing as the mounted police charged into the throng, piercing his hand on a spike and leaving a scar that reminded him for months of his cowardice. True Gandhians, he reflected, would not have panicked; they would have stood their ground and taken what was coming to them.

As petitions and letters of political dissent flowed from his pen, 'the same old crowd' would endorse them by adding their signatures. It was H. W. Nevinson, staunch defender of justice and freedom, who referred to such signatories as 'the stage army of the good – the people who opposed the Boer War, the people who stood up for Ireland, the people who backed women's suffrage and all the unpopular causes'. That phrase, 'the stage army of the good', caused Reg 'immeasurable joy. We could laugh at ourselves, seeing our small cast as the people who trotted on and off stage with a few halberds, trying to persuade the audience that we were a great army. But in the past the Stage Army had generally won in the end and would win again.' For Nevinson himself, Reg had respect and affection. It was said of him that he, more than any other man, had helped British women in the last round of their struggle to win the vote, and it was not cheap service, for he gave up a lucrative job on a Fleet Street newspaper in protest against its policy on the issue.

In the early and mid 1930s, pacifism was fashionable; cult figures Aldous Huxley and Gerald Heard were associated with the trend. The emaciated Heard, long-bearded and red nosed, invited Reg to his sumptuous flat where the 'Wellsian supermind' outlined a plan in which Huxley was also interested: self-training pacifist groups were to be established for a spiritual crusade. To Ethel Mannin, this sounded intolerably high falutin', but Reg, not a one to miss out, attended several meetings of one of the groups before realising that he was too essentially down-to-earth for such a transcendental crew. He wrote to Heard that he felt a misfit and Heard replied kindly: 'Probably you are right but in a way

I'm sorry. It was perhaps early to be sure of doubts as to value. What is more important, though, is to ask you, if you find what you are looking for, to let us know'. Reg thought these words were worthy of Gandhi himself.

Gerald Heard's *The Source of Civilisation* seemed to Reg to offer historical and anthropological justification for his own philosophy, and he was similarly taken with his friend Jawaharlal Nehru's *Glimpses of World History*. He wrote of both books in an article, 'What Can We Learn From History?', published in *No More War*, the journal of the NMWM:

'Nehru is a socialist – the leader of young India. He is a cosmopolitan, educated in England and widely travelled. But of late he has spent much of his time in Indian jails, as is the custom with the really great men of that country – and one that is likely to last as long as British Rule. In jail Jawaharlal was by no means idle. He read deeply and wrote charming letters to his daughter, and it is of these letters that a remarkable book has been composed – the first History of the World from an Asiatic standpoint.

The Indian leader has no illusions as to the possibility of an 'unbiased' approach to history. Every historian has his bias, and the least dangerous is the one who knows it, admits it and does not attempt to conceal it behind a cloak of impartiality. When we read of the Magna Carta we come across such a comment as this:

> It is interesting to think that this rule laid down in England over 700 years ago does not apply to India even in 1932 under British Rule. Today, one individual, the Viceroy, has power to issue Ordinances, framing laws and depriving people of their liberty and their property.

Gerald Heard, in *The Source of Civilisation*, attempts to examine the inner cause of many historical phenomena, dwelling rather specially upon the rise and fall of empires; for he notes that 'their periodic collapse is perhaps the most striking fact throughout history'. It is difficult, he says, to explain why violence should fail at the moment of success. Various theories have been put forward – those of Spengler, for example, and Gibbon's 'decline of martial virtues', the latter based on 'the heroic saga made to justify aggressive violence. The militarist argument really runs that the only way to preserve martial virtues is always to be fighting and always losing'.

*The Source of Civilisation* is as much as anything an attempt to discover a philosophy of history in the answer to this question. All social animals can 'scrap' and are liable to quarrel individually. But the man who values, and is valued by, the community will not make a real breach of the peace. He will not let his passion become homicidal:

> ·Man, then, naturally loses his temper off and on, but the rest of the community as naturally damps him down. What is not natural is for the

whole community not merely to lose its temper but in cold blood and with infinite arrangement to get ready to destroy another community.

This development Heard explains from its growth of unnatural relationships between individuals, 'so strained that the sword is drawn to "keep order", when men are already so divided from their fellows that they allow an armed master to keep and enforce division and inequality'. The community then becomes 'in the hands of the chief executioner . . . a weapon to divide, scatter and despoil other communities'.

Anthropological evidence is called in to prove that primitive man is not naturally war-like. The myth of the ferocious savage is an invention of 'those 19th-century evolutionists, who, we now see, were making a case to their conscience and squaring it with their comfort'. What, in plain fact, was 'Natural Selection' but an attempt to justify biologically the ruthless competition of the Victorian age and the cynical doctrine of *laisser faire*?

But the primitive in contact with 'civilisation' absorbs first whatever has most greatly impressed him. Is this culture, philosophy, religion or science? Is it even the physical benefits which civilisation can bestow upon him? No, his first contact with civilised man commonly results in his realising new powers of destruction, stirring up fear and the desire for self-defence. From civilisation he learns little but the art of war, which he uses first to defend himself and then to attack his barbarian neighbours and civilisation itself.

Empires fall for the same reason that they rise – because material 'progress' in the specialised field of war has so far outstripped moral development. They have 'no Sanction but the Sword' though they make frantic attempts to stabilise themselves upon a basis of religion and tradition ('prescriptive right').

In modern times new sanctions are sought. George Fox rediscovers 'the spirit which taketh away the occasion for all wars'. Woolman, following the same tradition, sought passionately for social justice because 'he could no longer consider himself a distinct and separate person'. But Quakerism, too, becomes corrupted by wealth, which is the most highly developed form of power.

The statesmen's way to peace Heard likens to the edicts of the Middle Ages when Days of Truce were promulgated 'like early closing days, to give the harassed workers a little rest', and bishops (who were specifically forbidden to use the sword) wielded a mace.

If we fail, it would appear that we have already too far infected the primitive races with the virus of social violence to hope for a new and better civilisation arising out of primitive society when ours has destroyed itself. Nevertheless there is still time and even a way out for our civilisation through an active pacifism'.

☆     ☆     ☆

In 1933, the NMWM moved from Doughty Street to two attic rooms in Long Acre. The Covent Garden porters would automatically send the odd-looking or extravagantly dressed stranger straight up the stairs to Reg; one was a Hungarian anarchist with a dark swirling cloak and a broad-brimmed black hat. The Movement's volunteers were kept busy folding circulars and stamping envelopes. They included Freda Jackson, then a student actress, and the amazing James Saunders, known to the office as 'Daddy'. For 40 years, Jim had been a manual labourer in Australia, New Zealand and America. He delighted Reg with his fabulous stories of gold-digging days, conjuring out of his weird stock of fantasies the character of Captain Barry who, in his rowing boat, encountered an enormous whale:

> So I said to the three other men who were with me, 'Now get your sheath knife ready and hang on to your oars whatever you do'. The whale came at us, and with one crack of his tail he smashed the boat to matchwood, leaving us struggling in the water. But we stuck to our oars and in a few minutes he had swallowed the four of us, oars and all. Then we slit two holes in each side with our sheath knives, put our oars out and *rowed* that whale into Port Chalmers.

Like Jimmie Whittle, 'Daddy' Saunders was a rumbustious raconteur, Reg's type of man. His 'almost Gargantuan humanity' was the perfect corrective to the blind fanaticism of some of the Communists with whom Reg was embattled.

Enticed to Paris, where the Anti-War Movement – the Interamsterdam-national, as he called it – convened a Youth Conference, Reg, as one of the British delegation, fumed helplessly as his efforts to engender concrete decisions were quietly sabotaged. He could agree, though, with the Conference's description of the League of Nations as 'the Board of Directors of the great victorious imperialisms. It is an institution whose aim it is to maintain the blood-stained and dangerous peace which crowned the large-scale industrial and commercial operations of 1914-1918'. The Conference's Manifesto dismissed the policy of uniting 'democratic' states against dictatorships. This was 'the most up-to-date manoeuvre of democratic imperialism'. In reality it meant 'huge business wars, a flag covering a vast commercial bargaining, which will end as always in the crushing of the masses'. But within a year came the somersault. Russia joined what Lenin had termed the 'Thieves' Kitchen' at Geneva, and entered into an alliance with France. Communists everywhere were instructed to work for a 'Popular Front' with Social Democrats and radicals, 'the most up-to-date manoeuvre of democratic imperialism' of less than 12 months before. Attacks against French imperialism were suddenly regarded as a betrayal of Russia; French colonials in revolt were denounced as 'fascists'; and the repugnance felt by this Communist double-crossing soon spread to Britain where intellectuals like the West Indian George Padmore, who had formerly been a leading exponent of Communist policy in the colonies, were compelled to re-assess their position.

Through Padmore, Reg was drawn into a circle of West Indian Negroes living in London. One of the most dynamic was C. L. R. James, philosopher, independence leader and Trotskyist. In Ethel Mannin's novel *Comrade, O Comrade*, written in 1945, three Trotskyists visit Mary Thane, a character used by Ethel to express her own opinions. The chapter 'Trotskyists At Tea' was from the life: Ethel had invited C. L. R. James to her cottage and he arrived with two of his friends in tow. They greeted her briefly, then they continued a discussion begun hours earlier. 'Sugar?' she enquired. 'Thank you, sister.' Their talk was interminable – Popular Front / French workers / Stalinist bureaucracy. An hour later they left, Permanent Revolution / International Socialism / Collective Security – still on their lips. 'Goodbye', said Ethel, which was only the 12th word she was allowed to utter to her preoccupied guests. The satirical *Comrade, O Comrade* was dedicated to Reg 'who has shared with me so many comradely adventures, and survived without loss of sense of humour'. A lowdown on the Left, it was aimed at readers whose political sanity had been preserved intact in an ideology-ridden society. Ethel and Reg were closely acquainted with the thinly-disguised characters – the anarchists who, almost on principle, started their meetings late, regarding even a clock as a form of central government; the surrealist partygoer who stood beside a hip-bath containing a cello with a woollen muffler tied round its neck; the Trinidadian Negro in Trafalgar Square who announced to the crowd for the umpteenth time that Mary Thane's door was always open to black and white alike and that the little lady's name was a by-word throughout British Africa.

This turbulent desperado, Chris Jones, an ex merchant seaman, Reg loved as he loved Jimmie Whittle and Jim Saunders. An incident relating to Chris which he recalled with pleasure occurred at a conference of delegates convened by a Communist-controlled organisation in London. Reg had long since abandoned working with the CP, but, with a few friends, decided to attend this particular conference on imperialism and to expose the organisers. He was voted one of the nominees on the Standing Orders Committee which admitted a fraternal delegate from a French colony, flown over at his and his friends' urgent request and unknown to the organisers of the conference. When the French colonial delegate spoke, it was of course to inveigh against the French Popular Front Government and their Communist supporters. Some Communists began shouting him down and Jawaharlal Nehru, the chairman, had to call for order, 'but the disturbance was nothing to that which followed when I spoke myself. I returned to the French delegate's theme, and began to elaborate it, but before I'd been speaking for 60 seconds my attempts were inaudible. The words 'lies' and 'liar' were about all that could be heard until an immense voice boomed from the back of the hall.

"It's the truth. It's the truth that yuh can't stand!" And there stood Chris, like an avenging black angel.' Reg seized this brief opportunity 'to inform Nehru that the rowdies were not, as he might have supposed, fascists, but defenders of democracy and free speech. (In those days I scorned tact and still enjoyed platform tactics which many of my pacifist friends rightly deplored.) Soon Nehru was appealing for order again, but I was hitting hard and when – for the third or fourth time – the meeting got out of hand there was another boom from the back of the hall."Ah'm wid you, boy", roared Chris above the tumult. And that, I think – for I was trembling with a mixture of anger and fear – is the most tender and grateful memory I have of Chris Jones'.

Chris, his white wife and their mulberry-coloured children used to visit Reg and Ethel, 'providing us with some of the happiest memories of the war years', and they in turn would visit the Jones's, once for the christening party of a son. George Padmore and Ethel were godfather and godmother while Reg supplied one of the boy's Christian names. On Chris's death, Ethel became treasurer of a committee which raised enough money to clothe and educate the Jones's children until they were ready to pay their own way.

Life aboard the political carousel was sapping Reg's strength, and his blood pressure failed to stabilise when Esmond Romilly, Churchill's rebel nephew, crossed his path. The 15 year old Esmond, with whom he was in correspondence, had escaped from his public school which disapproved of his editing an anti-war magazine for schoolboys. Now he materialised in Reg's office, his disappearance front page news. Reg phoned the *Sunday Referee* – 'Esmond Romilly is with me. You may interview him on condition that you don't say where you met him or in whose company, and Esmond must approve what you write before it goes to press'. He found him a room in a friend's flat close to the boy's mother and father, the last place the police would search for him. The *Sunday Referee* interview appeared, accurately written and reassuring to Esmond's family. Refusing to return to his public school, Esmond spent a term at a co-educational progressive school and, in spite of Reg's warnings, consorted with Communists. He fought in the International Brigade, then was killed, as a member of the RAF, in a raid over Hamburg. In his autobiography, Esmond referred to Reg as 'Richard Routledge', such was his love of mystery and anonymity.

☆    ☆    ☆

The NMWM was facing another financial crisis, so for six months Reg became an unlikely letting agent for a block of luxury flats which had not yet been built. In the evenings, he worked for the Movement without pay, but as soon as political fear and anxiety swept across Europe, he was brought back to full-time employment at Long Acre.

It was in January 1935 that he first met Ethel Mannin, thanks largely to the young Walter Greenwood. Greenwood had sent Ethel his short stories which she suggested he weave into a novel; the result was *Love on the Dole*; thereafter he called her his 'fairy godmother'. When the play of *Love on the Dole*, written by Ronald Gow, was rehearsing, Ethel took Greenwood to an ILP dance. Light-headed with influenza, she almost cried off going, but as she had promised various Party comrades that she would be there, and so as not to disappoint Greenwood, she finally decided to make the effort. Dancing with Fenner Brockway, she caught sight of Reg. Brockway introduced them and they spoke for a few minutes before Ethel, increasingly feverish, left for home. Reg wrote to her in July, reminding her that they had met earlier in the year and asking if she would address an anti-war meeting he was organising. This she declined, feeling unequal to the occasion, but, yes, she *would* meet Reg again, though it had better be soon as she was leaving town to complete some work. Their love affair had begun.

The following year, the 70 year old Laurence Housman was jubilantly exclaiming, 'The Victorian age is over at last. In one week the Crystal Palace has been burned down, Edward has announced that he will marry Mrs Simpson and my plays on Queen Victoria are to be licensed'. The Lord Chamberlain had previously refused to license his collection of one-act plays, *Victoria Regina*, but, by the intervention of the short-reigning Edward VIII, the plays could now be produced in the West End. With simultaneous productions in Paris and New York, Laurence felt ashamed at the vast amounts of money he was earning – 'the government will seize much of the money in death duties and that fills me with horror because the government spends most of its money on war preparations'. His solution was to give the money away, to his relatives and to every good cause – one of which was Reg; Laurence said that he could use his Bayswater flat, rent free. Ethel and Reg shared many homosexual friends. 'Laurence was homosexual like his brother', wrote Ethel to the present writer, 'and it was a great embarrassment to Reg in the Bayswater flat when he was constantly being requested to absent himself at certain hours as Uncle Laurence had what he called a "matinee". It was also *tiresome* for Reg. And sometimes on the way out he would meet the participant partner in the "matinee" on the way in, and it gave him the creeps. As he once said to me, "intellectually one is sympathetic to homosexuals – and it's all right as you don't have to think what they actually *do*!" LH's "matinee" partners were all gross types – abhorrent to Reg'.

Lively times with Laurence and livelier ones with Ethel could not deflect him from the growing divisions within the NMWM. The newspapers were self-righteously proclaiming that Mussolini was murdering the Abyssinians and confiscating their land, conveniently ignoring the fact that the 'democracies' had adopted these self-same tactics in the interests of colonial expansion; and as for bombing natives, the British were already conducting a war against the Afridis. Then, in the summer of 1936, came the news of the Spanish Civil War. Given its socialism, where exactly did the NMWM stand? In Spain, the popular left wing was in danger of being torn apart by the weaponry of the military right. What role could pacifists play? Relief work, said some, what else? To others, like Reg, pacifism, alas, had no effective answer. His view was that 'the oppression of the subject classes and races is worse than war. What does death matter to those who have never been suffered to live? To support the Great Powers and call it peace is to sell justice to the highest bidder'. He and his colleagues took the line of the ILP, which was anti-Franco and also anti-Communist, centring their hopes in the 'POUM', the Workers' Party of Marxist Unity, the Spanish equivalent of the ILP, a Marxist party independent of the Communist Party, and linked to the Anarcho-Syndicalists. Reg admitted that he did not know what pacifism was; it did not exist for him. He campaigned to exempt civil wars from the Movement's pledge, and when the resolution was defeated, he and the staff at Long Acre resigned in protest. This was the final nail in the coffin of the NMWM. In 1937, the Movement merged with its young competitor, the Peace Pledge Union, regarded by Reg at that time with contempt because of its emotionalism, nebulous thinking and playing down of the necessity for social change in removing the causes of war.

He was out of a job. His Gandhian ideas had receded into the background. Very much in the foreground was his sweetheart, Ethel Mannin.

CHAPTER VII

# Lovely Ethel Mannin . . .

Bob Mannin, Ethel's father, left school aged 11 to hold the horses' heads as goods were delivered at John Barker's. For 40 years, he was a post office sorter, working six days a week except every other week when he worked seven. 'He always said the day he retired', wrote Ethel, 'he would spit on the doorstep of Mount Pleasant. I hope he did!' Ethel was born in 1900 (she was five years older than Reg) in Clapham, the eldest of three children. She started writing at the age of seven; in 1910, at the Crystal Palace, the Queen of Portugal presented her with a prize given by the RSPCA for an essay on cruelty to animals. As a young schoolgirl she was shy and introverted, 'a well-behaved little prig'. Intensely religious, she held services in the back yard and conversed long and passionately with God, but her sanctity evaporated when a communist teacher fostered her budding socialism.

She wrote incessantly – poetry, essays, stories – and all they could think of doing with the girl was to send her to commercial school and then, if she was lucky, she might obtain a decent position in an office. At 15, she was employed as a stenographer at Charles F. Higham Ltd, Charles Higham's advertising organisation. An artist in the firm – a New Zealander, an anarchist and a conscientious objector – advised her to read the works of Shaw, William Morris, Upton Sinclair and Kropotkin, and it was he who told Higham that she was wasting her talents doing shorthand and typing. Accordingly Higham, eager to Give Youth A Chance, set the ambitious 16 year old the task of running two business magazines. By the time she was 17, she was publishing her own articles and verses in one of Higham's monthly journals. She wrote all sorts of copy, for tyres, oil-engines, brown bread; she designed layouts, and still only 17, was made Associate Editor of the theatrical paper *The Pelican*. – 'Noel Coward and Esmé Wynne-Tyson came to offer me contributions. I explained (I was 18 then, Coward 19 and Esmé 20) that I couldn't pay for contributions, but if they liked to give me anything suitable I'd be very happy to publish it. Esmé explained to me about homosexuality, apropos of Coward. I didn't really understand about it; I just vaguely knew about something unspeakable in connection with Oscar Wilde. Esmé and Coward called each other Stoj and Poj; she explained that they were like brother and sister and that he had no feeling for women as such. All very bewildering to the young E. M. . . .'

In 1918, she disposed of her virginity to a teenaged soldier in a frozen field near Penrith and, soon after her 19th birthday, married a Lowland Scot, John Alexander Porteous, a copywriter at Higham's and 13 years her senior. Their daughter, Jean, was born, and they moved from furnished rooms in Strawberry Hill, Middlesex to a semi-detached house of their own at Merton Park with a resident maid and a cook general. She disliked quite intensely the memory of herself when young – 'I was brash and uppity, and quintessentially of my times'. She wrote women's page articles for the London and provincial press – 'How to Manage Baby', 'Ways with Rice', 'What to do with Last Winter's Coat' – and also churned out cheap novelettes with such sultry titles as *Bruised Wings* and *The Tinsel Eden*. Her first novel, *Martha* (a girl who loved not wisely but too well) was published when she was 22, followed by *Hunger of the Sea* (a story of fisher-folk in old Hastings) which had a charcoal-drawing jacket by Laura Knight and was recommended for the Femina Prize. Her third novel, *Sounding Brass*, a satire on the advertising world, caused a stir in Fleet Street, its sales enabling her to travel to America, accompanied by a woman magazine editor.

In New York, fuelled by drink, she found herself in strange company and in strange beds. In London, inspired by the *corps de ballet*, she changed her hairstyle to the severe centre parting which almost became her trademark; one photograph of her was sent to 40 newspapers. Highly sexed, she helped to ring the bells of freedom for the young intelligentsia. She was always recognised at first nights – 'Lovely Ethel Mannin, striking in black, with a huge pink ostrich feather fan. . . .' As more of her novels were published, she was hailed as a 'modern Georges Sand, but *so* much better looking, my dear' and denigrated as 'one of the novelists who go too far'. Realising that she was temperamentally incapable of making a success of her marriage, and opting for independence, she left her husband when she was 28, later acknowledging that she had been both selfish and irresponsible.

She bought Oak Cottage in Wimbledon. As a child she had passed this 'rabbit's house in *Alice in Wonderland*', dreaming that one day she might own it and, incredibly, the morning she went house-hunting, Oak Cottage came onto the market. She fell in love with a narcissistic young man who, overwhelmed by their affair, committed suicide. In 1930, her *succès de*

*Ethel – an editor in her teens, 'an oddly exotic painted child'. She was also a teenaged mother – ' I didn't keep my little one "nice". I never worked on the principle of "here's a child, let's bring it up", but "here's a child, for God's sake let's leave it alone"'.* (Confessions and Impressions, *1930*)

*Reg at Oak Cottage, the year before he married*

*Ethel was criticised – or hailed – as 'the most shocking of the modern young women'*
[PAUL TANQUERAY – COURTESY: JEAN FAULKS]

*scandale, Confessions and Impressions,* appeared. Considered daringly outspoken and morally shocking, it produced a crop of libel writs which, luckily for her, came to nothing; among the people featured in the book were Dr Norman Haire, the gynaecologist who fitted the Gräfenberg inter-uterine ring, Jacob Epstein, Paul Robeson, A. S. Neill, Radclyffe Hall and Bertrand Russell.

After the suicide she sobered up, and as the bitter, disillusioned and dangerous 1930s progressed, her social conscience was reawakened. She wrote for the ILP's *New Leader,* and joined the Party. Already she was looking back on her *Confessions* as dated and tedious. For four and a half years, she lived with the writer James Stern – 'every single year since we parted he has sent me a birthday card and on my birthday in 1976 he wrote me a very affectionate letter in which he said he was glad to have known me'. She wrote most of *Commonsense and the Child,* containing her radical ideas on child education and child psychology, and for which A. S. Neill wrote the preface, in Paris. From here, too, she wrote a weekly social gossip letter which some of her more ribald friends referred to as her French letter. Then on to Cologne, Munich, Vienna, Salzburg, Majorca; the start of her friendship with Red Emma Goldman, the Queen of the Anarchists; in 1934, she flew to Russia, and the following year, made an illegal and fourth-class journey to Samarkand. With the USSR she had a kind of love-hate relationship, wavering between admiration and mistrust.

She had now fallen in love with Reg and, under his influence, was involved in the African and Indian freedom campaigns. Through Reg she met Laurence Housman and Verrier Elwin and basked in their exuberance and gaiety. She introduced Verrier – who lived in the Indian jungle among the primitive Gonds on an uncompromising level of equality – to A. S. Neill of the avant-garde, international Summerhill 'free' school where Jean was a pupil. 'Like Neill with his children, Verrier was on the side of the Gonds, and again like Neill, he realised the importance of rooting out fear. Neill and Reg were allergic to each other. Neill told me once that he thought Reg was jealous of him because he, Neill, had known me before *he* did – which was bloody daft!' Ethel herself was not entirely simpatico with H. G. Wells. When she lunched with him, she, preaching social revolution, was irritated by his innate liberalism and by his neutrality over the Spanish civil war. The irritation was not all hers. Wells was less than thrilled with what he called her 'native tendency to uncritical enthusiasm', 'crude beliefs', and 'antics and poses'. He also believed, erroneously, that she had wished to 'click' with him.

☆　　☆　　☆

86

Secker and Warburg – C. L. R. James, George Padmore and Jomo Kenyatta were on their list – had commissioned Reg to write *White Sahibs in India*, published in 1937 but banned, of course, in India. Most of it was written from his office in Long Acre – 'and when I look now at its bulk and the terrifying phalanges of footnotes I still wonder how the work was completed whilst I was doing a full-time job'. Jawaharlal Nehru contributed the foreword, commending the book for the author's knowledge and insight. (Reg was closer to him on matters of policy than he was to Gandhi though his devotion to Bapu as a man never faltered.) The sales of *White Sahibs* merited a second edition in 1938 and an abridged and revised version, published by the Socialist Book Centre Ltd, appeared in 1946. Reg felt that this book was probably his most effective service to the Indian cause. It certainly made large numbers of British people think seriously about India for the first time.

Some of the reviewers had a field day. *The Observer*, referring to his activities in India, said he was 'one of the Communist troublers of India at that time' when in fact every mention of the Communist Party in the book was critical. Harold Laski in the *New Statesman* accused him of claiming that 'everything Asiatic is right', a deliberate perversion of the truth as the book had a whole chapter on the crimes of Indian princes and landlords. For seven years, Reg had been goading the Maharaja of Patiala, a murderer and torturer, into taking legal action against him. When the Maharaja was in London, Reg addressed a meeting on India in Trafalgar Square:

> . . . and right in front of the crowd were two CID men, one taking notes, while the other held an umbrella over him. I began with 'Friends, Comrades and Gentlemen of Scotland Yard'. The crowd showed enthusiasm as I begged the Yard men to listen with extra care, as I was about to say a number of things for which the Maharaja of Patiala had every right to bring an action against me. After every actionable statement I would pause and ask the plain-clothes men if they had got it down correctly, repeating all references to murder, torture and even such peccadilloes as embezzlement of public funds. There was a resounding cheer when I concluded with the request that the notes should be copied in triplicate – one copy for the Maharaja, one for the India Office and one for the Home Office. Almost the whole of this material was used, in a last effort to expose Patiala and his British accomplices, in a long appendix to *White Sahibs*. The Maharaja, who had very able British legal advisers, maintained his silence throughout. He had bought a few MPs, but he was sufficiently well advised not to ask me my price for silence; which was a pity, as I had a nice trap waiting for him even on that front.

In German-occupied France, *White Sahibs in India* was plagiarised. A book was published under the title *L'Inde et l'Angleterre* with the name of Robert Briffault as author; it was little more than Reg's book rehashed – apart, that is, for the last chapter covering the war years, a period subsequent to the publication of *White Sahibs*. This chapter spoke of the Japanese 'liberators' of Asia; in other words, it was blatant Nazi propaganda. Reg was not surprised. Just as the exposure of Nazi horrors was used to glorify British Imperialism and Russian Communism, so did the Nazis make hay with Britain's colonial crimes and injustices.

In *White Sahibs in India*, Reg was concerned with the causes of historical events and social problems and their far-reaching consequences, dwelling on issues which were often relevant to political situations in other parts of the world. He said that impartiality in politics was impossible; he was partial to justice, to freedom, to humanity, and was prejudiced against oppression, robbery and cruelty. He did not think that most Britons had attained political manhood and considered the subject races better judges of their own needs than the British electorate could ever be.

> What I fundamentally object to [he wrote in the preface to the third edition], is the assumption that certain people are 'backward' because we (in our opinion) are 'progressive'. This is simply a variation of the old theme of aristocracy – the claim of the self-appointed 'best people' to rule those whom they themselves have designated as inferior. I find it peculiarly odd that the Labour Party which fought its way to power against this very injustice – the assumption of a ruling class that Labour was 'unfit to govern' – should apply the same self-made standards to others.

He described how the East India Company, formed in 1600, was destined to carry European domination to India; how the rulers of Bengal became the helpless vassals of the British merchants; how natives were forced to buy dear and sell cheap; how fortunes were accumulated at Calcutta while 30 million people were reduced to the direst poverty; how Indian industries were destroyed by the economic policies dominating 19th-century Britain.

> We did not [the Tory Lord Brentford had pronounced] conquer India for the benefit of the Indians. I know that it is said at missionary meetings that we have conquered India to raise the level of the Indians. That is cant. We conquered India as an outlet for the goods of Great Britain. We conquered India by the sword, and by the sword we shall hold it.

The Indian capitalist was encouraged to interweave his interests with those of the ruling race so as to ensure his support against revolution. The wealth of an ever-increasing number of Englishmen depended upon the taxation of Indian peasants; the extortion of revenue opened an age of growing famine.

It is impossible to say with certainty what would have happened if the country had been left to itself. The history of mankind is so full of unforeseen events that none can tell whether India's development would have been swifter or slower than that of the West. Few would have dared to prophesy at one time that the kingdom of the Pharaohs would become a dependency of an unknown island beyond the Pillars of Hercules. In more recent times Japan stood forth suddenly as the rival and equal of the Western Powers. And so the alternative destiny that lay before India must always be a matter of purest speculation.

During the 19th century, the British government waged some 111 wars in India. And what price peace in the 20th century, asked the Indian nationalist, combined as it was with poverty, illiteracy and disease. Peace bought at the cost of national degradation where generations were bred to be doormats for the British – what worse slander on peace's name? Peace was a manifest evil.

Gandhi's consuming passion was a desire to raise the masses. He largely succeeded through the Congress in changing demoralised and bullied Indian peasants into a unified people with self-respect and self-reliance, willing to sacrifice themselves for a larger cause. Reg quoted from his own memorandum written in 1930:

It was from the Congress hospitals, where Hindu and Moslem, caste and outcaste, lay side by side, victims of the lathi and the bullet, that Indian nationalism drew its inspiration, even when the police descended upon those hospitals and hurled the victims of savage and indecent assaults into the streets. And it will be in the villages and factories, where Hindus and Moslems suffer from the same robberies of rent and interest, that the social revolution will find its strength, superseding nationalism in the coming years as the spearhead of Indian liberation and racial unity.

Under British rule, canals built 3,000 years ago had fallen into disuse – 'What was achieved a thousand years before Christ the British government, with all the devices of modern engineering at its disposal, had not even the interest to maintain'. Poverty in India in the 1930s was the result of 150 years of extortion. It began with the robberies described in the early chapters of *White Sahibs*,

and a steady rise in the land tax in *ryotwari* provinces to double or treble the amount exacted by the Indian rulers. It progressed with the policy of annexation, whereby the revenues of Indian states were plundered on the pretext of defence. It was systematised in some of the provinces by the creation of an Indian land-owning class, which by the year 1900 was paying only 28 per cent of its rents to the government and keeping the rest of the plunder as reward for its loyalty.

In 1932, *The Times of India* announced the banning of 14 different films depicting such incidents as Gandhi's arrival in London and his visit to Lancashire. An American missionary told of how, in the United Provinces, women were raped and made to 'frog parade' through the streets. In one village, an old woman was mercilessly beaten by police because her son was a Congress worker. These were just two cases where Press Ordinances were used to stifle the news.

At the very time that the Labour Party was condemning Italian imperialism in Abyssinia, the British attempt to drive a military road through the Mohmand territory on the North-West Frontier had led to a war similar in origin to the Abyssinian war –

> In each case there had been 'incidents', and the British, like the Italians, claimed to be 'policing' a troublesome and uncivilised neighbour. Moreover, the Mohmands, like the Abyssinians, were accused of harbouring 'undesirable' refugees and agitators. But there were also important differences, for the Mohmands were few and ill-armed compared with the Abyssinians. They also had the misfortune not to be represented at the League of Nations. But their worst crime was that they were opposed to being bombed by the British, which was clearly quite a different matter from being murdered by the Italians. Hence it came about that the Labour Party at their (1935) Conference, perhaps a little embarrassed by their own past, found themselves unable to spend five minutes on a resolution condemning their own government for the crime they so loudly denounced in Mussolini.

Near the end of *White Sahibs in India*, Reg discussed India's most urgent problems to date,

> but, while imperialism remains, the national struggle diverts much of the energy of India's men and women, who fight, not primarily for specific social programmes but for the bare right of India to decide on such policies for herself.

He quoted Dinah Stock's 'the art of being governed by the British requires infinite patience with a multitude of irrelevant virtues', and added, 'It is just that irrelevance of our own virtues that we need to remember; and perhaps to be a little less conscious of the virtues themselves'.

☆   ☆   ☆

As *White Sahibs in India* was published, Secker and Warburg commissioned from Ethel the book *Women and the Revolution*. Reg was involved in the unsuccessful ILP effort to break Franco's blockade of Bilbao. Ethel had offered her entire savings for this purpose which now supported Basques who had suffered heavy bombardment.

Four thousand Basque children arrived at Southampton in the summer of 1937. Reg was one of a handful of volunteers at the Stoneham Reception Camp with its hundreds of bell tents. Isolation units were prepared for children with serious diseases. Food rations were soon exhausted: food had been scarce in Bilbao, and some of the refugees were hiding it in their pockets or inside their shirts. Most of the time it rained and the whole exercise was known to Reg as 'Basquing in the Rain'. Many youngsters caused trouble by drifting off into open country, by fighting over religious or political differences and by ignoring sanitary arrangements.

Reg dealt with the first 400 to leave the camp; they were bound for a Salvation Army Home. Each child was interviewed with the aid of an interpreter, papers were checked, and great care taken that members of a family were not separated –

> When I had finished I realised that the papers provided were very inaccurate, that there had been a good deal of confusion, and that there might be more if I could not explain a number of facts about the papers and my own hasty jottings to some responsible person. The key man, however, was 'not to be disturbed'. His secretary and other members of the (London) committee were, they assured me, too busy. I said with disgust, 'I'm leaving for good in 15 minutes; and if there's one hell of a muddle about this business it's not my fault.' I have often wondered since what it was at Stoneham that was so much more important than the children. That committee (that crowd of top-level obstructionists) had driven me as near to a nervous breakdown as I've ever been.

He wrote for the *News Chronicle* a lengthy report on the camp which, in spite of the committee and because of the patience of a team of genuine workers, managed to operate efficiently. As the most pressing task was to secure permanent accommodation for the refugee children, he had arranged to house a number of them in a large property belonging to his Clark relatives at Street.

☆　　☆　　☆

One day in August 1937, at three o'clock in the morning, Ethel received two cables informing her that Reg was seriously ill in the Copenhagen State

Hospital. (He had been stricken with a haemorrhage in one of his lungs during the Congress of the War Resisters' International.) She flew out to him from Croydon airport, and stayed in a small hotel room, visiting him every day, days full of fretting and grieving, until he suddenly began to recover.

He introduced her to the Dutch anarchist and pacifist Bartelemy de Ligt who, like them, believed that the road of anarcho-socialism demanded in the first place the moral regeneration of the people. People could be freed only by self-emancipation; their spirit of servility to church, factory, office, barracks, party, press was the way of bondage.

Reg entered hospital again in London, but as he was now surrounded by friends, Ethel fulfilled her promise to join her daughter Jean in Vienna. She completed *Women and the Revolution* and *Commonsense and the Adolescent* and since a Spanish foodship venture, for which she had offered £1,000, was dropped, some of the money she gave towards the subsidising of a Spanish film.

Reg, still shaky, was ready to start his convalescence, paid for by Laurence Housman. Accompanied by Ethel, he sailed for Bordeaux in a boat of 900 tons with one other passenger and a cargo of waste paper, old rubber tyres and empty barrels. Near Margate harbour a fierce storm developed. The propeller was lifted out of the water so that the whole boat shuddered and plunged. Reg and Ethel staggered up and down the swaying staircase and reeled on to the sodden deck. Then the battered hulk, with other vessels, went to the assistance of a Dutch oil-tanker on fire in the Bay. 'This is convalescence?' asked Reg ruefully.

In Bordeaux, they were exhilarated by the glamour of the Fair – the Grand Guignol of the 'headless woman', the 'world-famous' dancer naked among the lions, the fortune-tellers' tents, the terrifyingly steep switch-backs and the grinding music of the merry-go-rounds. They travelled on to fairytale Carcassonne, Foix, Toulon and Cavalière where Ethel made notes for her novel *Rose and Sylvie*, in one afternoon creating 13 delinquents and their case histories. For a month they stayed in Hyères. Here, in a side-street bar, they saw a beautiful young girl in a dressing gown, carrying her underclothes over her arm. Reg was bedazzled by her huge, almond-shaped eyes, the eyes of a 'sleepy tiger'. The vision passed through to the kitchen and reappeared in street clothes, her luxuriant hair unkempt. Ethel accused him of behaving like a love-sick schoolboy but she sympathised; she was equally intrigued. 'Why not ask her if she'll let us photograph her?' she suggested. The girl was delighted. They presented her with violets, they kept returning to the bar for a sight of her and they eventually escorted her to a tatty revue, a pale imitation of the Folies Bergère.

'One wants to do something for a girl like that', said Reg. 'She's wasting herself down here – with a lot of local louts and sailors.' 'Come, come, comrade', mocked Ethel. 'That's not exactly the party line. A man's a man for a' that, etc.' 'But for a lover or a husband for a girl like that! It's unthinkable! She should have someone who can *appreciate* her, see that she makes the most of herself, takes care of herself – you know how plump French women tend to become when they're about 40. Beauty ought not to be allowed to squander itself. It ought to be State property, State protected!' Ethel laughed, and agreed; she, too, was worried about the girl's possible fate. She had come into their lives as a mystery and one night, abruptly, and just as mysteriously, she vanished.

On returning to London, Reg planned a new project – his *Prison Anthology* – making a selection from the writings of prisoners and revealing how different types of men and women reacted to imprisonment. Laboriously he researched at the British Museum, and wrote the long introduction, but by the end of January 1938, overwork once more exhausted him. His friend Dinah Stock was glad to collaborate with him on the anthology while at the same time assisting Jomo Kenyatta. Reg came to know Kenyatta well. He believed him to be sincere in his political convictions and much maligned, though he detected in him a measure of conceit, snobbery and laziness.

He badly needed to recuperate again and, with Ethel, headed for the Dalmation coast. On the train from Vienna to Zagreb, they fell in with a cabaret act consisting of an American man, a Viennese boy and a Viennese girl. In Zagreb, they applauded the trio's display of acrobatic dancing, grew fond of them and parted from them affectionately. Sarajevo was the port of call before the medieval walled city of Dubrovnik which, said Reg, after a time became like living with a beautiful woman who had only her beauty to offer. Ethel began her novel *Darkness My Bride* (using the cargo boat/Bordeaux/Dubrovnik experience) and Reg resumed work on an unpublished novel he had struggled with in France. Ethel then broke off to write two short stories, *Cabaret*, based on the group they had recently met, and *Mistral Morning*, inspired by the girl in the bar at Hyères.

A telegram was delivered to them – PARTNERS LEFT SEND MONEY COOKS ZAGREB – signed by the American cabaret performer. They did as he asked immediately, and he wrote back gratefully, explaining that he had arrived one night at the Zagreb nightclub only to find his partners gone with all the stage clothes and all the money they had earned. Ethel and Reg wrote to the Viennese boy for his side of the story, hoping that the nightclub would forward the letter. The boy replied that the

American had been difficult to work with, had piled up debts and had drank away more than his share of their joint income. Feeling intensely sorry for the ragged little band, Ethel and Reg wished them well as they tried to rebuild their lives, but that was not the end of this adventure into show business.

Moving on to Split, Reg was enchanted by the shoddy shops and apartments built into the walls of the Palace of Diocletian; Ethel was outraged by them, they reminded her of the booths around Tamerlane's Samarkand. In a restaurant, they were surprised to see 'egg-plant' advertised on the menu. 'You'll be telling us next that you've even got tomatoes!' Yes, they had, said the waiter, so both were ordered, a rare treat after a surfeit of Yugoslavian pickled cabbage and white beans. When the dish was served it proved to be – a fried egg with tomato sauce. 'You get the egg all right', observed Reg, 'and the rest is a "plant".' They left by boat for Susak and were driven over the Italian roads to a hotel in Trieste where the cashier told them that 'there is no quotation for the Austrian shilling today – Hitler is in Vienna'. Next, it would be the turn of Czechoslovakia.

☆      ☆      ☆

Reg's *Prison Anthology*, published by Jarrolds/Hutchinson (Ethel's publishers), met with no great success. He was employed by Laurence Housman to do some research for him at the British Museum, and soon got embroiled with Emma Goldman and the anarchists. Red Emma had come to London to campaign to the British whom she despised for their non-intervention, and to raise money for arms for Spain. Ethel, roped in to help her, and dressed in flame-coloured velvet, would relentlessly coax pound notes out of her audience ('Come now – not enough yet even for one machine-gun!'). Reg also appeared occasionally on Emma's platforms, never to encourage violence, but, after the revolution was lost, to speak up for Spanish relief. Ethel and Reg were to find the anarchists as doctrinaire, bigoted and ruthless as any other political group but at least most of them recognised that in the lust for power, whether in capitalist or communist countries, lay the greatest danger. However, Emma Goldman, Reg would have it, was bitten by the power bug herself.

A Russian Jewess, Emma migrated to America in 1885 at the time of the pogroms. With the anarchist Alexander Berkman, she helped in the plot to assassinate that symbol of wealth and power, the chairman of the Carnegie Steel Company whose workers were on strike as their pay claim had been rejected. Political assassination she considered a noble ideal, a blow struck for the liberation of the people. Berkman's attempt to slay the chairman and then himself 'in the assurance that I gave my life for the people' was thwarted, and he was sentenced to 22 years' penal servitude. Emma, meanwhile, supervised the feeding of the homeless, led mass demonstrations against social injustices, served a term in prison, learnt nursing, opened a massage parlour, started a paper called *Mother Earth*, and was reunited with Berkman when his sentence was commuted to 13 years. Later, they were both imprisoned for two years and deported to Russia where they witnessed the betrayal of the revolution into the hands of bureaucracy. Leaving Russia, Emma lived and worked in Sweden, Germany, France and England, marrying the Welsh miner James Colton in order to acquire British nationality; after the ceremony she gave him 10 shillings with which to take himself 'to the pictures'.

Ethel had no illusions about the thick-set, square-jawed Emma. She knew that she lectured, never conversed. Her egotism was colossal. She would invariably rub up the wrong way the people most sympathetic to her. When Ethel poured her a cup of tea, 'that's too *much* tea', snorted Emma, so Ethel added water, but Emma took the cup from her, emptied its contents and poured herself a fresh brew. When Ethel had carefully chosen an expensive Rhine wine and asked her how it tasted, Emma drawled, 'Well, dear, it isn't *dry* enough and it isn't *cold* enough, but I guess it'll do!' When Emma stayed at Oak Cottage, Ethel filled her room with roses from the garden; Emma gathered up the vases and plonked them ungraciously outside the door. But she was sometimes capable of the sudden generous act, she was sometimes responsive to love and affection and no one, thought Ethel, could deny her utter honesty and unfaltering heroism in the face of persecution.

In *Women and the Revolution*, Ethel wrote a dedicatory letter to her:

My own revolutionary faith insists that despite the Communist International and its betrayal of the Revolution in Russia, its wrecking of the Revolution in China in 1927, and its sabotage of the Revolution in Spain in the struggle against Franco, in the interests of its foreign policy – the deterioration of the Marxian ideal into a dictatorship of the few over the many is not inevitable, and that by educating the masses through a truly free workers' democracy the ideal of the Libertarian Society of Anarchism may ultimately be achieved. For the purposes of the Revolution in Spain we have been comrades, and we mean the same thing when we use the word revolution in relation to other countries; we do not mean a dictatorship from the Kremlin; on that we are wholeheartedly agreed, however much we might disagree on the course the Revolution should take in the interests of preserving a living Freedom once the capitalist system was overthrown.

When the Spanish people had swept into the streets armed only with sticks and stones to confront the machine guns and rifles of the Right (the landowners, the Church and the Army), when they cried 'Viva la Republica!' and 'Viva la Fai!', when the troops refused to fire on them and went over to their side, when, within a week, throughout Catalonia, factories, transport, land and public services were under workers' control, Emma was in seventh heaven, she wept for sheer joy, for here was a classless society that had thrown off the shackles of the State. With the exception of the ILP, the so-called Left in Britain, obsequious to Soviet foreign policy, was downgrading the revolution. Emma would show them! In her American-Yiddish-Germanic-Russian voice, she bleated and bellowed about the sins of 'Frarnco' and the triumphs of 'our Spaan-ish kumrads'. She did not wish to be 'a damp sheet', no, she was 'a red cloth to the bull', so come on, you British, don't be so 'duck-hearted'.

Her rapture was short-lived. The vast anarchist trades union organisation came to terms with the Communists, and Emma was heartbroken – anarchists should never have anything to do with centralised government; the revolution had been stabbed in the back by Stalin's henchmen. Now, every meeting that Emma addressed was, to Ethel, an ordeal; they were little more than vicious slanging-matches. She was battered by Emma's dynamic energy and realised that she could never *feel* Spain as passionately as Emma did; for her, Spain was more an intellectual matter, part of a general revolutionary attitude. Then an international anti-fascist organisation was formed for Spanish relief and Emma was appointed its English representative with Ethel as its treasurer. Ethel wrote appeals for circulation by post but support was dwindling. Emma was incensed that Chamberlain and his umbrella were ousting her beloved Spaniards from British hearts.

Reg was one of the few comrades who dared to oppose Red Emma, and to his frequent criticisms, she always retorted: 'Don't listen to Re-eegie, he's a very sick ma-an'. He thought her quite hideously ugly and he detested her aggressiveness, her clichés, her self-importance and her humourlessness. 'She's a female Hitler', he would say. 'She's a mob to herself.' Nevertheless, her platform behaviour fascinated him, the way she fidgeted noisily while other speakers were on their feet and the way she passed notes to Ethel, who was usually in the chair, if a speaker overran his allotted short time by so much as a minute – *she* demanded a full hour which, to Reg, seemed endless, her invective inflamed by the whisky she kept in a flask under her corset.

Ethel's patience with Emma was a wonder to Reg. He admired her efforts to present a balanced picture of her in *Red Rose*, a novel based on Emma's life, but in *Comrade, O Comrade*, Ethel portrayed Emma as *he* saw

*Ethel aged 30, who had 'a terrible contempt for those women who from fear dabble on the brink of experience when their desire is to plunge into the flood. . . . Every woman of courage and intelligence has had numerous lovers . . . but . . . it is the attitude to life which counts, not the statistics; not the number of affaires, but the amount of living'.* (Confessions and Impressions, *1930*)

*Reg had a genius for friendship*

her. In one episode, a fight broke out between Communists and Blackshirts in the meeting hall, chairs were hurled about and the whistling and cat-calling was deafening. '*You* can't shout *me* down!' roared Emma as she stormed on for the inevitable hour. A long-winded ILP speaker followed her and then a Negro – Chris Jones – put the anti-imperialist case with special reference to Africa. Emma was dropped on. 'Does he know this is a meeting about *Spain*, dear?' she twanged into Mary Thane's (Ethel's) ear. Mary/Ethel was powerless to stop his river of rhetoric, his torrent of words. He had beaten Emma at her own game and, to her great annoyance, finished his tirade amid prolonged applause.

☆　　☆　　☆

Ethel and Reg spent time and money on Spanish anarchist refugees in London, helping them to settle into jobs. Ethel used her knowledge of them in her collection of short stories, *No More Mimosa*. One story, *Downfall of a Comrade*, though it purported to be fiction, was true. Reg had asked Ethel, the Hon. Treasurer of a new committee to raise funds for Spanish relief, if the accounts had been audited, an important point as Ethel's name was being bandied about to inspire confidence. The matter came to the attention of Emma Goldman, who exploded: 'No, there hasn't been an audit and there *won't* be! Auditing accounts is a bourgeois notion!' 'But Ethel is responsible for the money', countered Reg. 'It's her duty to insist on an audit and so should the comrade who's actually handling the cash, in his own interests. The position's as unfair to him as it is to Ethel!' The cash-handler, like Emma, did not agree. Comrades should trust each other!

Reg resigned from the committee but Ethel continued with the treasurership out of loyalty to Emma. In *Downfall of a Comrade*, the trusted Joe Bane (not his real name) was accused of embezzling funds. The narrator of the story – Reg – torn between pity and anger, looked on him as a pitiful wreck yet also as the most contemptible kind of crook. In Barcelona in 1937, when the communists and the police hatched the plot that finally smashed the revolution, Joe had been a useful dogsbody, duplicating literature and running hither and yon for coffee and cigarettes. Back in London, it was all one to him if he lived or died, his diving for shelter during bombardments, like his work for the movement, seemed purely automatic. Some enterprising anarchists had defrauded a 'Fascist' of thousands of pounds for the benefit of the movement, and Emma and a few others decided to avail themselves of part of this windfall by sending Joe to Mexico on a gun-running expedition. At the last minute, however, somebody informed, the guns were seized and Joe dodged the police in the nick of time. Next, he was sent to Morocco with several hundred pounds 'bribe money' to get a comrade out of jail, and he succeeded – good old Joey. Then it was discovered that the comrade had escaped from jail before Joe had arrived in Morocco. Joe made himself scarce, but was tracked down. 'I got into a jam', was all he could plead, 'I've gotter live'.

'So have we all', Reg told him, 'but not at the expense of others, not at the expense of comrades. That money belonged to the movement, collected from working people. Now there are thousands of our comrades in the French concentration camps who need this money. Stealing money given by the poor for the relief of the helpless is to sink about as low as it is possible to sink.' Reg said goodbye. He held out his hand to Joe who whimpered: 'Try not to think too badly of me, comrade'. Reg hardened and walked off. If only Joe had expressed one word of remorse, it would have redeemed him in Reg's eyes, but there was only truculence flavoured with self-pity. Soon after the war started, Reg saw Joe again in a London pub. He was boasting about his exploits. Reg slipped out without Joe spotting him.

Emma, Reg learned, just dipped into the movement's funds as it suited her –

a startling thought when one recollected all those passionate clichés about the Spa-anish people. Here at last was the explanation for Emma's fury at our suggestion of an audit. Ethel had said that, as treasurer, she would like to be able to say in public how the money we raised had been spent – even this request had been evaded. Anarchists don't call in the police when such things happen – and, principles apart, they would not have dared to do so in these complicated circumstances. Nobody seemed to blame Emma – they said she 'had to live' but against the embezzling comrade there was a cold fury.

CHAPTER VIII

# Art Thee in Trouble, Friend?

INDIA STILL PREOCCUPIED REG. When Clement Attlee wrote in 1938 that 'there is no particular gain in handing over the peasants and workers of India to be exploited by their own capitalists and landlords', Reg publicised the fact that Attlee applied a very different standard to the situation in Britain where the foundations of class collaboration were already being laid. Attlee had claimed: 'It is no good telling the ordinary Briton that it does not matter to him whether he is ruled by British or foreign capitalists. He does not believe it. He is right'. Indians, wrote Reg, felt similarly, but they were evidently wrong, an ingenious argument which somehow justified the Labour Party in its policy of holding hands with British capitalists and helping to suppress India to their advantage.

Ethel did a stint of film criticism for the *Sunday Dispatch* before taking a holiday with Reg in Ireland. Never had they laughed so much or drank so much or been so carefree, but afterwards, with the world news worsening, they were sickened by the feeling that they had experienced freedom and beauty for the last time. In Dublin they dined with W. B. Yeats and Fred Higgins, the manager of the Abbey Theatre. Ethel had met Yeats in the early 1930s.

He was distinguished in appearance and manner [she told the present writer], and somehow lived on a 'higher plane' than ordinary mortals – all poetry and dreams and Celtic twilight. But he had flashes of wit and a *bawdy* sense of humour. For three years, I knew him *intimately*. I went to a party once at the Soviet Embassy and I was to call for Yeats later as he wanted to dine with me. At the Embassy, I drank with Ernst Toller who also wanted to dine with me. I said I couldn't, as I had a date with Yeats. This gave Toller an idea. He wondered if Yeats, who'd been awarded the Nobel Prize for Literature, could recommend that the German writer Ossietsky, in prison in Germany, receive the Nobel Peace Prize. If he were to get it, he'd almost certainly be released from prison but he must have a recommendation from some other Nobel

100

prize winner. Toller and Yeats discussed the matter, but I knew that Yeats would refuse – he had no truck with politics. Toller started to cry, said this was a question of life and death, the question of a man's life. I started to cry as well, a mixture of my feeling for Ossietsky, for Toller, and the vodka. I argued with Yeats, too – and he was very uncomfortable but he said he couldn't become involved, it was no part of an artist's business, he was very, very sorry. We parted from Toller, and Yeats said he'd fully explain his political position to me – but he never did.

The 1938 reunion with Yeats was followed by a riotous soirée with the surgeon, scholar and wit Oliver St John Gogarty who lamented the passing of Irish roisterers and bawds. Then, through Emma Goldman, they met the indomitable Hanna Sheehy Skeffington whose pacifist husband had been shot in cold blood by an English officer in 1916. In America, Hanna had lectured on the injustices of British rule in Ireland and the murder of her Francis. 'It would be a poor tribute to my husband,' she said, 'if grief were to break my spirit. His death speaks trumpet-tongued against the system that slew him'. In England, she was arrested as a militant Irish republican, and in Ireland, was harassed by house raids. She edited *The Irish Citizen*, the organ of the Irish Women's Franchise League; she saw women's rights, not as an isolated issue, but as part of the whole struggle of the labouring classes to banish capitalist exploitation and imperialism. She fought for the abolition of the death penalty: 'Can you imagine that we actually import the English hangman whenever there's a job for him?' To Reg, she was one of the Grand Old Girls. It amused him to watch her sitting so demurely and in a soft purring brogue come out with such gems as 'I didn't really approve of what he was doing, but he was breaking the law, which I always take to be a good thing'.

The great war scare of 1938 ended the Irish holiday. Ethel and Jean saw a performance of Emlyn Williams' *The Corn is Green* in the West End; after the second interval, a radio was brought on stage, the announcer reporting that an agreement had been reached at Munich between the Four Powers.

So the days became normal again [wrote Ethel in *Privileged Spectator* (1939), her second volume of autobiography]. And there was room again for the Palestine question, and an enormous amount of conscience money poured into the fund for refugees from Czechoslovakia. Odd the things people get a conscience about. Nobody gets a conscience about Arabs whose homes are blown up by British troops in Palestine, as disciplinary measures or reprisals. Nobody talks about the betrayal of the Arabs, or gets hysterical about proposed mutilations of their country. Few people even bother to remember that it is, after all, their country, the property of neither the British nor the Jews.

But the fact that an artificial state called Czechoslovakia had about as much right to Sudetenland as France has to Alsace-Loraine, was lost sight of in the uprush of anti-Fascism. It is easier to pity the Jews and the inhabitants of a small remote place like Czechoslovakia than Arabs, Negroes, Indians; we have nothing to lose by feeling sorry for those who suffer under Hitler. Besides, whilst people are busy being rabidly anti-Nazi, attention is distracted from the innate fascism of all Imperialist governments. So let's talk about Jew-baiting in Germany and keep off such domestic affairs as nigger-baiting in Africa, bombing the Afridis, blowing up the Arabs. Let's feel hot about the other fellow's evil-doings, believe all the atrocity stories about his administration, and indignantly deny any he may utter about us. Disgraceful that benches in the Vienna boulevards should be labelled 'for Aryans only' – never mind the fact that there is a similar segregation for coloured people in England in regard to hotels, restaurants, lodging-houses, even the renting of unfurnished rooms. And nobody gets excited because in South Africa Negroes may not ride in the same compartments of trains and trams as Europeans; or the Indian settlers bathe from the same beaches. Democracy, truly thy name is humbug.

In October 1938, Ethel supported the platform against the Eton beagling, and a newspaper referred to her as 'Miss Ethel Mannin the well-known anti-beagler', which she thought made a nice change from 'Mr Jack Hobbs, Miss Ethel Mannin and other well-known sportsmen'. Also in October, she and Reg received a letter, postmarked Algeria, from the American of the Zagreb cabaret trio. He had joined the French Foreign Legion, had 'got tired of being kicked around the consulates of Europe', and was now dancing 'for the boys'.

Ethel was corresponding with Llewelyn Powys on her work for Spanish relief. Visiting him in Clavadel, she wrote that he combined 'the austerity of a saint with the zest of a pagan', words which could equally have been applied to Reg. She was back in England for Christmas, a season she hated for its tawdriness, commercialism and sentimental cards. Her old boss, Sir Charles Higham, was dangerously ill. She had written to him that though their ways lay in different directions, she regarded him with affection and esteem, and she treasured the little seed pearl brooch he had given her when she was 17. He died on Christmas Eve. She went to his memorial service in the Savoy Chapel as a farewell tribute – and she remembered the girl she once was, the girl who had hero-worshipped him, who had shyly placed blue cornflowers on his desk in thanks for his kindness and encouragement.

☆      ☆      ☆

102

Two days after Christmas Day, Ethel and Reg were married. Earlier in the year, when her divorce from John Porteous was finalised, she had written to W. B. Yeats:

I am very angry today because the *Evening News* ran my picture on the front page last night, all about the divorce, and that has started the whole press avalanche. My picture on the front page of the *News Chronicle* this morning with the co-respondent named. Last night a *Daily Herald* journalist tried to make me give him an interview, and the *Star* sent me a wire – which I ignored. How foul it all is! What is it to do with anyone else? I hate it all for Jean's sake and my parents, and Reg's nice old Quaker parents. It's all very disgusting.

Recalling the marriage, she told the present writer:

With Reg named as co-respondent, elders of the Society of Friends had visited him and asked him, 'Art thee in trouble, Friend?' But Reg wasn't having it, he was not going to make a confession of guilt. In answer to the question, he said cheerfully: 'No, not that I know of, why?' Quakers prided themselves on their broadmindedness and Reg was determined to give them something to be broadminded about! We neither of us really believed in marriage, so why did we make this concession to convention, when we didn't even want to live under the same roof? It was entirely my own fault that my first marriage didn't work – I was too emotionally immature and I knew, anyway, that conventional marriage wasn't for me. So I left a perfectly good husband, not to live with anyone else, but just to be free.

Reg had had the first of his series of haemorrhages, and it was thought to be tubercular, but then it was found that the haemorrhage was caused by high blood-pressure. When it was believed to be t.b. we thought that he might have to spend a large part of his life in a sanitorium, and it seemed to us both that if I had the status of lawful wife, it would simplify things and I asked the husband with whom I hadn't lived for years for a divorce. But long before the divorce was through, we discovered that Reg wasn't t.b. and I said, well, there's no reason to marry now. However, Reg said it would be 'nice to be legal' and that it would be a 'vote of confidence'. That was fine by me, so long as there was no question of living together – my freedom was precious and Reg, too, liked his independence. He was happy as long as he had one room stacked with books and dust, didn't need to worry about regular mealtimes, and could take off to visit his friends without having to consult anybody. Reg wrote that marriage to me was the right thing to do because it left him all the freedom he needed. I needed solitude and he needed to be near libraries and cafés, and he said that this semi-detached marriage was ideal for both of us, which was true. It certainly, long after 'passion's trance was over-past', left us each other's Best Friend.

I married Reg at Paddington Registry Office where the Press lay in wait. Our witnesses were his mother and my housekeeper. We all went off to lunch, saw his mum and the housekeeper off, and, for a lark, the two of us celebrated the wedding by seeing some horror films.

As I said in *Commonsense and Morality*, and I still hold to it, between two people who've had great pleasure in each other's bodies and done innumerable things together, a friendship is established which should outlast sexual passion. If the man or the woman develops outside sexual interests, this doesn't mean that it detracts in any way from the deep feeling they have for each other. Reg and I were devoted to each other to the end but to remain 'in love' is for most of us a psychological impossibility. If a man and a woman are separated by force of circumstances and have a brief affair with someone else, that affair is purely ephemeral, and their devotion to each other unimpaired. Jealousy and guilt are morbid, selfish and destructive. Love is free, whether we like it or not. It can't be regulated within a prescribed code. Freedom was the basis of the relationship between Reg and me, and it had nothing to do with mere legalisation.

☆    ☆    ☆

Ethel had added her signature to public demands for the lifting of the arms embargo on the Spanish government. She had stood before hundreds of people and asked for their money to provide the Spanish republicans with weapons, so intolerable was the thought of brave revolutionaries falling into the hands of Franco. But now with increasing Fascist aggression, now that horror was being piled on horror's head, her ingrained pacifism broke bounds and a pacifist she remained to the end of her days. The logical conclusion to pacifism, she reasoned, was non-violent anarchism, de-centralised *order*. Anarchism was the abolition of the State, of centralised governments, the governments that create wars – 'since violence is a violation of the human personality, logically your anarchist should be also a believer in non-blood-spilling methods for the resistance of tyranny and the achievement of revolutionary purpose'.

The newly-married lovers enjoyed a few days of relaxation, joining in the choruses of bawdy country songs at a Suffolk inn –

> Hey dingle-dangle, dingle dangle doe,
> Never let your dingle-dangle dangle in the snow!

104

Reg sang a version of the traditional Ram of Derbyshire, and the pub rose to

> Here's to *the* cock as treads the hen,
> And flaps un's wings an' treads agen;
> Here's to *the* hen as never refooses
> To let un tread whenever he chooses.

Sitting on the grass outside the inn, they ate bread and cheese and drank brown ale. It was an afternoon 'straight out of the *Earthly Paradise*'.

Reg still lived in Laurence Housman's Bayswater flat. (Laurence was mainly in Street.) Laurence shared with Ethel's father, Bob Mannin, a supremely generous nature, a pure-in-heart, a sea-green incorruptible socialism, a delight in Low Life, and a passion for books, an insatiable thirst for knowledge. Bob's father, a drunken stonemason, would thrash his studious young son with a belt each time he caught him with a book. Bob's socialism, said Ethel, went far deeper than party politics; it was the authentic socialism of the Early Christians, the true communism of 'all things in common'. Priests were 'sky pilots' and 'Bible-punchers'; church he attended just three times in his adult life, for his marriage and for the christening of his first two children. His abiding principle was 'cast your bread upon the waters, for it shall return to you after many days'. Admire any of his possessions and he would urge you, 'Take it! Have it!' When, in 1940, Ethel, as a pacifist, refused to register for national service, Bob foresaw the possibility of her being 'on the run'. He raised £100 on his life insurance policy and should she ever need 'some ready cash at a moment's notice, it'll be there. Don't forget, girl, there's £100 lying there whenever you want it.' In 1943, he wrote to her: '70 years old. Born and bred in a slum, now by favour of the gods and your splendid generosity, living on the fat of the land in a miniature mansion with half an acre of land and many trees. Glory be!' (the 'mansion' was a six-roomed house in Surrey that Ethel had bought for her parents). Ethel's mother kept the house spotless and shining; Bob declared that when she got to heaven she would polish God's golden throne and the haloes of all the angels. He once told Ethel as they walked in her garden that she should not have put stepping-stones through the wooded area because it would discourage the Little People – their faery feet slip on stones.

Bob ('Dad' to Reg) and Reg ('ole Reg' to Bob) were a mutual admiration society. Reg never tired of hearing Bob recount his stories of Victorian London, the London of stewed eel shops, side-shows, music halls and the underworld. He noted that Laurence Housman, as a penal reformer, had made friends with criminals, but Bob had grown up amongst them. He would tell of the 'leery boys' pushing people off the pavement, of how he and his mates grabbed a copper by the ankles and pitched him over a bridge into the river, and of how the victim of a shop raid stocked his till with razor blades, with bloodcurdling results. To his dying day, Bob would 'find' a few bricks or a piece of wood, for there were some things it did him a violence to pay for, and he saw no wrong in depriving the affluent of their surplus provisions. His humour was invariably coarse but never salacious; with Ethel's mother out of earshot, Reg would request from him a rendition of yet another raunchy song. From Bob's Irish ancestors and his gift for story-telling sprang, Ethel believed, the writer in her. Like father like daughter, the police were always suspect to them, and the underdog and the dispossessed were always to be supported.

Since editing his *Prison Anthology*, Reg had corresponded with prisoners and ex-prisoners in many countries, and this had led to people in trouble with the law arriving at the flat. He had the knack of greeting them as if they naturally belonged there, as if he had all the time in the world to listen to their problems.

Whenever he helped me [said one], it never somehow seemed like help – it was as if I'd thought of the solution all by myself, but that was Reg's way. That's why so many people adored him – he never said things that were 'good for you', he always mentioned his own foibles so that you immediately felt at ease, as if you were the one person he really wanted to see, and God knows, I must have been a trial to him. . . . However dire my circumstances, the evening always ended in laughter and a marvellous feeling of 'all's right with the world'. If you needed food, Reg would empty his larder for you, and go without himself. If you were short of clothes, he'd hand you his jacket and jumper. Nothing could shock him – it was as if he'd *been* there, he *knew*. If he had the money, he thought nothing of taking taxis – it was a poor man's extravagance, he said – he knew all about how the poor must sometimes make what seem to the 'sensible' wasteful gestures – he knew they have to do that to keep sane. I'd call Reg a saint, you know, but a saint who had a ball. He was so much 'of the world' and that's why he could get on with anybody, from tramps to high society. He made you *glow*, and when you think how wretched he must have felt a lot of the time, with his illnesses. . . . I've seen people – the helpless, the hopeless – just gravitate towards him and he'd embrace these total strangers – a kiss for the leper sort of thing, with never a trace of the goody-goody. If ever a man lived out the teachings of Jesus, that man was Reg. And yet – oh, he could be naughty – rubbishing some politician, for instance – no, that wasn't very Christ-like – but even there, he'd watch himself enjoying himself, rabbiting on and on, and he'd poke fun at his rhetoric and he'd start to tell stories against himself and of course I'd be limp with laughter.

Reg and Bob Mannin were the men Ethel loved and revered most, and as she often said, they were in many ways two of a kind.

☆ ☆ ☆

Ethel and Reg both felt that Zionism was a racket.

We felt the more strongly about it [wrote Reg], because it exploited the sympathy of decent people for Hitler's victims and diverted it to the justification of an outrage perpetrated on the Arabs of Palestine. We felt even more keenly because professing socialists were mostly taken in by it. Just because Hitler regarded all Jews as evil, anti-fascists were prone to assume that no Jew could ever, in any circumstances, do any wrong – which was equally absurd. And, finally, as we became drawn into controversy, we bitterly resented the hysterical denunciations of all opponents of Zionism as 'fascists'. The irrationality of the taunt was no less galling than its unfairness to people like ourselves, who had done what we could to help Jewish refugees.

In *Women and the Revolution*, Ethel had written of Jewish nationalism as being the tool of British imperialism. Arab nationalist leaders had been deported to remote islands in the Indian Ocean without trial. The women's movement in Palestine had pledged itself to work for the mitigation of the sentences passed on nationalist political prisoners, protested against the importation of firearms into Palestine for arming the Jews, and demanded the establishment of a free, self-governing democratic state.

By 1939, Reg was writing on Palestine for *Peace News*. Reviewing the book *No Ease in Zion* by 'an intelligent Zionist', T. R. Feiwel, he quoted Feiwel's chapter heading 'The Arab does not exist' by which words 'nine-tenths of Zionist attitude toward Arabs could be qualified'. Feiwel told of a fair at Tel Aviv where Jewish workers strode 'in unbroken line toward the observer, conveying, as intended, an impression of irresistible penetration – the new army of Jewish conquest', and an English pro-Zionist had remarked: 'And then they wonder why the Arab reaches for his rifle!'

'For 20 years', wrote Feiwel, 'the Zionists, relying entirely on British aid, have tried to ignore the Arabs and camouflage the issue by confused propaganda, in which Palestine was Jewish by historical and international right.' Reg observed that some, such as Ben Gurion (leader of the Jewish Labour Movement) had even greater ambitions; he had proposed a scheme for sending another 5,000,000 Jews to colonize almost the whole of the Middle East.

'The dependence of all such policies on British imperialism is also made clear,' wrote Reg. When the Arabs revolted in 1936, Ben Gurion had offered the British government an army of 50,000 Jews to keep order in Palestine, and a Zionist Labour newspaper had appealed for British aeroplanes 'to deal with the situation'. Of Jewish youth in Palestine, Feiwel said that 'they are brought up on endless Zionist processions. The propaganda din is incessant. Arabs are both neighbours and enemies, more Jewish immigration means more strength, life is insecure and it pays to organise, particularly on military lines. These few crude ideas suffice. Everything else is rejected'. 'Is it necessary to comment,' added Reg, 'that, by altering a few words here and there, this would serve for a description of fascist youth in Germany? On much less evidence Mr Feiwel continually imputes "fascism" to the Arab nationalist movement, whilst in one place he even says of the British officials that "they tend today to wear the green pork-pie hat denoting Fascist mentality".'

In the *Peace News* article 'The Promised Land', Reg explained that now the British government had at last published the correspondence with the Sherif Husain in 1915,

> we know that Palestine was promised during the (first world) war to the Arabs who lived there and to those Jews who wanted to go there. Like the promises to the Arabs, the Balfour Declaration was dictated by the military requirements of the moment. Whatever may have been the government's intention at the time, it had to decide one day which promises to keep and which to break. Eventually it appeared that the solution of this problem was to remain in Palestine ourselves, creating 'a little, loyal Jewish Ulster' as a bulwark against Arab nationalism. At least, that was the expression used by Sir Ronald Storrs, who was Governor of Jerusalem at the inception of the Mandate, to describe the policy of Zionist immigration. Political Zionism thus came to overshadow completely the Zionism of many early visionaries who had not thought in such terms.

The British authorities had not ignored the Arab people.

> They were so well aware of their existence that when they first entered Palestine they dared not publish the Balfour Declaration, though all the rest of the world knew its terms. On the contrary, they gave quite a different impression to the Palestine Arabs. The Palin Commission of 1920 reported that: 'As late as June 1918, active recruiting was carried out in Palestine for the Shereefian army, our allies, the recruits being given to understand that they were fighting in a national cause and to liberate their country from the Turks. The real impression left upon the Arabs generally was that the British were going to set up an

independent Arab State which would include Palestine'. Similar evidence is to be found in the proclamations, which, said the Palin Commission, were dropped on Palestine from British aeroplanes calling upon the Arabs to join the national movement for independence. No wonder the Palin Report was suppressed!

Not until September 1923 did the Palestine Mandate come into force.

At the 11th hour, the government was warned by its Chief Administrator in Palestine, that 'approximately 90 per cent of the population of Palestine is deeply anti-Zionist. This opposition comprises all Moslems and Christians and a not inconsiderable proportion of Jews'. But no facts or arguments could break the government's determination. For years it had anticipated this mandate, administering the country on the authority of a 'Draft Mandate' – that is to say, on a hypothetical assumption of what its authority *would* be *if* at some later time that authority were delegated to Great Britain. During the interregnum amazing transactions took place. For example, a certain Mr Rutenberg, acting on behalf of a Jewish Agency which had not been established and a Company which had not been formed, was granted by this government with 'draft' authority a monopoly of the two principal waterways of Palestine – the Jordan and the Auja – in respect of all use of those rivers for electrical power and irrigation! Palestine is an arid country where water is bought, leased and even pawned. The principal reserves of this precious supply of water were thus made a private monopoly. It was a hard blow for the 'existing non-Jewish communities', as the Balfour Declaration somewhat tactlessly called the Arab population.

It is this background of high-handed and fraudulent transactions which alone makes the present situation in Palestine understandable.

At weekends, Reg supped with Ethel and their Arab friends at Oak Cottage. He resigned from the inveterately Zionist ILP. During the annual conference in 1939, he had tried to get a vote of censure passed on John McGovern and his anti-Arab speeches:

My tactics on such occasions (to forestall any attempt to shout one down as a 'fascist') were simple enough, and I followed them in this attack on McGovern. The resolution was moved by an anti-Zionist Jew and I seconded it. McGovern flatly denied having used words which I'd attributed to him. I was sitting a few feet from the rostrum with *Hansard* open in front of me, and the objectionable sentence underlined – exactly as I'd quoted it. I jumped up and pushed the Parliamentary Record under McGovern's nose, inviting him to read his own words. He swept the Record aside, blustered on, and received

109

the solid Clydeside vote which could always steam-roller any ILP conference.

His resignation marked the end of his involvement in party politics. He planned to write a book about Palestine, 'the clearest and yet the most commonly misunderstood of all political issues' but the war intervened and all he was to know at firsthand of the Middle East was a short spell in Cairo, at the outset of his African journey in 1953, and a visit to the Gaza Strip. It was left to Ethel, a few years after his death, to appeal for understanding of the Palestinian case in the guise of a travel book, *A Lance for the Arabs* – 'Reg, with his wider and deep knowledge, would have done it "straight", and better'.

Why had they remained members of the ILP when they were professing anarchists, regardless of their opinion of some of their colleagues in the movement? 'We believed it to be more likely to bring about social revolution in England than were the anarchists who had even less following,' said Ethel. In early 1939, she was speaking on a pacifist platform in Wales and the ILP tried to expel her, pacifism being un-Marxist; the *Daily Express* immediately printed an untrue story that she had in fact been expelled and was standing for Parliament as an Independent. Soon, however, she did leave the ILP as she believed it was far too uncritical of the USSR.

☆      ☆      ☆

In 'Let Us Put An End To Empire', another article for *Peace News*, Reg asked, whom do the colonies pay?

They pay the Settlers, who buy land cheap from the government, which steals it from the natives (eg Kenya). Native reservations being insufficient, wages must be earned to pay taxes: that means cheap labour. Taxes again are spent disproportionately on Europeans.

They pay British Investors, who obtain concessions for mining, railways, etc. Government contracts tend to go to British firms.

They pay British manufacturers, merchants and shipping companies. Once more these are government contracts. Also tariff preferences . . . about one third of total colonial imports in 1937 were British. Without political control, would any *single* country have obtained so high a proportion?

They pay British banks, which finance these ventures and profit on the exchange because London is the clearing house. The Rupee is so tied to the Sterling that every Rupee converted into (say) francs brings 'us' a profit.

They pay an army of British officials receiving salaries often much higher than that of a British Cabinet Minister, and always utterly disproportionate to the average among the natives – which is much lower than it is here.

In my book *White Sahibs in India* I analysed all this in detail, citing the evidence in relation to that country. The huge dividends – often hundreds per cent per year on the capital – speak for themselves.

And now for the Debit Account – Imperialism does not pay those who suffer or will suffer from 'Coolie Competition'. For some years now factories have been growing up in the colonies, worked by cheap labour and free from restrictions which a democratic government would be compelled to impose upon them. Hence the jute industry leaves Dundee for Calcutta. Iron and steel are beginning to follow. Unemployment in Britain results, and a downward trend in wages 'to meet competition'.

It does not pay the colonial peoples, who produce the wealth from which the profits are made, whilst living themselves in scandalous poverty.

It does not pay the ordinary tax-payer, who, with only a very indirect 'interest', if any, in Empire, must pay for vast armaments in order to protect somebody else's dividends in Hong Kong or Jamaica.

It does not pay the millions of young men who will be killed, in all parts of the world, in the next war to decide who shall bring peace and civilisation to these ignorant savages.

And finally, it will not pay those who want democracy at home and despotism abroad. The Moors of Spanish Morocco decided that it made no difference to them who was in power, because Spanish democrats behaved as autocratically as Spanish fascists – where the colonies were concerned. When Franco offered them bribes and promises to march against Spain they felt that they were just 'getting their own back'.

Let us get rid of the idea that the Empire is a 'trust'. It is no more a 'trust' than Abyssinia was 'entrusted' to Mussolini; and if we have a 'duty to remain' merely because we happen to be where we are, then the Italians have the same duty in Ethiopia and the Japanese in China. I know the excuses. The colonial peoples are 'children' and must be 'educated for self-government'. We are all children and all in sad need of that education; *but why should the children with the most dangerous toys, after robbing their brothers and sisters, suddenly set up as parents and teachers?*

'But if we left the colonies, some other country would seize them.'
Quite possibly, though it does not follow. If I do not rob my neighbour
or murder him, someone else *may* – but even if it were a certainty it
would not be a justification for *my* doing so.

The small minority of us in this country who repudiate the
domination of nation by nation or of race by race can proclaim it from
the housetops and make clear that ours is the only *realist* solution,
because all others lead to oppression abroad, the decay of liberty at
home and endless vistas of war *in which we shall refuse to participate.*
The emphasis of this final point which may be made into a powerful
deterrent is the most practical contribution which we can make at the
moment.

Ethel was also writing for *Peace News.* In 'Pacifism and Politics', she
attacked the majority of pacifists who

> sit in the ivory tower of their simple pacifist doctrine, complacently
> relegating the problem of the colonial peoples to the Mandate system
> and a bigger and better thieves' kitchen called the League of Nations.
> 'Our business is to refuse to have anything to do with war', they say,
> smugly. 'We aren't interested in politics.' What are politics if they are
> not the conduct of human affairs? How separate the problem of peace
> from the problem of war, and the problem of war from the problem of
> the whole capitalist-imperialist system under which we live? Can any
> honest, thinking person oppose war yet support a government which
> maintains a military dominance over millions of people whose labour it
> exploits to the point of slavery, and whose lands it stole and continues
> to steal? You are not prepared to join in the class struggle for the
> building up of a society in which war becomes impossible? You are
> content to be merely negative, not cooperating in a war, but also not
> cooperating in the revolutionary struggle for a better, safer world?

She had no use for such 'pathifists'.

> Give me a thousand times rather than such sentimental pacifism the
> anti-militarist who opposes all imperialist wars, but is prepared to go to
> the barricades if need be for the wild, mad, impossible dream of
> smashing by such tactics the system that breeds wars. About such a
> man there is no hypocrisy. The simple pacifist doctrine of Dick
> Sheppard (of the Peace Pledge Union) is a very good starting-off point
> for pacifists, but the revolutionary anti-militarism of Bart de Ligt is
> where the consistent pacifist should ultimately end. End? The real
> peace movement – as opposed to a negative, milk-and-water, war-is-
> horrid 'pathifism' – only begins there.

112

*Reg (right) with more friends*
[COURTESY: FRIENDS SCHOOL,
SAFFRON WALDEN]

*Ethel inscribed this photograph
'For Reg, his Best Friend, the old
woman, with everlasting love,
Mary'*
[PAUL TANQUERAY – COURTESY: JEAN FAULKS]

Reg then shattered 'The Illusions of Power', giving as the first illusion 'the fact that few of us will admit power to be an end and not a means. Those who have no power share this illusion with those who have'. Power was not commonly desired – by the successful businessman, for instance – as a means to a specific goal, but for its own sake. The desire for popularity was a desire for power – 'popularity is a form of power, and unpopularity is its negation. Hence a man who will twist you in a business deal will stand you an excellent dinner out of the proceeds.' The second illusion of power he defined as 'the belief that certain people have "power" over us, when their "power" is mostly the measure of our own acquiescence. The power of one man or one group over a community exists just so long as the community on the whole believes in it'. He quoted the artist Joseph Southall: 'People talk about the workers getting power into their hands. They've already got it; it's in their heads that they want it', and illustrated the point by citing an unemployed British working man who boasted of 'our possessions in China' when he himself did not possess even a flower pot of his native soil. Power, itself an illusion, was shared by those who in no way exercised it.

The illusion which presented the greatest problem was the tendency for movements, originating in the wish to eradicate oppression, to create new oppressions, and for social discontent to become the lever to power for unprincipled opportunities or for honest leaders to become corrupted by their own success. This illusion, 'the belief that power, used unscrupulously and for selfish ends, must be overthrown by power which will not be used unscrupulously and for selfish ends', did not recognise that 'power itself is the evil – the power of an indiviual or group over the community'. Illusions of power could be dispersed only

> by a great task of regeneration – the reinstatement of social ethics as the basis of progress. If power is ever to be challenged, only a profound conviction of human rights can make that challenge effective. Only the same conviction can prevent the replacement of one form of oppression for another. Peace, justice and liberty are only possible where the pursuit of power is abandoned. I believe that Marxist socialism has failed to make headway because its protagonists have forgotten the universal truth of the saying that man does not live by bread alone. Actually the hunger for idealism is so great that if people are not offered good ideals they will follow bad ones – hence their willingness to die for Adolf Hitler or the British Empire. We say that all men are equal before the law; and that law we must aim not to destroy but to fulfil. It is not by sneering at democracy that we shall achieve that end, but by pushing it forward to its utmost political and economic limits. And the end of that path, for those who have the courage to follow it, is universal anarchism.

Reg was invited to contribute an essay for an anthology of reflections on the life of Gandhi. He quoted from W. G. Hole's poem, 'The Fools of God' –

>His fools in vesture strange
>    God sent to range
>The World and said: 'Declare
>Untimely wisdom; bear
>Harsh witness and prepare
>    The paths of change'.

He had read the poem a few months before he went to India and doubted if any words had made a more lasting impression on his mind. The poem told of God's instructions to his Fools: 'Be deaf; defer to none, and ever perversely shun the prudent way'. 'Faith-befooled', they claim

>To see the light that rings
>Men's brows and makes them kings
>With power to do the things
>    Of righteousness.

Within a few months of discovering the poem,

I met – may I say it with all respect – Public Fool Number One, Mahatma Gandhi. And it did not take me long to discover that the vivid description in the lines that had so moved and inspired me fitted this man to the last detail.

In spite of all that has been argued to the contrary, I do not think Gandhi is a *clever* man. Since I first came to know him, 10 years ago, I have often felt extremely critical of his words and his actions. His claim to greatness would, in my mind, be a slender one if it had to rely upon his political sagacity. It is by other standards that he must be judged.

In his right place the Puritan is but a stern physician who prescribes abstinence and a strict regimen for a patient who is sick from a surfeit. Wherever great movements of social reform or revolution are found, a strain of Puritanism can be discovered. It is part of the discipline of men and women who have to give up much in order to concentrate their energies on one thing. That the leaders of modern India should be Puritans and the chief of them all a rigorous ascetic is therefore no accident. A revolt against imperialism could make no headway unless it struck at the fetters and blinkers which kept the people of India ignorant, indolent, caste-ridden and superstitious. Gandhi was able to lead the movement for political emancipation because he opposed the power of the priests, the evils accepted by the orthodox, 'Untouchability', the inferior status of women, child marriages, neglect of public

115

hygiene, religious intolerance, wasteful expenditure on marriages, the use of opium – in short, the social corruption which had produced political inertia.

It was Baül who said – as a warning to myself and others who with our little learning try to appraise the incalculable –

A goldsmith, methinks, has come into the garden:
He would appraise the Lotus, forsooth,
By rubbing it on his touchstone.

Judged by the standard of the goldsmith the lotus was valueless. Our familiar measures may often prove equally deceptive when human wisdom sits in judgement over the Fools of God.

# CHAPTER IX

# War, Prison and Loos

FROM THE TIME OF THE SPANISH CIVIL WAR until 1945 (the year of Hiroshima), Reg did not consider himself to be a real pacifist:

A real pacifist loves the human race and his anti-militarism is only an incidental expression of this attitude. My own opposition to militarism arose from a dislike of all governments; and if I did not exactly hate the human race I generally felt exasperated with it. I hated Hitlerism and I hated Zionism; I hated Communism with more consistency than the Tory statesmen who were so soon to welcome the Russians as allies; and I had spent many years in the struggle against imperialism – especially that of my own country.

I am no good at choosing between two evils, partly because I regard 'lesser-evilism' as the line of perpetual retreat, but partly because I find it difficult to decide which evil is greater – it implies a pre-vision of ultimate results and a confidence in one's own infallibility which I don't possess. Before the war was six months old I'd decided that the only solution for anyone holding my views was to find something to do that was intrinsically useful, concentrating temporarily on those 'ameliorative' activities which I'd always despised because they solved no fundamental problems. And then, of course, there were ideas that one believed in, which still needed to be kept alive until something practical could be done about them.

But for the first few months I could not accept this view. I was a member of an anti-imperialist organisation and some of us had romantic ideas about using Ireland as a base for propaganda against both sides if war broke out. Ireland had impressed me favourably, but when I returned to explore the possibilities I found no support of any practical value.

For three weeks, Ethel and Reg rented a near-derelict old Irish house where damp streamed down the walls and rats scuttled in the wainscoting – 'Ah, sure, they're in every room', said the stoic landlady. Ethel worked on her satirical novel, *Rolling in the Dew*, based on a pie-in-the-sky summer school she and Reg had attended in Switzerland. Reg read the book chapter by chapter, making criticisms ('to the most modest and receptive of authors') and helping to create new cranky characters.

*Rolling in the Dew* was dedicated, in part, 'to George Orwell who so abominates "the bearded, fruit-juice drinking sandal-wearers" of the "roll-in-the-dew-before-breakfast" school'. The representatives at the school were all in search of the eternal verities. Everywhere you turned they were pontificating on the Cosmos, the Libido, the Infinite, the Absolute. They were like people in films, stopping to embrace when the ship is sinking and each moment counts. There were earnest women in hand-woven smocks and folk-dancing men in bathing slips. There was Frau Thistlebloomer playing leapfrog with an elderly cove in horn-rimmed glasses and little else. There were shrieking enthusiasts rolling in the wet grass, toning up their nerves and muscles. There was a woman revolted by the sight of an onion – onions were stimulants, don't you know, and not consistent with the true *Brahmacharya* of body, mind and spirit. There were pre-supper nudist showers and discussions on the correlation of historical chronology with social evolution. They thought they wanted the simplification of life but what they most enjoyed, in an orgy of self-indulgence and passionate proselytising, was the complication of life. Their cerebral fornication had no roots in reality. They believed in everything from cold water to psychoanalysis, in everything but honest-to-goodness *action*. They groped in the clouds instead of on the earth. Never mind. Have pity on them now in wartime. Keep them safe in their ivory towers.

Ethel and Reg returned to London but, by January 1940, Ethel was back in Ireland, in Connemara in the west of County Galway, the country of the O'Mainnín clan. Her aim was to rent a cottage near Mannin Bay of which her father, proud of his ancient Irish lineage, had often spoken. She had every intention of spending most of the war in London, however, before the war had started, she had pined for a retreat where, periodically, she could work undisturbed. The outbreak of hostilities gave her added impetus: if the bombs destroyed her Wimbledon home, there would still be something left in Ireland. The three-roomed cottage she found, set amongst bogs, boulders and mountains, was above an estuary five miles from Mannin Bay. She rented it for five shillings a week and through February, made it habitable. She created a garden, brought sand and fine shingle from the seashore in a donkey-cart to build a drive up to the front door and, with a local lad, whitewashed, distempered and painted. Her neighbours recognised her as the mad English writer who had had two husbands and was reputed to have had nine. Reg joined her in March and they left together in April on receiving the news of the sudden death of Reg's mother. Ethel was unable to get a permit to return to the cottage until 1945 and then, anxious that her landlord might sell it to one of the English flocking over to Ireland to buy meat denied them by the rationing at home, she bought the property.

Early in 1940, Reg wrote for *Peace News* again on Palestine, one of the 'A' Mandates, which, according to the League Covenant, had reached

a stage of development where their existence as independent nations can be provisionally recognised by a Mandatory until such time as they are able to stand alone. The wishes of these communities must be a principal consideration in the selection of the Mandatory.

He hardly needed to point out

that the 'independence' of Palestine has never been recognised, either 'provisionally' or in any other way; that the people were never consulted as to their choice of a Mandatory; that the Mandatory Power, in fact, selected itself; that Palestine comes under the control of our Colonial Office and that the latest White Paper on 'Colonial Development and Welfare' gives a jolt to the whole fiction. In it you will find the significant parenthesis, following the term 'colonies': 'in which term are included for the purpose of this statement protectorates and mandated territories'. So I am right enough in considering Palestine as a colony *de facto*.

Due to the issue of the Land Transfer Regulations,

land sales have no doubt profited both the Arab landlords who sold and the Jewish settlers who bought; but they have left in their trail a story of evicted Arab tenant farmers whose numbers, in the words of *The Times*, 'threaten the disastrous swelling of a landless Arab proletariat'. What is really interesting is not that the government should have taken this action, but that it should have taken it *at this time*. Our government has an unfortunate habit of rarely moving forward unless it is somewhat aggressively pushed from behind. Yet we are continually assured that all is peaceful and happy in Palestine. Hence the pointed question put to Mr MacDonald by Major Cazalet, who said: 'Why has the right hon. gentleman chosen this particular moment, after six months of war and six months of peace in Palestine, for the first time for the last six years, when all sections of the community are working loyally with the government in that country, to introduce a measure

119

which will exacerbate Jewish opinion not only in Palestine but throughout the whole world?'

Why, indeed? Mr MacDonald endeavoured to assure the House that everything in Palestine was just as the gallant Major had described. The Arabs had suddenly swung round to frenzied enthusiasm for the Union Jack. Nevertheless (for fear they swung back again) this measure was urgent, so urgent he couldn't even wait for the League of Nations Council to consider it first.

Other politicians felt that

it was proper to obtain the sanction of Geneva before it could be decided that the Arab peasants should not be driven off their land. But in face of such a conscientious internationalism, I found it curious that no one asked *whether the permission of Geneva had been sought before Palestine was turned into an armed camp by a belligerent Power*. If we are *not* using Palestine illegally as a mere cog in our own war machine then we have a right to know and a duty to ask *what is happening there which makes these sudden concessions on the land question an urgent diplomatic necessity and also necessitates the maintenance of an enormous standing army on the spot?*

He did not often agree with the *Evening Standard* but one of its leaders aptly summed up what needed to be said about Palestine and the general colonial position: 'Those responsible, it seems, are hesitant in making known facts which might be used by German propagandists. This is a plausible doctrine: *We believe it is also highly dangerous*'.

Following the deaths of Ernst Toller and W. B. Yeats, Emma Goldman died in Canada, and Ethel was free to write the biographical novel which she and Emma had discussed in the Ivy Restaurant: *Red Rose* was the story of Emma, her ex-lover Alexander (Sasha) Berkman and his young mistress, 'Emmy'. Emma had been glad to put England behind her. '*Yew* English people!' she would growl at her audiences as they meekly passed up the five pound notes that Ethel had wheedled out of them for arms for Spain. Stuffing the money into her black leather handbag, Emma would shake with fury at the 'miserable sums' extorted from the British 'bourgeoisie', and fruitlessly would Ethel protest that raising as much as £200 at a meeting was, for England, good going. Near the end, Emma had lost the power of speech, for which relief much thanks, thought Reg uncharitably. Ironically, she was only allowed to return to America, which she regarded as her home, after she was dead. She was buried in Chicago where thousands watched the hearse heaped high with roses and carnations. The funeral procession was more like a May Day demonstration. 'The most dangerous woman in America' drew the audiences she craved at last. For Ethel, she always had affection and respect and, in spite of all, those feelings were reciprocated.

☆    ☆    ☆

Through the death of his mother, Reg was in closer contact with the Society of Friends. He was guided into living and working for some months at Spiceland, a large house in Devon, used as a training centre for Quaker relief workers. His course included community service, first-aid, building, camp-cooking and farming; and Ethel visited him for weekends at Honiton, Cullompton or Sidmouth. Dramatic events soon upset his schedule. After a bout of renal colic, he underwent a kidney operation at Bart's Hospital. While he was there, a barrage balloon came adrift one stormy night, dragging its cable over the top floor flat he shared with Laurence Housman; the cable smashed the chimney which fell through the roof, Laurence narrowly escaping from his bed.

Reg convalesced at Oak Cottage, salvaging what remained of his belongings from the rubble of the flat. There were no vehicles available for removals, railways were being bombed and bus queues stretched into infinity, so he often walked the last four miles to Wimbledon, carrying heavy loads of damaged books and papers. He also managed to rescue a beautiful inlaid wood gaming table which he had bought in his youth with money borrowed from his father for the purchase of a bed, his old camp-bed having collapsed. He had searched the secondhand shops for a cheap replacement but when he spied the table, there was no contest, the money went on that, and he continued to sleep on the floor.

He proudly showed the table, acquired for such a small sum, to visitors at Oak Cottage, and learned that it was a valuable example of the handicraft of a family in Kerry. There was a sequel to the story. To Ethel's shock and horror, he decided one day to part with it – he was broke and 'I could probably sell it at Christie's for £200'. 'But it's your one material treasure!' she exclaimed. All right, he said, he would hold on to it for a while, 'but such is masculine perfidy that as soon as my back was turned, he removed the table and took it to Christie's. Later, he sent me the catalogue in which it was listed. I was very upset; it seemed so very sad that he who was always so generous to everyone, far beyond his very limited means, should have parted with his one treasure'. Unbeknownst to Reg, she asked a friend to bid for the table up to £50; as some of the inlaid shamrocks were missing, that was all she thought it would fetch.

121

On the day of the sale the only bidder other than my friend was a dealer. He offered £2.10s. My friend got him up to £8 – and secured the table which, for the time being, he took to his flat. In due course I heard from Reg. He was very fed up, he wrote; his table had fetched only 'a miserable eight quid'. I wrote commiserating with him and meanwhile my young friend continued to house the table, grumbling from time to time about it being in the way and what an infernal nuisance Reg was. I had planned to take the table back to Ireland – a year or two might well pass, I thought, before Reg would be there again, and by that time it would be easier to break it to him that it was I who had bid, by proxy, at Christie's.

But her friend wanted rid of the encumbrance and she finally decided to bring it to Oak Cottage.

Then one evening, when we were returning from town together, I told Reg I had a surprise for him at home, adding that I didn't know whether he'd be pleased or angry. Then I opened the front door and as he stepped inside he saw the table which I had placed in the little hall. 'My table!' he gasped. 'How on earth – – –?' 'I couldn't bear for it to go from us so I had Alan bid for it', I told him, adding quickly, 'Please don't be angry. But for that you'd only have got 50 shillings for it'. 'I'm not angry. I think it noble of you. I also feel a bit of a fool.' 'The moral', I said severely, 'is always give me the first offer of anything you want to sell. You'll get a better price.'

Spiceland claimed him for the winter. Riding his bicycle at nearby Blackborough, an hour before daylight, he was apprehended by a special constable. 'You've got no light', he accused. 'But there's a full moon and a clear sky', said Reg. 'I can see a good 100 yards ahead.' No matter; he was guilty. In court, he was fined seven and sixpence and nine shillings 'costs'. 'What is the alternative?' he enquired. 'Seven days in prison!' Good, he thought, winking at Ethel who was sitting at the back of the court. Now he could say 'When I was in prison – – –' rather like the left-wing weekenders who used to pay brief visits to Spain and casually drop the remark, 'When I was in Madrid during the Civil War – – –' A police inspector murmured to Ethel, 'Miss Mannin – don't you think *men are unwise?*' (the title of her novel about mountaineering). 'Not at all', she replied. 'It's a matter of principle!' Several farm labourers had caught it in the neck for the same reason, when everyone knew that in bright moonlight the semi-blacked-out light on a bicycle was less than useless. 'They've been run in', Ethel told the inspector, 'through the officiousness of the special constable and they've all tamely paid up! *Someone* has to make a stand!'

122

It required a car and two policemen to convey Reg to Exeter prison –

Odd it seemed to me that the State, because it could not extract 16s 6d from me, was prepared to spend so much more on making my life (and its own) inconvenient. Of course, I had emptied my pockets before leaving for the court because I had heard of fines being taken from people who forgot to do that. So I knew they'd have to pay my fare back from Exeter. The more I thought of it, the clearer it seemed to me that the State was fining itself and that I was to be rewarded for my wickedness.

A spokesman for the farm labourers who had paid the fine mumbled sheepishly to Ethel: 'I hope you won't take offence but if Mr Reynolds has gone to prison because he can't pay, we'd be glad to pass the hat around'. She thanked him warmly and tried to explain that it was the Principle of the Thing, you see, as he shuffled out, bemused.

'Wotcher in for, mate?' asked fellow prisoners at exercise time. 'Riding a bike without a light.' If only, thought Reg, I could have said I was in for batting the missis or for rape, they'd have respected me. (In prison, the bigger the crime, the greater the prestige.) A warder brought to his cell, in which he languished for 14 hours at a stretch, an armful of coarse canvas – 'Have you ever sewn mail-bags afore? No? Well, nah's yer chance ter learn!' During air-raids, prisoners were locked in, the possibility of their deaths not so disastrous as the possibility of their escape.

After five days, he was released. Once again, he was riding his bicycle to work, this time with the regulation light, when he narrowly missed running into a farm labourer. He skidded badly, fracturing his femur, and was taken to Exeter General Hospital. Wrote a Spiceland wit:

> Ethel has no Mannin.
> He's gone in a van in
> To Exeter
> to see a leg-setter.

With his leg skewered and slung up by means of weights and pulleys, he was informed by two policemen that he was suspected of colliding with the labourer deliberately, in the mistaken belief that this innocent citizen was the special constable who had been responsible for his arrest. Reg assured them that that was not the case and the policemen departed with an air of 'We believe you – thousands wouldn't'.

He spent three and a half months in hospital, Ethel staying for weeks at a local farm whence she stumbled some six miles over steep and frozen roads each visiting day. Then she went back to London, travelling down to Exeter every Sunday morning and returning to Oak Cottage in the evening. In hospital, Reg reviewed his recent imprisonment. From the financial point of view, it had been profitable: he was able to sell two articles about his experiences and, with the saving of the fine and costs, plus the Discharged Prisoners' Aid half-crown, he had made a net profit of about £13. He had found only one amiable warder – the rest were brutal.

> A man goaded as prisoners are goaded by perpetual insults [he wrote], will not always think of the frightful punishments reserved for assaulting a warder. That first evening of monotony I paced my cell and learned something about prison nerves the next morning, when a dejected face looked in at my door. It was a neighbour on his way to empty his slops, and he said: 'If you must walk up and down, mate, wear your slippers. It's an awful row – it's depressing'. Yes, prisoners have nerves; but they must have an iron control of them to make rioting as rare as it is. I was given no soap and only obtained a piece after two days of persistent requests for it. During that time, I had to wash as best I could with tooth-powder. The eating utensils were dirty, the basin caked with filth, and the slops had not been emptied.

Ethel urged him to write to the prison governor but how, he asked, could the governor possibly accept the word of an ex-prisoner when all his warders were sure to tell a different story? However, he had no objection to Ethel writing, and her letter resulted in the gentlemanly governor escorting her around the prison to convince her of her wrong-headedness. The forewarned warders were, naturally, on their best behaviour, and convinced she was not.

☆    ☆    ☆

Reg was released from hospital in March 1941 with his right leg in a steel caliper. 'No more *bicycles*!' said Ethel, as she helped him lurch out of the ward.

Her *Christianity – or Chaos?* was published, with acknowledgements to Reg for research, suggestions and criticisms.

> This book [she wrote] contends that though men were good before Christ, as they were wise before Buddha, and 'God' may be the Christian conception, or the Judaic, or the Islamic, or the Hindu, or the nameless emanation of Pantheism, Christianity gives the fullest expression to the doctrine that God is love, and that to seek to live in the imitation of Christ is the highest ideal to which Man can aspire. [She stated at the outset that] intellectually, so far as any personal Deity is

124

concerned, I call myself an agnostic, even an atheist, a rationalist, but when I set out in war-time to cross the Irish Sea I prayed for a safe journey, and when I reached the other side in the grey morning I felt a deep compulsion to give thanks. The religious impulse – call it superstition if you like – goes deeper than intellectuality – which is a sterile thing at best. Religion, deeply felt, is a matter of the emotions, and the emotions are the source of creativeness, of all that is vital and potent in life.

War was the greatest of all evils, 'greater than any evil it may set out to fight'. To deny life was 'to deny all goodness, the supreme goodness which is God. I can respect the argument that *the ultimate end* justifies all the horrors and sufferings of warfare, including the mass sacrifice of human life, but find myself totally unable to accept it, or to reconcile it with Christian teaching, though I am aware that the Church finds no difficulty in doing so'.

She paid tribute to the revered Verrier Elwin:

Elwin's sainthood lies in the fact that here is a cultured, highly civilised man, a man who enjoys the good things of life, good wine, good food, comfort, the conversation of people as cultured – in the Western sense – as himself, who voluntarily adopts a life of poverty, hardship, and suffering, in the jungle. For years his health has suffered, with fever after fever. I asked him once why he went about wrapped in a blanket in the cold winter months of that high altitude, why he did not take out thick shirts and pullovers from England. He replied that he could not afford to equip everyone with such warm clothing, and that that being so he did not feel entitled to indulge himself in such comfort. This, I submit, is the essence of Christianity, the spirit of Christ in practice. [Elwin did not preach Christianity; he lived it.] And he does not missionise. The Gonds have their own ideas of God and Creation, and from this springs their folklore and primitive culture which Elwin is very anxious they should preserve.

Europe, she maintained, had never recovered from the gradual growth of nationalism due to the development of 'national' churches out of the great schism of the Reformation:

The seamless garment of Christ was rended. To speak of 'The Church of England' is surely a contradiction in terms, for the Church is essentially catholic, as universal as God. Its power is essentially spiritual; it can have nothing to do with the State, whose power is purely temporal, whose values are not of God, that is to say as enunciated by Christ, but of the stock exchange and the market-place.

There were two kinds of nationalism in the world today, and had been throughout history.

There is the *liberating* nationalism of a nation's struggle for independence, as in India, Ireland, Palestine; and there is the *imperialist* nationalism of fascism and Zionism – the latter cannot even lay claim to a distorted form of socialism; it is through and through capitalist in its imperialism.

What the political revolutionary almost always overlooked was 'the importance, the absolute necessity for revolution in the heart of man – the triumph of the religious heart over the materialist heart; to use Gandhi's language, of soul-force over brute-force.'

She took a swipe at the Quaker William Penn, founder and first governor of Pennsylvania:

In view of the fact that the keeping of slaves was sanctioned by the constitution framed by him for his 'Holy Experiment', and that he was himself a slave-owner, it is not unreasonable to doubt whether his treatment of the Indians was inspired by humanitarian motives so much as expediency. The Indians, unlike the Negroes, were not helpless slaves.

If Penn and his followers were not to be exterminated and were to do business with the Indians,

their approach to them had necessarily to be very friendly. It would be easier to believe in the purity of his motives where the Indians were concerned had he shown any brotherly love towards the Negroes. But he was never interested in Negro emancipation.

Intellectually, she granted, Quakerism was ahead of Catholicism:

it is essentially sane and reasonable and free from bigotry, [but spiritually], from the point of view of universal human satisfaction, it can never catch up with Catholicism, despite its basic principles of the Inward Light. [Perhaps because of its very reasonableness] it has never swept human imagination with the force of the Catholic Church; in a sense it may be said to be too 'materialist', too much of a rationalisation of the Divinity of Christ and the inspiration of his teachings. For deep spiritual satisfaction, it would seem, humanity demands a *faith*, out-topping reason; it has need of a more profound mysticism than Quakerism can offer.

She approved Herbert Read's definition of anarchism as a reaffirmation of a natural freedom, of 'direct communion with universal truth', of the rule of reason and the release of the imagination. Anarchism was not to be confused with anarchy, which was chaos and confusion. 'Anarchism is *cooperation*, the replacement of the individual struggle for existence with the

126

natural law of *mutual aid*. Anarchism in its modern interpretation connotes control of each industry by the workers in that industry – anarcho-syndicalism.' That an anarchist system of society demanded a very high ethical standard was obvious:

> It demands complete loyalty to the cooperative ideal; it demands the utmost personal integrity; it demands that the ultimate end, the good of the community, shall always be applied to the ethic of individual conduct; in a word it demands *Goodness*, the selfless serving of that Supreme Good which is 'God' and which alone can effect the Kingdom of Heaven on earth. It involves the whole of the *positive* creed of Christianity – Thou shalt love thy neighbour as thyself; thou shalt love thy enemies, do good to them that persecute you. Thou shalt love, thou shalt forgive, thou shalt serve. It embodies the whole philosophy of Christ's supreme command, *'Love one another'*.

How much of that entered into the existing systems of Christian society?

> The very nature of a competitive, capitalist society is opposed to it. It is a system entirely incompatible with the practice of Christianity. Either we abandon all pretences at Christianity – in which case we lapse into barbarism, or we have the courage and the vision to go forward to a new way of living that is yet as old as Christianity itself.

Only painfully, inharmoniously, was it possible to live in the imitation of Christ within a capitalist society.

> By selling all our possessions and giving to the poor we become homeless outcasts dependent on a society which is a negation of all Christian principles; the position is untenable. Only through complete reorganisation of society can this equable distribution of possessions be effected to good purpose. Then, when each is giving to society service according to his ability, and taking from it according to his needs, the evil of riches and of private ownership is disposed of and a natural equality achieved. A stateless, cooperative society of goods in common not merely makes Christianity a living reality, instead of a hollow mockery as it is today, but makes the *spirit* of Christ's teaching a reality. Equality, cooperation, goods in common, these are the material aspects of Christian teaching; they could exist in a communist, socialist, communist-anarchist, anarcho-syndicalist, society without the application of the *spirit* of the Christian law; they could exist, that is to say, purely as part of an economic system. The USSR, freed from its bureaucracy, could be such a society, whilst at the same time completely denying Christ. Such a society lives in the imitation of Christ only by the application of the Christian principle of universal

love – without which the principle of nonviolence cannot be made effective. The application of the principle of nonviolent resistance to evil can only be effected through *the spiritual revolution*, the 'change of heart', implicit in Christ's teachings.

☆     ☆     ☆

In the late evening of Passion Sunday 1941, a young man, with whom Ethel and Reg had been corresponding, turned up on the doorstep of Oak Cottage. He was a merchant seaman who hated the idea of being part of the war effort. He had climbed through the porthole of his ship, having explained in a note to his captain his reasons for absconding. He asked Ethel and Reg to take him in, which they willingly did, thus making them technically guilty of the crime of 'harbouring' a deserter. The next day Reg, in pain and still limping, visited the shipping company and pleaded the boy's youth and sincerity. The company, behaving with restraint, insisted that the boy return to sea, but while he was waiting for a ship from the wartime 'pool', he registered as a CO, appeared before a tribunal, and was employed in land work until 1944 when he died of a cerebral haemorrhage. Found in his jacket pocket was a letter addressed to Ethèl, telling her that he had changed his views and was planning to apply for a job in the Air Force. She was relieved that he had delayed posting it as she would have written to him bitterly and he might have received the letter on the day of his death.

Acquaintanceship with this young man spurred her into writing *Commonsense and Morality* – 'there seemed to me no better time to consider the question of morality than when surrounded by the vast immorality of war'. She would like to see Christianity liberated from the Church in all its denominations:

> I have no use for the Church, but every use for the Sermon on the Mount. If I am told – as I am – that Christianity is a great deal more than the Sermon on the Mount, that it involves belief in the Immaculate Conception and the Virgin Birth, in Original Sin, Transubstantiation, the resurrection from the dead, and the life everlasting, I reply that I am not interested in the mythology of the Christian religion, which a very little research shows to have existed in one form or another thousands of years before Christ, but considerably interested in the ethics of Jesus and their practical application to modern life. It may seem blasphemous to some, but nevertheless to me it seems unimportant whether Jesus was the Christ or not. The Christian ethic, to my mind, can get along very well without the impositions of either Judaism or pagan mythology.

128

On the far-reaching effects of a revolution in the heart of man over and above any political revolution, she wrote:

Political revolution involves a change of government – very seldom of an entire social system; when we get a change of the social system, as in Russia, unless it is accompanied by the greater revolution of the change in the heart·of men it is doomed to failure in the end. Can Russia, a member of the League of Nations, be said to have fulfilled the promise of the October revolution? Can Jesus be said to have achieved a revolution in the heart of man when men still exploit and murder each other whilst calling themselves Christians? Jesus failed and Lenin failed; Paul succeeded Jesus and Stalin succeeded Lenin. You may admire Paulianity and Stalinism, but it is not to be pretended that they are the same thing as Christianity and Communism. The need is for the Christian communism of the early Christians, but it must steer clear of the State if it is to survive, avoid every form of centralised government if it is to preserve its integrity – its Christian communist integrity, that is to say its essential anarchism.

Reg, his leg healing, was finding it difficult to get a job. He kept going by writing and placing an occasional story or satirical verse, and was still contributing articles to *Peace News*. One of them, 'Who Is For Liberty?' illuminated the fact that

Socialists for many years talked a great deal about organisation, which was obviously going to prove inevitable, and very little about *who was going to do the organising* – a question by no means pre-determined. Perhaps it was part of their Marxist heritage that the inevitables of economics attracted them much more than the ethical issues, which the materialist conception of history could not decide for them. It appears that men in the mass work more enthusiastically for a cause that is promised *inevitable* triumph, though one might have expected such 'inevitability' to make a Communist lazy in his work and a Calvinist lax in his morals. Once more human nature shows itself inexplicable in terms of logic.

The result of that teaching could be seen today:

The Fabian end of socialism completely captured the Labour Party, whilst similar influences dominated the social-democratic parties on the Continent. Socialists formed minority governments or entered into coalition with the older parties in order to obtain office.

The result could only be socialist organisation on a capitalist basis – that is to say, as much coordination of industry as capitalists would permit – but always the old profit motive kept intact. The war has

129

accelerated that process and shown us just what 'the inevitability of socialism' really means. It had to come, even if there had been no socialists.

But now that we are rapidly getting just what many socialists spent their lives fighting for, startling facts come to light. The first is that *whichever way we start out, we seem to reach the same end*; and that it is not, after all, a very pleasant end. The Bolsheviki set out in the opposite direction from the Fabians. They would have no coalitions or compromises. They had their revolution and their revolutionary dictatorship.

The Nazis again, disgusted alike with Social Democracy, capitalist individualism, and Communism, tried yet a third path. F. A. Ridley (in *Fascism – What Is It?*) compares them to the Jesuits, who met Reformation with Counter Reformation. And yet Britain in the year 1941 is racing to meet Russia and Germany on a common level – that of the totalitarian State.

Behind this convergence of systems lay a convergence of ideas, or lack of them.

In spite of all the recent talk of liberty and democracy in Britain, it has never occurred to the Labour Party that efficiency and organisation were two-edged weapons, capable of being used for two purposes.

A community that organises itself collectively, owning corporately and controlling democratically the means of production, extends its own freedom by its greater efficiency – that is to say, by its more scientific mastery of nature. But a community organised by others for the benefit of themselves becomes nearer to slavery with each advance in efficiency. The fewer the masters, the greater the tyranny. The tighter and more efficient the organisation, the greater is the servitude of the individual.

Socialists had preached organisation as the cure for waste and chaos in a rotten economic system.

Hitler offered them organisation and *delivered the goods*. Socialists had been authoritarian, either coming to terms with the bourgeois State (as the Social Democrats did) or preaching the 'dictatorship of the proletariat'. This propaganda admirably prepared the way for the Nazis – for, after all, if you are going to trust somebody else with absolute power to do something that you are too lazy to do for yourself, why not one man as well as another?

No one who had given thought to the problem of freedom and how to maintain it

130

could have failed to see that the greater the collectivisation of industry, the greater would be the threat to liberty, if power remained concentrated in a few hands. We cannot too strongly emphasise the need for liberty, the meaning of liberty, the intimate connection between liberty and every other social or political need. We cannot too zealously guard whatever liberty is left to us, press for the return of liberty taken from us, and agitate for liberty which we never yet possessed. To show what freedom means and what it could bring to this diseased world, to replace with hope the despair and disillusionment on which future dictators feed, that is the greatest task before us, and more than enough for our strength.

Reg completed his convalescence at the home of relatives, one of whom drew his attention to a literary competition which he entered and won. Philip Unwin, the publisher, wrote to him asking if he could produce anything equally amusing in the way of a book. If I wrote a book at all, replied Reg, stressing that he was really a serious political writer whose views were unpopular, it would be a history of the water-closet, as he believed that the best part of mankind went down the drain. He supplied Unwin with a synopsis and a specimen chapter, and started work on *Cleanliness and Godliness*. When it was published in 1943, it sold out rapidly, was taken up by Doubleday and Company of New York, and was reprinted twice.

His exuberant style reminded reviewers of Burton and Sterne. John Cowper Powys was transported by the book, calling it a 'poignant interrogation in the manner of the author of *Finnegan's Wake*.' A. S. Neill's verdict was 'fine, lovely, something unique, most subtle in its politeness about what ain't considered polite'. Laurence Housman enthused:

Bless Thee, Bottom, Thou art translated. . . . Neglect of sanitation has probably destroyed more human lives than the spectacular Scourge of War, both nuisances surviving owing to lack of commonsense. Sanitation is the second revelation – the revelation of science – and its progress is the subject of Mr Reynolds' learned and highly entertaining treatise. One proof of our advance is the improbability that, either from police-court or pulpit, will there be any attempt to head off the beneficial career of this book.

☆ ☆ ☆

To Reg, the romance of sanitation, its progress among the ancients, decline in the Middle Ages and revival as an integral, but neglected, aspect of the Renaissance, was the Intimate History of Man, beginning some 3,000 years BC with the elegant privies and elaborate drainage systems of India and Crete, and, in Britain, with the Neolithic jakes in the Orkneys – small oblong enclosures, let into the thickness of the wall. The hero of *Cleanliness and Godliness* was an Elizabethan, Gloriana's godson, Sir John Harington, poet, courtier, soldier, wit and inventor. His inventions were the achievement of an ancient civilisation that found rebirth in his imagination, so true was he to the Renaissance tradition; for his prime invention was the valve water-closet, the apex of Minoan culture. He called it Ajax and wrote his *Metamorphosis of Ajax* to tell the Elizabethan world that salvation was at hand. (At Richmond the Queen installed a model of the new contrivance, with her godson's book hanging nearby). In Victorian times, the Sanitarians led a great reform movement, for with industrial towns spreading like cholera, and cholera spreading like the towns, it was a question of drainage or death. The reformers fulminated and the vested interests in dirt blustered and protested. They said the reformers were bureaucrats and enemies of democracy. They said the old cess-pools had been good enough for grandpa. They said that sewage and offal in the streets created employment, because periodically it had to be carted away. They went down fighting.

Reg discovered, in the lavatory of a famous London building, a disgruntled person's record of his sojourn:

I do not like this place at all,
The seat is too high and the hole is too small

Below the couplet, a critic had written:

You lay yourself open to the obvious retort:
Your bottom's too big and your legs are too short.

Clearly, thought Reg, it was Man who was at fault: he was utterly unworthy of the seat which Science had provided for him.

*Cleanliness and Godliness* was the first attempt to write a comprehensive work on sanitary matters since the *Metamorphosis of Ajax*. The overall message of the book was – Take care of sanitation, and civilisation will take care of itself. We read that, in ancient Egypt, the women stood erect to make water, while the men squatted; that the decline of Rome was politico-hygienic; that the Chinese made thrifty use of excrement; that the Duke of Wellington, having learned from the Hindus the habit of daily bathing, was considered in this respect a fanatic; that the Welsh, in the 12th century, rubbed their teeth to a dazzling whiteness with the leaves of the hazel.

Concerning the 'Nastiness of Natives and the Filthiness of Foreigners', was it not true that the Moslem and Hindu religions enjoined the most meticulous rules of personal hygiene? Why, then, did such filthiness exist in the East where the traditional culture was founded upon an exacting standard of purity?

Why, you say, there is nothing remarkable in such a proposition, for the whole of Christian civilisation is based *de facto* upon the systematic breach of the Ten Commandments and the ethics of the Galilean. Did we build an empire by turning the other cheek? Do not the Kings of the Gentiles still exercise lordship over them, and are they not called Benefactors? Are the disciples of Christ known today because they love one another? Do not the Pharisees still devour widows' houses? Did our settlers in Kenya possess themselves of African land by too nicely observing the Eighth Commandment? And can we defend this Empire in war by a rigid adherence to the Sixth? Are fortunes made by those who fare without scrip, sword or wallet, having given all their goods to the poor and even their surplus coats to him that hath none? Is My Lord the Archbishop a pattern of Christian humility and Holy Poverty? Or can nations that sound their own praises with fife and drum *walk humbly before God* when they are drunk with their own pomp and circumstance? Why, you would think, if you did not know better, that you had come among idolaters to see the worship lavished upon a swastika or a Union Jack, to say nothing of Mammon's graven image on the filthy lucre of Caesar.

Well, I know one honest staff-sergeant who but recently turned Mohammedan because he thought it better to follow openly the Prophet who carried the Sword of Islam than to make a pretence of loyalty to the Prince of Peace.

British rule had destroyed the ancient system of village self-government in India to the detriment of agriculture. Now, half-starved villagers were being forced to offer food free of charge to an 'Uplift Committee'. Now, Indian peasants were being taxed to the tune of £67,500 to pay for sanitary fittings in the Viceroy's house.

To speak truth, there is not a Great Power in Europe which has not taken a share in the oppression and robbery, the urbanisation and degradation of primitive peoples, making slums where there were once forests and prairies, and all the while boasting of its health services and civilising mission.

The Anal-Erotic Complex was delved into, and the stratagem of two spinsters who were obsessed with a urinal behind a restaurant from which men emerged adjusting their dress. When, during the war, the restaurant was closed and the urinal deserted, the disappointment of the spinsters was intense and bitter.

There was an ingenious privy in Norway. An acquaintance of Reg's had occasion to pass the night in a *saeta*, where he arrived after dark.

And being moved to relieve himself after he had breakfasted, he sought the house of office where he was about to seat himself when he was astonished to spy daylight through the hole beneath him. Looking downwards, he was horrified to discover that the place overhung a precipice of some 2,000 feet, and that he was looking into the distant waters of a *fjord*, where a large ship appeared as a small object framed in the *chaise percée* (like the picture of Queen Victoria which an ignorant artisan framed in like manner, thinking so fine a piece of polished wood could hardly have been intended for so base a use). When I enquired of this person what were his reactions, he replied that his principal desire was to feel his feet upon *terra firma*, and that he therefore withdrew in haste from the place without attempting to transact his affairs. But surely, said I, such places were expressly devised to precipitate business by the emotion of fear, which may well have proved a stronger and cheaper medicine than *Enos*, and account for the excellent health of the Norwegians. To this, however, my friend only replied that he would sooner suffer from habitual costiveness than expose himself daily to such peril and to a matutinal fantasy of breaking timber swaying over such an abyss, however much it might *encourager les autres*.

The book included sections on people who had died in privies, and on curious *pots de chambre* such as the lavatory of a restaurant in Soho, *sur les toits*, for which reason Reg always called it *Café René Clair*. He told the story, as verified in the *Nuremburg Chronicle*, of a Baron who, having defied a proud prelate, was besieged in his castle by the Bishop.

And when the Bishop could not prevail either by the temporal means at his disposal or by the powerful weapon of excommunication, he had recourse to a stratagem revealed to him by a page-boy, the servant of the Baron, who (in dread of the ghostly powers of the Church) escaped from the castle to advise the Bishop on this matter. Acting, then, upon information received (as our police are wont to say) the Bishop placed two cross-bowmen in a privy place at an hour indicated by the page; and things falling out as the boy had said, the Baron received a couple of bolts in his posterior what time he made his morning ejestion upon the battlements (being a person of regular habits), for they shot straight up the shaft that led into the Baronial jakes. And this, as I suppose, was an event of some importance to all concerned, and shews that an understanding of my chosen subject may help even a Bishop to prevail, where neither temporal power nor spiritual threats have availed him.

He reported on a rampant feminism showing its resentment at the payment of one penny for the fulfilment of the natural function which was gratis to the other sex. This discrimination, according to one woman, could be easily abolished if women organised an intensive anti-penny campaign by always using the gutter and going to jail if necessary. There was a saloon bar in New York where saddles played the part of stools, the doors leading to the toilets labelled *Colts* and *Fillies*. There were perforated toilet rolls which played tunes when pulled, and devices to start chimes or to release a shower of confetti. There was an engine contrived in Britain

> whereby a person sitting upon such a seat caused the National Anthem to be played; whereat he was compelled (if a patriotic person) to rise again, being unable in this way to conduct his business peacefully.

'How a Young Gallant should behave himself in an Ordinary', was a piece of advice from Thomas Dekker. You may rise (said he) in dinner-time to ask for a close-stool, protesting to all the gentlemen that it costs you £100 a year in physic, besides the annual pension which your wife allows her doctor; and, if you please, you may, as your great French lord doth, invite some special friend of yours from the table, to hold discourse with you as you sit in that with-drawing-chamber; from whence being returned again to the board, you shall sharpen the wits of all the eating gallants about you, and do them pleasure to ask what pamphlets or poems a man might think fittest to wipe his tail with.

On the absence of modesty among the Japanese, Reg gave as an example a traveller who, coming to a house, was offered a bath, which he gladly accepted.

> But seeing that his host's family sat around to keep him company, and being unable to speak their language, he indicated as best he could by means of gestures his need for a screen. This they brought, a little thing about two or three feet high, such as they thought necessary, no doubt, to protect him from draughts. And when he showed by signs that he would have a high screen, they removed the small one and brought him another, fully seven feet in height, which was made of glass.

A Japanese emperor, keen to ape the West, once attempted to import modesty, decreeing that bathers in the sea should wear a minimum of clothing instead of bathing nude, as they had in the past,

> which decree the Japanese obeyed very literally, playing naked upon the beach until such time as they were ready to enter the sea, when they covered their shame appropriately. And from this one may see how utterly devoid these people are by nature, culture and tradition of our own most cherished virtues, like that child who was seen by a friend of

135

mine coming up the steps of St Mark's, in Venice; who, finding herself without a hat, threw her skirts over her head as a perfunctory act of *modesty*.

He recollected that a man, having informed a lady that he had to see a man about a dog, was asked what sort of dog; which threw him into such a state of embarrassment that he replied, a dachshund with four puppies.

Such are the traps we make for ourselves by our feeble efforts at deception. Or there was that English woman who sought for a certain place in a Paris restaurant, *soi-distant se laver les mains*, and, finding it repeatedly locked, complained to a waiter. How cruelly were her foolish pretences shattered by his intended words of comfort, '*Courage, madame, j'entends déjà le craquement de papier!*'

Reg admitted to his readers that he always decorated his lavatory with the most indecorous photographs he could find of our Cabinet ministers; and he hoped that he had given them enough levity to carry his heavy cargo. This cargo was nothing less than a terrible indictment of Man. Man was an extravagant accelerator of waste. He had swept into the sea soil-fertility which only centuries of life could accumulate, fertility which was the substratum of all that lived. Man had destroyed food on the preposterous excuse that it was necessary to maintain its price. But there were signs of hope. He described in detail the success of a Sewage Disposal Works as a Centre of a National Industry of Organic Fertiliser Manufacture, and of a campaign for Sewage Sludge as a Manure. Why, then, this continued waste, if local effort had achieved so much? The answer was two-fold. Firstly because

the *interests* opposed to scientific utilisation of sewage are enormous. Do you suppose those who own the vast capital invested in companies providing chemical fertilisers are unaware of the peril in which they stand? Do you imagine they will allow such competition to *extinguish their traffic altogether* without resorting to all means open to them as honest merchants or manufacturers? Only imagine that you are the possessor of a few hundred thousand shares in a firm manufacturing chemicals, for the slaughter of human beings in time of war and the corruption of the soil in time of peace, and you will construct your syllogisms from very different premises.

But the second reason had to do with the failure until recent years to find a cheap and efficient method of manufacturing from sewage the best and most easily portable product.

Now, however, Fertilising with Sewage was no longer an experiment but an achievement. The producers of chemical fertilisers, on the other hand, were the druggists of the soil, offering quick results, dearly bought in the final reckoning. [He pointed to] the heritage of the chemical fertiliser, the once-fertile fields of Europe, where for 30 years now, since the first stimulus of these drugs ceased to be effective, the production of crops has declined, while the fields of China continue, even after a decade of war, to nourish her vast population. [The fertility of the earth was being destroyed through the commercialism of agriculture. So long as Man continued to exploit the soil for profit, he sowed the seeds of his own destruction.]

By sanitation [he went on], we were saved from unknown horrors as our world became industrialised and urbanised, nay, more, for life has lengthened, the old and known diseases have been slowly driven back upon all fronts. But slowly, insidiously, while we have battled with deadly bugs, a new enemy has intrenched himself behind our lines; and in the struggle for health we have become like those wretches who bind themselves to a domestic tyranny in order that the same thing may not be imposed upon them by a foreigner. This new enemy is STERILITY: the sterility of our soil and therefore of our crops; of our crops and therefore of men and beasts. In vain we build Maginot Lines of hygiene against the hordes of harmful bacteria: slowly but inevitably Life itself is on the ebb. Mankind is so surely dying that generations to come may like enough grow their first hair grey or white, and every child among them need spectacles from infancy.

Ever-increasing quantities of vegetable matter are made into cloth or paper, the ultimate fate of which is that it is cremated in the name of Refuse Disposal, that is to say (once more) of Sanitation. Yet Sir Albert Howard shewed that all such matter, when composted with sewage, could be used to feed the land from which it came, which otherwise must starve. What are we then doing with these vast *destructors* and *incinerators* but burning up the land on which we live?

And now, to mock our tragedy of greed and ignorance, a campaign of *salvage* is proclaimed. Salvage for what? Is it intended that anything should be saved in order to conserve the wealth of the world for the use of the people? Had it been so, we should have heard this talk of salvage long before the present war drove us to it. But the word has now also undergone a metamorphosis, emerging as *destruction*; for what else can it be truly named? Hitherto paper was burnt, but now we are to save it for the making of cartridges; and by diligent application to this programme in both Britain and Germany it is optimistically proposed that instead of merely destroying × tons of paper annually we shall destroy the full tonnage of paper plus an incalculable number of human lives.

Note well, however, the patriotic organ of public opinion which appointed itself the Big Noise of this paper *salvage*. Observe its imperative demands, that we should *forget our past*, give up treasured letters and diaries, books, sheets of music and everything we kept for mere *sentiment*. Are you not, were you not at the time, astonished at such unexampled impudence from the hired hacks of Fleet Street, whose ephemeral scribbling eats up each day acres of good forest land, turned into wood-pulp to make a penny platform for their antics?

A stern Marxist accused Reg and his subject of being exceedingly decadent, displaying the inherent escapism of the bourgeoisie of which he, Reg, was a hideous example. He replied:

Why, are you not dialectician enough to know that if one escapes far enough one comes full circle, approaching Reality by the North-West passage as demonstrated by Galileo and Einstein? For though you may represent truth in a crude, two-dimensional form, like Mercator's Projection, to obtain a better view of it, I assure you that it moves in circles like everything else; and if you go far enough in any direction you will come back to where you started, taking your opponents in the rear.

And this is what he had done. He had begun the book to escape from a world that wearied him, 'but I have come back through space and eternity to expose one of the worst *rackets* in the world, by which I mean the trade in chemical fertilisers'. 'What!' said the Marxist, 'in 1942 and with a war on?' And I told him 'yes, in 1942, and *because* there is a war on. For the neglect of dung was never such a grave matter as it is today'.

## Stately Pleasure-Dome

In a report to the Aberdeen Cleansing Committee, Mr William Alexander said: 'Our city fathers of the past, with narrow Victorian mentality, thought that public lavatories should be built in mean side streets. . . . The public toilets of the future should be standing side by side with the big business concerns in our principal streets, brilliantly lit'.

(*Glasgow Daily Record*)

> In Barrhead did Inventor Shanks
> A strange, new-fangled jakes decree
> So Clyde, between its sacred banks,
> Bore effluent from sewage tanks
>     Which served each WC
> In No Mean City's meaner streets
> The public sat on private seats,

138

But with no gardens bright, no sinuous rills,
For Art was blighted by inherent ills
Of cramped Victorian mentality.
Cheered by no host of golden daffodils
The urgent pilgrim paused but momently.

Ancestral voices, up at Aberdeen,
Wailed for the like, to keep their city clean;
So from each jakes (with ceaseless turmoil seething,
As if this earth in fast, thick pants were breathing)
A mighty stream meandered endlessly
Down to a sunless sea.

A toilet with a neon sign
    In a vision I have known:
It stands beside a Woolworth Store,
The Radio chanteth evermore
    And flicks are freely shown.
Could I produce in marble
So sumptuous a Gents,
The Muscovites would cease to garble
The tale of our predicaments;
Kruschev would cry: Behold! Behold!
These silver chains! These seats of gold!
Make a treaty with these guys,
    For though the bourgeoisie remains
    The Proles are happy with their chains
And flush the pans of Paradise.

                                    (from *New Statesman*)

139

# CHAPTER X

# The Fallow Ground of the Heart

ON ACCOUNT OF ILL-HEALTH, Reg was barred from working with Quaker relief teams. While still at Spiceland, he had registered, reluctantly, as a Conscientious Objector, two words he hated for their smugness and inadequacy and because, like Ethel, he had little patience with many of the woolly-minded, unctuous and priggish people so labelled. Wanting to avoid the futility of prison and to work in a socially useful capacity, he appeared before a CO Tribunal and asked for unconditional exemption. 'Conditions' were unacceptable to him. He regarded the right not to kill as a moral absolute which could not be dependent on the will of others.

The Tribunal refused him unconditional terms, and the Ministry of Labour blocked his every effort to obtain employment. Finally, he joined the Chelsea Borough Civil Defence as a rescue driver, persuading a surgeon to certify that his leg could cope with strenuous tasks. He soon discovered that it could not; during his first few months in Civil Defence, he had two accidents, one of them up a ladder. He searched for the bodies of 16 children from a bombed site, he drove for a Mobile Hospital Unit, and in off-duty periods he researched for and wrote chapters of *Cleanliness and Godliness*. He later became an Alsatian dog trainer, the dogs being used to scent out buried or trapped bomb victims. He was often on duty for 24 hours at a stretch.

Occasional visits to Ethel at Oak Cottage provided much-needed laughter. One of their neighbours in Wimbledon was Bentley Purchase, the St Pancras Coroner. He asked them what they thought of 'these new-fangled things Jerry keeps sending over'. They replied that they didn't care for them. 'Neither do I', said Purchase, 'they bring the war down to the Woolworth level.' Ethel once phoned Purchase, who was responsible for local fire-watching arrangements, reporting to him that a bright light was showing at the window of a nearby house, and what did he propose to do about it, this beacon for a German bomber? Instead of notifying the police or the First Aid wardens, the distinguished coroner, huge and high-spirited, climbed up to a turret at the top of his house and peppered the offending window with ammunition from his son's air-gun. He achieved his object – the light bulb shattered. On another occasion, in the garden of the house of the light bulb, a tipsy man pursued his equally squiffy wife, threatening to kill her. Ethel shared her worry for the woman's safety with Purchase who sent a note to the villain of the piece: 'Dear Sir, In common with all your neighbours, I have noted your intentions with regard to your wife's future and shall be happy to give the matter my professional attention'. When Reg went to borrow a saw from Purchase, he was offered one that was ideal, he was assured, for 'chopping the old girl's bones into suitcase length'. Hearing of the remark, Ethel was not totally amused.

☆    ☆    ☆

In an unpublished essay, *William Blake – Revolutionary*, written in 1941, Reg said that 'Blake belongs by right to the anarchist tradition, if he was not one of its originators'. Instinctively he mistrusted Law, just as he mistrusted organised religion: 'Prisons are built with stones of Law, Brothels with bricks of Religion'. He also saw and fore-saw the dangers besetting a revolutionary movement, and in his analysis was typically anarchist:

> The hand of Vengeance found the bed
> To which the Purple Tyrant fled:
> The iron hand crush'd the Tyrant's head
> And became a tyrant in his stead.

Which might have been written as a direct answer to the theory of 'Proletarian Dictatorship' and as a description of Stalin.

'When I was a boy, those magnificent lines from Milton, beginning 'And did those feet in ancient time', sung to Parry's music, were a sort of revolutionary hymn, only heard where idealists of 'left' opinions were gathered together. So, at least, I remember it. For this reason it was a shock to hear them recently on the radio, at the conclusion of some sort of sabre-rattling rodomontade. How modern patriotism gets over the 'dark, Satanic mills' I have no idea; but I suppose it is by some process analogous to the bland singing of 'Sufficient is thine arm alone, and our defence is sure', or the complacent sing-song with which a congregation asks to be forgiven as they forgive others, or a hundred other anomalies of religious worship.

But Blake, curiously enough, meant what he said. True he loved England, just as John Ball and John Lilburne had loved England, as Babeuf

141

loved France, as Tolstoy loved Russia and as the Spanish anarchists loved Spain, when they died to save her from the hirelings of Rome, Berlin, Moscow and Burgos. Blake's 'patriotism', however (if such debased coinage can still be used without a suggestion of something fraudulent) was itself of a revolutionary order. He believed in 'Albion', in what England could become. But of the England that he saw before him, imperialist and bloody-minded, he wrote:

> Is this thy soft Family-Love,
> Thy cruel patriarchal pride,
> Planting thy family alone,
> Destroying all the World beside?

When Albion's spectre 'tore forth in all the pomp of War', Blake saw him as Satan. The visionary Jerusalem 'fell from Lambeth's Vale' and the poet painted thus the deeds of Albion:

> The Rhine was red with human blood,
> The Danube roll'd a purple tide,
> On the Euphrates Satan stood
> And over Asia stretched his pride.

Beyond this evil world, of which he was so deeply conscious, the poet could see, however, the end of 'the war of swords and spears', and unlike many of the present day, who passionately desire peace, but appear to have no conception of the conditions in which it is possible, he visualised those conditions:

> Where the son of fire in his eastern cloud,
>> while the morning plumes her golden breast,
> Spurning the clouds written with curses, stamps the
>> stony law to dust, loosing the eternal
>> horses from the dens of night, crying,
> 'EMPIRE IS NO MORE! AND NOW THE LION
> AND WOLF SHALL CEASE'.

Nor is it too fanciful to suggest that the sickle which 'sang in the fruitful field' and could not be subdued by the 'song of death', sung by the sword, is the symbol of toil and therefore of the worker and the peasant, by whom war will ultimately be outlawed.

'Mercy, Pity, Peace and Love' were the sovereign values of spiritual regeneration as Blake understood it. But lest these things should be corrupted, like other Christian virtues, by the smug charity of the propertied classes, his 'Devil' is always there to remind us that:

> Mercy could be no more
> If there was nobody poor;

142

And pity no more could be
If all were as happy as we.

Blake's religious ideas were as subversive as his social criticisms and attitude
to accepted 'morality': with his Angel-Devil he reads the Bible 'in its
infernal or diabolical sense, which the world shall have if they behave well'.
The world has not behaved well and by neglecting Blake has missed this
treasure; but I like to think there was prophetic insight in the abrupt
observation which follows: 'I have also the Bible of Hell, which the world
shall have whether it will or no'. This in turn is followed by the apparently
disconnected aphorism 'One Law for the Lion and Ox is oppression'. But
surely, when one considers the meaning of this saying, it *is* the Bible of Hell
– the diabolical maxim on which Western Civilisation was to be based in
later years.

The farce of 'equality before the law', when a poor man cannot afford to
sue, and may be ruined in defending himself; the burlesque 'democracy'
where one side controls all the vehicles of information and opinion, together
with the means to bribe all but the staunchest champions of the underdog;
the doctrine of *laisser faire* and 'the weakest to the wall' (corrupted from its
courteous medieval sense); the 'equal chance' of war, where increasingly
the products of 'Satanic mills' overwhelm human valour – was not all this
summed up in the Lion and the Ox?

It is not difficult to understand the contempt with which Blake regarded
those who were 'not capable of a firm persuasion of anything', the withering
bitterness of so many of his epigrams, the pride with which he could say of
my namesake and his contemporary: 'I certainly do thank God that I am not
like Reynolds'. For Blake had colossal pride, the kind of pride without
which a revolutionary might as well be dead. The Jesus of his *Everlasting
Gospel* was proud, and Blake glories in his rebukes to his parents, his
defiance of the Pharisees, his speaking 'with authority'. . . . And the poem
ends with a reminder of the utter inadequacy of 'good intentions'. (How
often, when I first crossed swords with imperialism years ago in India,
people would hurl at me the utterly irrelevant information that Lord Irwin –
then Viceroy and now Lord Halifax – was 'a good man.')

And Caiaphas was in his own Mind
A benefactor to Mankind

says Blake, closing the matter finally, beyond the necessity for further
discussion. 'But thou readest black where I read white', he concludes.

Today, when poetry deliberately apes journalism in its anxiety to be 'on
the spot', it may seem odd that a revolutionary poet should have had so little

143

to say that *specifically* applied to his own contemporary world. That he was in touch with events we know from his close personal association with the revolutionaries of his age; but his work, with the doubtful exception of the poem *America*, does not reflect this fact. In many ways, contemporary progressive movements only antagonised him. He hated their coldness, their dependence on 'Reason' and lack of vision.

Certainly, he spoke in parables to the Blind. It was a method he explicitly approved. A lucid poet or prophet is like a man explaining his own jokes. Half the satisfaction to be had from a good poem, a good epigram or a good joke lies in its sublety – and in the exercise of the reader's own knowledge, intellect and imagination. And if he is not prepared to use these he is not worth talking to. (Jesus as good as says so.) But even for the lazier mind there are simple instructions and visions, like the vision of the just man's course through the vale of death:

> Roses are planted where thorns grow
> And on the barren heath
> Sing the honey bees.

There is still poison in 'Caesar's Laurel Crown', and above all,

> The Nations still
> Follow after the detestable Gods of Priam. . . .'

Glad you got along with Reg's Blake essay better than I did [wrote Ethel to the present writer]. I don't think that essay showed Blake as a *revolutionary* somehow. When I read it again last night, I decided it was full of ponderous pieties. I thought my *Lover Under Another Name* did more for Blake. Reg was more endemically *Quaker* than he knew. Any way, if I hadn't read Blake, that essay would put me right *off* him, it would.

Ethel's novel, *Lover Under Another Name* (1953), was the story of Tom Rowse, a modern St Francis, for whom Blake was his source of inspiration both as a sculptor and seeker after truth. Rowse was disgusted by the immorality of the money market. Money degraded art and life and made a mockery of Christian precepts. Even a loser in a prize-fight earned more from one night in the boxing-ring than a miner earned in a lifetime – it was senseless. As Jesus said, as Gandhi said, all who had more of this world's goods than they needed for their subsistence stole from those who had not. There were two kinds of being, the Prolific and the Devouring. To the Prolific belonged all creative impulses; to the Devouring all that demolished, materially and spiritually, such as wars, production for profit, orthodox religion. Trying to reconcile the two meant that you sought to destroy existence.

144

Rowse had rejected comfort to live the life of an artist. Only in a free world, where people were liberated from exploitation, from the profit motive, from wage-slavery, could the artist indulge in creativity without assuming privileges denied his fellows. Rowse had seen reproach in the eyes of a dying loved one; nothing he could create could erase that or transmute it into mercy, pity, peace; that blessed trinity had to be sought in the labyrinth of living. He had to be purged of all pride, vanity and ambition, not as a penance but in the hope of achieving peace through humility. He aimed to identify with those for whom life was unremitting hardship. Only so could he make his contribution, however minute, to the Vision of Christ. He would sleep in common lodging houses, give money to those who had less than he had, make friends of prostitutes and thieves. He could then look the world in the face, owning nothing, with no man's need on his conscience.

It is not hard to find aspects of Reg in the character of Tom Rowse.

☆    ☆    ☆

After hill-scrambling in the Lake District with Jean, Ethel began a novel, *Sleep After Love*, taking as a 'text' for the title-page, 'Sleep is a reconciling, A rest that peace begets'. The title was salacious, said *The Sunday Times* in 1942, and refused to publicise the book. The title must be changed, said Ethel's publishers, but, while seeing the point, it still seemed to her an outrage that sleeping after love, conceived in the style of 'sleep after toyle, port after stormie seas', should be construed as titillating. The story, set in the mid-19th century, concerned an Irish captain, leader of the peasants in their revolt against the landlords. Since she was banned from using the title of her choice, she decided on the innocuous *Captain Moonlight*, and if that was an exceedingly romantic title, she no longer cared.

The Foreign Office would not allow her to travel to her cottage in Ireland; Ireland was being pressurised about leasing its ports and this was no time to issue a permit to a well-known pacifist. She drafted another Irish novel – *The Blossoming Bough* – and, for *Peace News*, was writing:

> People frequently say to me, in varying degrees of anger and impatience, 'You don't seem to realise that if we lose the war people like you will be in concentration camps'. To which I reply a) that I am not at all convinced of that, and b) that even if this is so it is no reason for supporting a campaign for murder.
>
> · If one is primarily concerned with the saving of one's own skin, then obviously one cannot be a pacifist; but if one claims to be a pacifist, that

is to say, one who believes that war is evil in all circumstances, then equally obviously one's own wretched skin cannot be regarded as all-important.

The attitude that we've got to fight this war, and win it, because it'll be worse for us if we don't is the hate attitude rooted in fear, and in all propaganda for support of war every government, necessarily, trades on this fear.

Hitler tells his people that if they don't win the war it is their death as a nation; our government assures us that we shall be serfs and slaves if the Nazis win; on each side the hate of the people for the enemy intensifies with their fear. And hate they must, or they have no will to fight.

Before the USSR became respectable, joining the League of Nations and hobnobbing with capitalist powers, Bolshevism was regarded as the red menace, something to be feared, and therefore hated. Then it was the unspeakable 'Bolshies' who cut off babies' hands and ran bayonets through children, and committed all manner of atrocities only equalled by the Spanish Inquisition.

Should Russia win the war to an extent unbargained for by our politicians and represent a 'Communist menace' to capitalist interests, once more these stories will quite certainly be revived. So long as there is nothing to fear there is nothing to hide. But threaten the British possessing classes with communism, and see how much it will want to save Soviet Russia!

Does anyone for a moment suppose that if the Japanese were on our side they would be anything but a chivalrous and lovable people? Even if it were reported of them, then, that they bayoneted all their prisoners, it would be accounted a noble ruthlessness commanding admiration – like the Australian soldier last year who was awarded the VC for his 'heroism' in silencing a German machine-gun post by bayoneting the crew. He hateth most who feareth most – and a great deal of fear in wartime is a combination of superstition and ignorance. The pacifist has first to cast out fear in himself, and then to the best of his ability in others.

Young pacifists write to me continually, expressing horror and dismay at the rising tide of destruction and hate and asking despairingly, 'But what can we *do*?' The answer, as I see it, is that we can keep our heads and our faith in the midst of the inferno, and make propaganda against war wherever we happen to find ourselves. We can do no more at this present time, but certainly we can do no less.

All this atrocity and retribution propaganda should be regarded by pacifists as every bit as evil and dangerous as the Vansittart hate propaganda, and countered on every possible occasion as part of their general 'sowing of the seed' of their pacifist faith. It is an extremely insidious poison, particularly when coming from people who have such a following as Dr Temple and Cardinal Hinsley in their respective Churches. Their retributive utterances are a sad reminder of how far is the Church from the teachings of its Founder. Those teachings, it would seem, were not too profound for human comprehension; but too simple – too simple for complicated humanity's acceptance!

'Deliver us from blood-guiltiness, O Lord', and from the futile mockery of a vengeful Church.

Ethel's and Reg's mail was intercepted for inspection and would arrive, several posts late, bearing the obvious signs of having been officially opened. Reg moved into a small basement room in Jubilee Place, Chelsea. Ethel volunteered for fire-watching in Wimbledon and submitted to a course of training, crawling round a smoke-filled hut on all fours and learning how to manage a stirrup-pump. She was issued with a tin helmet and allotted duty days. When she was 'on', as soon as the siren sounded, she donned her helmet, ran up to the firewatchers' headquarters, took a disc with the letter F imprinted on it from a box in the porch and rushed back home to hang it on her gate. Her on-duty periods were known to her friends as Ethel's nights for F-ing. One night, though, she was caught napping. Her F disc was missing from her gate and she was reported. Her neighbour Bentley Purchase, the coroner, smoothed matters over. 'Nonsense', he said. 'You can't do that to our Ethel!'

With Reg, she went regularly to Holloway Prison to visit inmates interned under Emergency Regulation 18b, by which suspects were held in prison without trial. (Such visits, thought Ethel, were far more useful than F-ing). They had got involved with Resi, a young German Jewish girl. Resi lived in the same building as Reg and worked as a commercial artist. At the request of a left-wing revolutionary with whom she was in love, she had faked two identity cards. Her crime was discovered, she lost her job, and was summoned to appear at Bow Street where she was given a sentence of 10 months. Reg, realising that the girl had only acted out of romantic folly, consulted with a lawyer friend who was largely responsible for her sentence being quashed. Reg found her another job as a commercial artist and they lunched together to celebrate the event. He escorted her back to her office. A police car was waiting there. The police had persuaded Herbert Morrison to intern her under the Emergency Regulations.

147

Ethel and Reg campaigned to obtain her release but she remained incarcerated in Holloway and later in the Isle of Man. A socialist, and Jewish, she was now thrown among fascists.

I don't mean that all the people who were interned under the Emergency Regulations were fascists, of course [wrote Reg]. Some were victims of private grudges. Yet there *were* fascists – plenty of them – among those detained in His Majesty's prisons and in the camps. A fascist fellow-prisoner, such is the paradox of shared suffering, was kind to Resi. And when Resi left Holloway she asked us to visit this woman sometimes, as she had nobody to care for her. Apart from a feeling of gratitude, we were willing enough. Ethel and I detested fascism, but for the same reason we also detested this barbarous business of interning people against whom no charges could be brought which would have satisfied any court of law. It was only by degrees that we learnt of the grosser injustices and of the infringement even of their own regulations by the highest authorities. Ethel and I found ourselves, step by step, drawn into sympathy even with self-confessed fascists who were the victims of this system. At least they did not pretend to believe in democracy and were to that extent guiltless of hypocrisy.

Beginning with Resi's friend at Holloway, they soon became increasingly concerned with these victims of a vicious system:

What we found hard to overlook, in our enthusiasm, was the fact that many of the people we befriended were tiresome and some not personally likeable. It was a curious test of principle, but we floundered through that phase of life as we had through others, and I'm glad that we did what we did. There was indeed something of that sort needed in a country where the Council for Civil Liberties protested against the release of Sir Oswald Mosley – not, that is to say, demanding that he be brought to trial, but that he be interned again without one. I had often thought Mosley the worst thing in British political life, but I realised then that there was something worse still, which was the Mosley principle masquerading as the defence of Civil Liberty. My only regret with regard to that particular flounder is that we were never more isolated and ineffective than we felt in those days.

☆     ☆     ☆

*The Blossoming Bough* completed, Ethel worked on her collection of stories, *No More Mimosa*, and a new novel, *Proud Heaven* which, she admitted, 'bears the influence of an acute attack of Henry James'.

In 1943, as his contribution to a collection of essays, *Non-Violence for the West* (Peace Pledge Union), Reg said that he had never understood the term 'non-resistance' – 'If a man refuses to become a soldier I should say that he *resisted* conscription. If he gives in and becomes a soldier I should say he was a non-resister. But this does not seem to be the usual meaning of the term'. To him, as to Ethel, the ideal pacifist was an anarchist,

> since the best kind of State assumes some form of coercion. One can resist a State by pacifist means, but one cannot 'govern' by pacifist means. This is the last and most essential problem for pacifists; and few of us have passed beyond the stage of saying 'Lord, I believe; help thou mine unbelief'. I confess to a great deal of unbelief myself, because (though temperamentally an anarchist) I see the necessity for order, and cannot conceive of order without some minimum of coercion. This only emphasises, however, the need for a profound spiritual revolution, because it is only with very different people from ourselves that order, equality, justice and freedom could be maintained without that 'minimum force'.

In Britain, Pride, Greed, Brute Force and Oppression were such an integral part of our national tradition 'that *no* system will stand a chance without the Big Stick until there is a radical transformation of character and outlook. What is a good programme in an oppressed country is here (at present) irrelevant: the British need to learn, not how to resist, but how to leave go – not so much the lesson of Gandhi as that from which the Rich Young Ruler "turned sorrowfully away"'.

When, in the latter part of the war, Arthur Ballard asked for his help in buying the Socialist Book Centre in the Strand, Reg put up some money inherited on his mother's death. Ethel also became a partner, together with the cartoonist, J. F. Horrabin. To Reg's surprise, Ballard made the shop pay,

> and we were suddenly confronted with unearned dividends from the sale of Socialism, which made us feel so uncomfortable that Ethel and I gave our share to our current Good Cause, the Indian Freedom Campaign. Eventually Arthur bought out all his partners before selling out himself. Whatever other capitalists say in their defence I do know, as a simple fact, that the only successes I ever had in business were the rise in shares in the family business, in my youth, which happened in spite of my help, and the profits from this shop, which depended on the fact that I was a sleeping partner and took no active part in it. From this I deduce that if I had been born with a little money I could have got on very well without brains, ability, hard work or effort of any kind.

149

He wrote numerous verses in off-duty moments at Civil Defence. One of his fans was H. J. Massingham. He, on his part, delighted in Massingham's vehement humanism,

> yet he was a Tory, a defender of the old squirearchy by an amazing chain of reasoning, which led him from the denunciation of those responsible for the 'enclosures' to the defence of their present heirs. In some odd way he had come to see in them the only force capable of resisting the advance of bureaucracy.

Reg gave Ethel a copy of Massingham's *The Tree of Life*, inscribing it 'for my beloved one who is *my* tree of life'. It was a book they both admired, especially for its philosophy that people needed to rediscover the synthesis of religion, nature, craft, husbandry, all in one.

Ethel's brother, a Commander in the Royal Navy, was decorated with the OBE 'for distinguished services in the Normandy invasion'. She was pleased that he was honoured, 'for such things belong to the world of soldiers and sailors and statesmen, but not, surely, to the world of writers and artists, for whom public acclaim should be honour enough, if honour be wanted'.

Her new book, *Bread and Roses*, a survey of conceptions of Utopia, from Plato to the present day, drew the pacifist-anarchist conclusion, and then she made a start on *Lucifer and the Child*, the novel about witchcraft, and revised *Commonsense and the Adolescent* which was to appear in a new edition. During this time, a man of German origin but naturalised British, wrote to her from Brixton Prison, asking her to send him some of her books, as he had read all the Mannins in the prison library. He was a member of the British Union of Fascists and for three years had been interned under Regulation 18b. She could not help but admire his honesty and courage in refusing to recant. She visited him and, on his release, despite her protests that she was unable to pay him properly, he appointed himself her secretary. One day, working in the garden at Oak Cottage, he wore his BUF shirt. 'Please change it', she said, 'it's a symbol of something I detest.' 'Don't be so narrow-minded and bigoted,' was his reply. When he left her employment to 'better' himself, she often wondered if he still wore the little gold swastika under the lapel of his jacket.

Paris was liberated, but between rockets and fly-bombs and raids, sleepless Londoners felt that their chances of survival were slim. Ethel turned over in her mind the idea for a novel, *The Dark Forest*, set in an occupied country, to be dedicated to her Fascist secretary. Towards the end of the war, Reg applied to join a relief team on the Continent and was turned down because of his high blood pressure. Civil Defence men were required to report to their local Labour Exchanges to be 'directed' into new jobs. Unwilling to submit to this thinly disguised form of slavery, 'I didn't go. I received various formal messages and replied with flat refusals'. Then he learned that an official called Smith 'would esteem it a personal favour if he'd call here some time at his convenience'. Smith had Reg beaten: 'Much as I hate officialdom, especially when it is trying to treat human beings as unassembled parts in a machine, I'm always touched when any official shows that he is human – and courtesy demands and evokes courtesy in others'. He went next day and explained his attitude to 'conditions' and that his work in Civil Defence had, from his point of view, nothing to do with the law, tribunals, conditions or anything but his wish to do something useful. Now that his service with Chelsea Borough was nearly over, he intended to take up writing again and he was certainly not going to be 'directed' into doing anything else.

However, the law did not lie in Mr Smith's hands. When the Civil Defence was disbanded, Reg's papers were transferred to Wimbledon Labour Exchange from where a letter informed him that he was to work as a hospital porter. 'This letter reached me in another hospital where, far from being a porter, I was at that time a patient.' He had suffered a serious haemorrhage soon after the atom bomb fell on Hiroshima. 'The two events were not unconnected, for I'd done little since the Hiroshima tragedy except think, talk and write about this new horror. In hospital they'd brought my blood-pressure down considerably and the letter from the Labour Exchange sent it rocketing up again.' Ethel intercepted the next letter from officials at the Labour Exchange and wrote to them saying that she was destroying it, and would destroy any future letters in order to protect Reg's health. Months later, he was released from the 'conditions' he had never accepted.

Late in 1945, a joint letter from Ethel and Reg was published in *Peace News*:

We have now been told officially that the Government will not allow us to contribute voluntarily from our own rations towards the needs of millions who are starving in Europe. . . . For centuries we have celebrated the feasting in the inn, until the stable and the manger are almost forgotten. . . . To many of us the situation is completely intolerable, because it appears to take away from us the opportunity of even the smallest, the merely symbolic gesture of giving from our own sufficiency to those in terrible and urgent need. We are told of our rations having been cut to a minimum, but we know, as the whole world knows, that this is not true. It is with bitter shame that we realise our real condition – well fed, warmly clothed and yet unable to share

151

these benefits with those whose needs are so much greater than our own. There has been no proposal for a general cut in rations – only that those who wished to give should be allowed to do so. Without that opportunity the coming Christmas celebrations will be a gigantic sham in which we cannot possibly participate. The idea of stuffing ourselves with food in the name of peace and goodwill, with people starving outside the door, is indecent and macabre.

They took every opportunity to arouse the consciences of readers and meetings on this and other post-war matters, but it was the disaster of Hiroshima that continued to obsess Reg, a disaster which brought him a renewal of faith.

☆    ☆    ☆

His pamphlet, *The Fallow Ground of the Heart* published by *Peace News* in 1945, might have been called, he wrote, 'The Atom Bomb and the Only Answer', and pacifists, he now profoundly believed, *had* the only answer.

We have long said that war would destroy man if man did not renounce war, and the full proof of that statement has now appeared in the headlines of the press. But we appeal from this deadly logic of destruction to the living truth that is in the heart – to the truth that was taught by the old prophets of Israel, without this new terror before their eyes. That truth lies deep in the fallow ground of which Hosea spoke – 'Sow to yourselves in righteousness, reap in mercy; break up your fallow ground: for it is time to seek the Lord, till he come and rain righteousness upon you. Ye have plowed wickedness, ye have reaped iniquity; ye have eaten the fruit of lies: because thou didst trust in thy way, in the multitude of thy mighty men'. [Hosea X, 12 and 13.]

Reg felt that a great light had shone for his awakening, and 'that light was the death glare that blotted out the city of Hiroshima'. From such events, outside ourselves, yet bringing a violent shock to our moral nature, humanity could learn something: 'I believe that the moment has come when mankind must turn from material force to moral force, because there is no other way of survival'.

He had come to realise that parties and politicians 'were only a reflection of "public opinion" and that it was no good hoping for cleaner politics until there was a new morality to be reflected by a new type of leader'. Politics was a breeding ground for intolerance,

but a disillusioned dabbler in politics must either learn to be tolerant or become a complete cynic. So, in the end, I began to learn personal

152

tolerance for people whose political principles I detested – and I found it the hardest struggle I have ever known.

The publication of *Cleanliness and Godliness* had resulted in appreciative letters from many 'reactionaries':

> At one time I could not have considered friendship with such people, but now I could see no objection. If people of the 'Left', with whom I disagreed fundamentally, could be personally lovable – and even sincere – why not those of the 'Right'?

He had formed a number of friendships with Conservatives and often found them more truly liberal than the 'radicals':

> Being more consistent, they were also easier to understand. And while the fundamental difference between us did not disappear, I learnt a great deal from these 'reactionaries'. (It is an odd paradox that the land-owner who exploits the farm labourer may have more respect for him as an individual than the Marxist who wants to 'emancipate' the labourer, but regards him as a stupid clod who should fall in line behind his 'superiors' – the industrial proletariat.)

Though men and parties were so imperfect, things *could* move in the right direction:

> When I was in India the Simon Report was published. It was a miserable document, advocating the pettiest reforms, and it bore the signatures of representatives from the three big parties in Parliament – including that of the present PM Mr Attlee. Twelve years later that document was on the scrap-heap; and Churchill, leader of the Die-hards in 1930, was sending Stafford Cripps to India to offer terms that the Labour Party would have dismissed as Utopian a few years earlier. Yes, they were refused – and, as I believe, rightly. But how came this advance? Why do we stand now on the verge of a settlement likely to give India at least the substance of political independence? Because India has ceased to be such a paying proposition? Partly, perhaps – but is that all?
>
> Principally, I think, it is because of the long, non-violent struggle of the people of India, which has shamed her rulers and stirred, however slightly, the conscience of this country. There has been a slow, but perceptible, change in British opinion and in the attitude of most Europeans in India.

Something had happened – '*something that may prove to be more significant than the release of atomic energy!*'

The pacifist's task was to try to leaven society with a new spirit, *'and it is not impossible, because humanity is ready for that leaven.'* But great predatory powers remained, and

> there is no reason at present to assume that they are drastically changing their way of living and thinking. There are still many who, like the rich young ruler, 'have great possessions'; and it is in these possessions, where they conflict with the rights and needs of others, that the great Quaker prophet, John Woolman, saw the seeds of war. In the redemption of humanity what is our prospect of converting these few who have now such infinite power for evil?

He recalled an ancient legend, the story of the man who was supposed to have taught mercy to God himself, bargaining with him for the lives of the people of Sodom. Were there not 10 worthy of salvation in the city of Hiroshima? In the hatred and revenge generated by war, the light of charity was forgotten, but it was still there:

> It will come back to us, and we shall know individually that this must never happen again. The common people began this war with a general belief that they were fighting ideas – an evil spirit and an evil system. There was long an insistence on this; and long after it had ceased to be true the conception of 'precision bombing' still seemed to justify war's most ruthless weapon. We ended with 'obliteration' of cities; and then – this final horror. If it proves the atrocity to end atrocities then, in an unforeseen way, this has indeed been the war to end war.

There was a man who persecuted the Christians, just as the Nazis persecuted the Jews. He watched the martyr Stephen calling out, as he was stoned to death, 'Lord, lay not this sin to their charge', and still the man breathed out threatenings and slaughter. Conversion was not always without its cost. *'Was not such a man past all hope?* He is still about his grim business when he sets out for Damascus; and then . . . he lived to write the loveliest words about Christian charity that have ever been written.'

The Church outlived the empire of the Caesars just as the work of Copernicus outlived the power of the Medieval Church, and today, the threatening forces of modern science were themselves

> *witnesses to the strength of ideas against the power of rulers.* And the moral forces which must yet master and control the inventions of science can triumph by the same token; for all that is human is subject to moral force, once it is applied in earnest – with the thoroughness we give to its opposite.

He recounted the story of the Jewish girl, Resi, some of whose 'enemies' – interned Fascists – had proved real friends:

a miracle if ever there was one. In some degree they and she and I myself had undergone 'conversion'. It was difficult to see people after that as black or white, good or bad. They all seemed to be different shades of grey. [And in every case they had] that vital spark that *could* respond to the same spark in themselves. Is it because we, on our part, have kept that spark hidden that we so often find our 'enemies' so intolerant and intolerable, beyond conversion or redemption?

The untilled field of the heart had been so long neglected in our over-cultivation of knowledge and power. It was time for the message of love that casts out fear. In his *Decay and Restoration of Civilisation*, Albert Schweitzer had written prophetic words:

A new public opinion must be created privately and unobtrusively. The existing one is maintained by the Press, by propaganda, by organisation, and by financial and other influences which are at its disposal. This unnatural way of spreading ideas must be opposed by the natural one, which goes from man to man and relies solely on the truth of the thoughts and the hearer's receptiveness for new truth. Unarmed and following the human spirit's primitive and natural fighting method, it must attack the other, which faces it, as Goliath faced David, in the mighty armour of the age.

This was *our* responsibility – yours and mine, said Reg, not one to be delegated to a Member of Parliament. 'Let us break up the hard ground of our own hearts.'

155

# CHAPTER XI

# The Alternative to Politics

ETHEL AND REG BELIEVED THAT THE PACIFIST MOVEMENT was in a parlous state, from the 'emotional and unthinking' Peace Pledge Union to the stance taken by the editor of *Peace News*, John Middleton Murry. Murry, they found, sneered at democracy and at Gandhi, and indulged in anti-Russian propaganda worthy of the gutter press. According to Murry's biographer, Frank Lea, who succeeded him as editor, Reg made a rude attack on the conduct of the paper at the 1946 Annual General Meeting. A few months later, Murry announced that he was no longer a pacifist, which was little surprise. When the satirist B. J. Boothroyd became editor, Reg was asked to join the Board of Directors, 'but during the war years it was natural enough that one should prefer the company of courteous, friendly and intelligent "enemies" to "friends" whose God was Middleton Murry'.

Ethel's publishers were disturbed by the epilogue of her novel, *The Dark Forest*. Was she suggesting that one occupying army in a neutral country behaved much like another? Indeed she was. Under protest, she deleted offending passages, feeling nonetheless that the book would speak for itself despite emasculation. Good news followed. At last she was allowed to return to her cottage in Connemara, though the battle for Reg's permit went on for months. The rough peasant existence with no running water, no drains and no means of cooking except an open fire was offset by the joy she took in the rolling brown bog and the quality of the light and the solitude. Her fingers swollen and sore from gardening, she played the music of Johann Sebastian Bach on her gramophone, while Reg, permit secured, chopped wood or heaved stones about to construct garden seats.

She reflected on the thousands of human beings wandering homeless and starving. In England, 70,000 people had volunteered to give up part of their rations so that food might be sent to Europe. It can't be done, said the 'Socialist' Minister of Food. Oh no, echoed others, we can't have folks

156

pestering other folks to surrender their meagre allowances. In fact, no one was asked to surrender anything, but many – including Ethel and Reg – sent hard-earned money to organisations for the relief of Europe. Massacres, mass evictions, plunder and disease continued – the ghastly aftermath of war that was in some ways more ghastly than the war itself, and an inevitable part of it.

She reflected, too, on that grossly misused word, passion:

> A passionate nature, in the true sense, is capable of a passionate celibacy; passion is something, whether it is sexual desire or anger or hate or love, deeply felt; that the passionate person is strongly sexed goes without saying, but passion and promiscuity are poles apart. The truly passionate nature knows nothing of sex debased to mere recurrent appetite; the passionate nature cannot be trivial. In Dante's unconsummated love for Beatrice was more passion than was ever dreamed of in Casanova's amorous philosophy.

D. H. Lawrence's 'Lady Chatterley' and her gamekeeper lover were passionate people in the true sense

> in that their sexuality was intense, and *because* it was intense involved periods of chastity, what Lawrence makes Mellor in a letter to the woman which is perhaps the finest thing in the whole novel, call 'the cool between-whiles', of which the Casanovas (of both sexes) with their perpetual surface desire know nothing, and which is their physical as well as their spiritual loss.

She did not need to be a great deal with those she loved: 'I have only to know that all is well with them and I can stay contentedly apart for months. I have never believed the sentimental assertion that absence makes the heart grow fonder; absence merely demonstrates that one can get along very well on one's own!' Such wide-ranging thoughts found their home in *Connemara Journal* (Westhouse, 1947). In Reg's copy of the book, Ethel inscribed: 'For darling Reg, with utmost love from his Connemara Comrade'.

They both fell in love with *Kathleen*, a 12-foot sailing dinghy which Ethel bought, secondhand, for £24. After studying a handbook, *Sailing for Beginners*, Reg, with a local lad, tested *Kathleen's* seaworthiness and soon, all three were using her as a rowing-boat and catching mackerel in the estuary.

So intent was Ethel on being a part of the Irish way of life, she read a number of Catholic works, conversed with priests and attended Mass, but she was quite incapable of the willing suspension of disbelief. In Dublin, she visited her beloved Hanna Sheehy Skeffington. How the dying Hanna

*Ethel with the pearls Reg
gave her in wartime*
[PAUL TANQUERAY –
COURTESY: JEAN FAULKS]

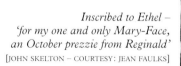

*Inscribed to Ethel –
'for my one and only Mary-Face,
an October prezzie from Reginald'*
[JOHN SKELTON – COURTESY: JEAN FAULKS]

*The hairstyle, inspired by the corps de ballet, which Ethel wore from 1926 until her death*
[PAUL TANQUERAY – COURTESY: JEAN FAULKS]

*Inscribed to Ethel – 'Just off some place. Mr Rinnolds smiles as his train leaves the station. For Mary, with everlasting love, from Reginald'*
[JOHN SKELTON – COURTESY: JEAN FAULKS]

would have disapproved of her next novel, the best-selling *Late Have I Loved Thee*, the story of a modern St Augustine, of a conversion to the Church of Rome! Working on the theme, Ethel was in a state of spiritual disintegration, no longer knowing what she believed, and, as a deflection, she and Reg walked some 20 miles a day. To her dismay, when it was published in 1948, she learned that *Late Have I Loved Thee* had led to conversions and was several times used by priests in their 'instruction'. Her Catholic phase was now over, much to Reg's relief – 'Ethel saw the red light this side of Vatican City' – and she was unclear whether she believed in God or not. To a young man who had taken the book to heart and who came to see her, she explained that the wording of the dedication made it plain that she was not a Catholic and, partly as a result of their discussions, he abandoned the idea of joining the Church and got married instead, to a woman old enough to be his mother – 'there is symbolism here for the Freudian-minded'.

In London, she spoke at public meetings against the Partition of Ireland and was later elected chairman of the West London Area of the Anti-Partition Committee. She also participated in a debate at London University, proposing the motion That Modern Poetry is Punk. The motion was defeated by 21 votes to eight, 'in spite of my readings from the works of T. S. Eliot in support of my contention'.

At the beginning of 1946, Reg was writing to *Peace News* that politics in Britain meant coercive action.

> It also means a confusion of issues, because the support of any existing party involves one in support of many things to which a pacifist should be firmly opposed. A limited objective *can* be sought by political means, *given certain conditions* – as Gandhi has shown – without sacrificing pacifism. But in Britain much individual work must be done before we can hope to see the human material with which a party could be built to which I, personally, could give even a limited support.

How support any party which denied the subject races the liberty he desired for himself, or which used (even in self-defence) the force which he was not personally prepared to employ? 'If my liberty really depends upon coercive methods, I believe that I should be prepared to lose it – or my life – rather than seek political "protection". If I wish that "protection", I must take my share in maintaining it by armed force.'

Ethel was incensed by a suggestion in *Peace News* that German prisoners of war, for years behind barbed wire, might be cheered by having parties of pacifists sing hymns to them. *She* suggested that it was high time that pacifists stopped being so infernally pious:

If any pacifists can sing good German songs (preferably drinking songs!) in German, and sing them *well*, these members of the most musical nation in Europe might derive pleasure from such singing. But a party of pious pacifists bleating hymns in English – really, really! What the men want is cigarettes and food – and a departure date.

Reg contributed his thoughts on the Nuremburg Trial to *The Friend*:

– – – – What is it to those who have lost their dearest friends and nearest relatives that a few men, whom they regard as scoundrels, should be hunted to death by a mockery of legal justice? The important thing is not the perverted judgement, but the uncharitable heart that demands it – not the rationalisation of vengeance, but the spirit of vengeance itself. [He was certain that] until the heart is purged of bitterness, the reason is incapable of judgement in human affairs. And the heart cannot be purged of bitterness except by the positive power of love – love that may begin, in such cases as these, with a tiny spark of pity, or the faintest spirit of chivalry to defeated enemies. [Only when we had learnt mercy were we fit to judge], but *when* we have learnt mercy we shall find that the desire to judge others has left us. 'He that is without sin among you let him first cast a stone.' Half the significance of the saying is that Jesus alone could have claimed that right; instead of which he is the advocate of mercy – the mercy that 'rejoiceth against judgement', as the accusers vanish from the scene 'convicted by their own conscience'.

He had found that mercy and truth were coupled together continually in the Old Testament. 'Of these references quite the most illuminating occurred in Proverbs xvi, 6: "By mercy and truth iniquity is purged". It is an amazing saying – a perfect recipe in seven words for the Christian attitude to evil. Truth without mercy gives us a harsh law and a cold morality. Mercy without truth becomes sentimentality. One condones evil; the other antagonises the evil-doer and gives us an excuse for imitating him, on the pretext of punishment. But when the two are brought together, when "righteousness and peace have kissed each other", then indeed we shall find the way whereby "iniquity is purged".'

☆   ☆   ☆

Some of Reg's verses that had appeared originally in the *New Statesman*, *The Weekly Review*, *Commonwealth Review*, *Adelphi*, *The New English Review*, *Forward*, *Plebs*, *Lilliput* and *The Countryman* were published in book form in 1946 by Allen and Unwin, with drawings by Quentin Crisp. *Og and Other Ogres* managed a crack at, among other targets, planners and

161

pre-fabricated houses, militarists, chemical manures, Philistines, Sabbatarians, bankers, Churchill, telephone girls, T. S. Eliot, white bread and the Conservative and Labour Parties.

John Betjeman admired the collection. 'His satire is deadly. At the heart is humanism, discovered by a laugh that may be wry or sardonic, but it is always salutary,' wrote *Cavalcade*, and *Poetry Review*: 'He remains the master of his temper and his art no matter what provokes his ridicule and so his strokes are the more apt to convince the victim'.

Satire cannot be kind [said Laurence Housman in the preface], and a poet, when he takes to satire, must leave kindness behind him. Reginald Reynolds is a man who feels it to be part of his mission to skin people. Once, having heard him perform the operation very efficiently at a public meeting, I expressed a certain apprehension as to what he might be doing to me someday, if ever we were to differ on some matter of faith or morals; and he was good enough to say, in recognition of our long-standing friendship and agreement, that if he ever felt it his duty to skin me, he would do it in private, not in public. On a later occasion, when he felt it his duty to put his hook into the mouth of a man who was also a friend of mine, he promised that he would do it as Izaak Walton counsels us to do to the harmless necessary frog – 'as though he loved him!' When I heard the outcome of that promise publicly delivered, I prayed Heaven to keep me from any similar manifestation of his love.

Yet Reginald Reynolds is not an unkind man; he is full of kindness; he is only fanatical. And there – having (affectionately) stuck my hook into him – my criticism of him ends. [Even his intransigence had virtue in it] because it is always in the right – that is to say the unpopular direction – in its assertion and defence of values which are in very present danger of being lost. Of all his well-pointed satires the one I like best (because it amuses me most) is also the simplest – the one in which, sitting 'with abject apologies on the shoulders of A. A. Milne', he records the electoral debacle of Winnie the Pooh!

*When We Were Much Older*

Herb, Herb
Morrison, Morrison,
Said one day to Clem:
  'Can't you get in
  To that show at Berlin
  Without going in with *them*?
For if I may say so without any malice
We're changing guard at Buckingham Palace'.

162

Then, when
They had an election,
Up spoke Winnie the Pooh:
    'If you miss the bus
    You can go with us,
    But we *aren't* going there with *you*'.
(A face looked out that wasn't the king's –
Just Laski, keeping an eye on things.)

Dubb, Dubb
The British elector
Rose one day from his bed;
    He missed his view
    Of delphiniums (blue)
    But there were geraniums – red!
But what should he find at the foot of the stairs
But Winnie the Pooh *who was saying his prayers*.

(Very softly)
H*rb, H*rb
M*rr*s*n, M*rr*s*n,
Said next to Clem:
    'Now you can go
    To Uncle J**
    While I look after *them*.
But just between me (and L*sk*) and you,
What *is* the matter with W*nn** the P**h?'


*Prayer to the Lord God of Lesser Evils*

    O, Lord God of Compromise, pillow and crutch of the weak,
    Soften our spirits to bear with the flesh and its fears;
    Give us thy Guidance and help us to find what we seek:
        *An easy way out, without tears.*

    We pray not for vision too far in advance of mankind;
    It is not Utopia we humbly beseech thee to bless,
    But that waking each morning the Evils of Life we may find
        Becoming progressively less.

    May statesmen sign pacts by degrees to abandon all war
    (As burglars by stages are weaned from the practice of crime)
    May nation rob nation and men rob their brothers no more –
        But certainly *not in our time.*

163

We pray for Thy Kingdom where rich men
    and poor men live at peace,
And the eye of a needle is broad for a camel to pass,
*Where prophets no longer are stoned, but respectfully cease*
*From stoning our houses of glass.*

(From *Og and Other Ogres*)

☆     ☆     ☆

Ethel followed *Late Have I Loved Thee* with another novel with an Augustinian title, *Every Man A Stranger*. Loosely based on the career of William Joyce, the story was about a man who betrayed everybody, but concerned, like Reg, with the Christian principle of redemption, she made the man love, without himself being loved, and for this love make the greatest sacrifice – the sacrifice of life itself.

By 1947, starvation in Germany and Austria had reached horrific proportions. When it was allowed to send a limited number of food parcels, Ethel and Reg found ingenious means of exceeding the quota. Ethel went further: under the unlikely sponsorship of the *Daily Mail*, she set out for Germany with rucksack, typewriter and a heavy bag of foodstuffs for distribution.

In her book *German Journey*, she described her visits to the needy people she and Reg had helped. Herr X lived with his wife, who had been raped by a Russian soldier, in one damp room, their home destroyed by shellfire.

Whenever I hear of a British housewife complaining of how 'difficult' the food situation is, and that in England we are 'half-starved', I have a sudden picture of the supper to which Herr and Frau X were returning from work that evening – the evil-tasting soup, black bread, and dry at that, and rhubarb cooked without sugar. And of a young man in Vienna, assuring me that he had lunched well, having had half of a tin of sardines I had given him, saving the other half for his supper. And of Fraulein Y sharing her rations with her father. And then I think of all the millions of adults who will not spare so much as a bar of chocolate to go in a parcel for a half-starved German child; then it is difficult not to feel a little bitter.

She contacted various relief organisations who were willing to receive the large clothing parcels which she was determined to get to destitute Germans and Austrians in all zones and sectors. She travelled to the Russian sector of Vienna to call on the cabaret dancer whom she and Reg had met on the train from Vienna to Zagreb 10 years previously. Franz had joined the Austrian army. His mother had been raped. He was hungry and despairing. He had had his fill of politics:

164

they have only run me into trouble. Before the war I was supposed to be a Red; now I am supposed to be a Nazi; I was conscripted to fight a war in which I had no interest; now all I ask is to be left alone until I am forced into a uniform once again.

But she also made friends with young people who were working towards the eradication of the old nationalist ethic and the development of an international spirit essential to the new democratic German republic. 'Every food parcel from England', she wrote in *German Journey*, 'is propaganda for democracy. And every time a German POW in England is received as a guest into an English home.' The essence of democracy was contained in the axiom which could never be too often asserted, 'I loathe your ideas, but would die for your right to defend them!' 'It is good that Nazi Germans should know that not all British democracy is hot-air and humbug; but it is also good for British democrats to learn that not all Nazi Germans are depraved and sadistic. It is good for us all to learn that labels are one thing and human beings quite another.'

She returned to Germany in 1948, staying with a Bavarian family from which experience she wrote the novel, *Bavarian Story*. In England, she appealed for people to send more food parcels. In Galway, she addressed an association of Women Graduates whose provisions were sent from Ireland through the Irish Red Cross.

☆    ☆    ☆

Reg was exposing the fallacy of measuring wealth in terms of cash instead of commodities. 'There is still a tendency to think that making money is making wealth, which is the reverse of the truth', he wrote in *Peace News* (1947). 'Making, saving or earning money is merely the means whereby we obtain a legal right to *dispose* of wealth – whether we have added to it or not.' The essence of the pacifist philosophy was trust:

In international politics this means no frontiers and no armies, no colonies and no 'security' except goodwill. In economics it means no 'employment' for the profit of shareholders, no protection of 'private property', except the goodwill which allows to each person reasonable enjoyment of things for his personal use and the raw materials necessary for his personal labour for the community. That is economic pacifism and in it there is no room for a money system. [Money power was the greatest obstacle to the fullest development and use of man-power.] Do we really want *things* (food, clothes, houses, books, etc.) and *services* (transport, education, medical attention, etc.) or do we

165

want a parlour game of playing about with chips to decide who shall have what? If we still insist on the parlour game, one thing is certain – that, no matter how much we juggle, fight, scramble, cheat and pile up the chips, there will be a shortage of real wealth, because money power, like war, is a great parasite that eats up the products of honest labour. The more people employed by Mammon, the less there is to buy, because less people are producing. [The pacifist movement] should surely advocate the commonwealth of mutual service and mutual trust which is implicit in an unarmed world. It should teach the simple commonsense gospel of work as a vocation and a means of service – not of personal profit.

He accompanied Ethel to a dinner party given by the Women Writers' Club of Dublin in honour of *Late Have I Loved Thee*. All the foreign publishers except the French adhered to a literal translation of the title, though Reg insisted that the Italians called it *Tardy Tomato*. Ethel was presented with a leather-bound copy of the book, inscribed by such guests as the Earl of Wicklow, Sean Macbride and Kate O'Brien, and lastly Reg signed it, 'Ole Reg, he was there, too'.

Days later, Ethel's father died in the public ward of a hospital. She was inconsolable, and not until 1951 did she find a way of easing her grief when, at Reg's suggestion, she wrote a tribute to Bob Mannin, *This Was A Man*, sending the proceeds of the book to an East End boys' club. She continued to feel 'that infinite regret which I suppose assails more people than not when someone close to them dies – that inescapable burden of remorse for not doing more whilst there was still time'.

Allen and Unwin published Reg's *The Wisdom of John Woolman* (1948), the book he cared most deeply about. It was reprinted twice, under Quaker auspices, with a preface by Ethel. Neither a biography nor an anthology, it was rather an exposition of Woolman's ideas. Ethel remembered well Reg's intense excitement at rediscovering Woolman's *Journal* which he took with him to hospital shortly after the Hiroshima tragedy. The *Journal* made a profound impression on him. 'As he tells us, it was as though Woolman had reached out of his century and stood beside him, "pointing to the inevitable climax of materialism, of the idolatrous worship given to machines, of the neglect of spiritual values and the degradation of human personality".'

John Woolman the tailor, born in West New Jersey in 1720, was the oldest boy in a Quaker family of 13 children. For Reg, he was an example of pure Quakerism:

By the non-participation of Friends in government and their non-cooperation in coercive measures, the unlimited growth of Quakerism in its pure form would undoubtedly bring government to a standstill. It would be replaced by a system of voluntary personal and corporate discipline, unequalled in the history of the State. Pure Quakerism is rarely found: but where it is, as we find it in the life of Woolman and a few others, it offers a complete alternative to politics. It is not merely the negation of politics, as found in the doctrines of anarchist theoreticians. It does not so much destroy, as replace, the machinery of coercion; and where it conflicts with the authority of an existing State, its emphasis is not so much on the necessary act of disobedience, but rather on *obedience* to the voice of God, on service to humanity, on voluntary cooperation for common good.

Oppression in more refined appearances remains to be oppression [Woolman wrote, and Reg commented]: One could not condone or support slavery and justify one's actions by working for better conditions on the plantations; though it might appear, superficially, to be the 'practical' and cooperative course. And the difference between his time and ours is that his attitude was understood for what it was, even by those who disagreed with his premises; whereas today he would have found plenty of support for his premises, but a complete lack of sympathy for his consistency and clear-headedness. His identification of himself with the oppressed would be regarded as a piece of obstructive individualism and a failure to cooperate with the good intentions and elaborate plans of the oppressors. We simply do not understand a man who really and literally *does* 'seek first the kingdom of God and his righteousness' nor can we believe that it is 'practical' to follow that instruction.

In his journeys, Woolman often stayed with Friends who were slave-owners,

and here arose one of the trials of that 'superficial friendship', of which he was so wary. He had to be at the same time the guest and the critic of such people, to be, as it were, the public conscience and the private friend. He could, and did, deal charitably with such hosts – but he could not afford to place himself under obligation to them, still less to accept the unpaid services of their slaves. He found his own characteristic solution by insisting on leaving money in payment for these services – a gentle, but practical, reminder to his hosts that they were daily accepting the same services without renumeration. The slave-owner, perhaps a proud and wealthy host, was thus confronted by his humble guest with the true facts of the situation – and, indeed, of all wealth built upon the labour of others – that it is the parasite who is

167

really 'pauperised' by poverty, living like a beggar on the largesse of labour, and, like a beggar, giving nothing in return.

How would Woolman have felt about the way land had been stolen from the people of Kenya,

> and the people of that country compelled by poverty, taxation and actual forced labour to work for the profit of those who have disinherited them? The parallel case of the Red Man, about whose interests he felt so keenly (though they fared much better than these African natives) gives us the clearest indication of what we might expect. What would he have said about an ordinance in Trinidad (sanctioned by the Labour Government) re-imposing the punishment by flogging of a black man who stole potatoes from a plantation?

There can be no doubt that Woolman would have regarded all such crimes against humanity as burdens upon his own conscience – that in regard both to the sufferers and those who caused the sufferings (the oppressed Negroes, the plantation owners and the acquiescent Labour Government) he would have felt that he could 'not consider himself as a distinct or separate being'. This was the kind of collective guilt in which he believed – not the imposing of vindictive punishment upon the innocent, but the willing acceptance *by* the innocent of responsibility, the burden of the guilty. It should not be necessary to demonstrate the complete contradiction between these two conceptions of collective guilt; in fact it is clear that the more we vindictively 'punish' innocent people for the sins of others, the less they are likely to accept this voluntary burden and its responsibility.

The more Reg looked at politics, the more he was convinced of the necessity for work on the personal level (the Woolman way) in order to create a new public opinion.

> Not only is force still the accepted sanction *in extremis* of almost all parties and politicians, but I am continually confronted by examples of party politicians who 'support their characters as just men by being just to a party'. Few politicians today can survive without a party, and no party can survive which is far in advance of public opinion – a state of affairs which would not be so serious were it not that public opinion is *impar congressus Achilli* (totally unequal to the menace of an atomic age). Elections, in such circumstances, are inevitably conducted (if the candidates seriously seek election) on the lowest possible level, the greatest moral issues being sub-ordinated to expediency, in the form of narrow and often purely local 'interests'.

Famine in India during the war meant very much less to most British electors than a cut in the meat ration or the suspension of dried eggs in 1946. The life and liberty of many millions in the British Crown colonies would weigh very little in an election if balanced against measures affecting local housing or unemployment. The smaller issues may be real enough, urgent enough; but while they hopelessly outweigh infinitely bigger ones, for which the electorate is equally responsible, our elections can be nothing but political auctions where politicians bid for support.

Throughout the social teachings of Woolman ran the simple criterion, 'How would I approve of this conduct were I in his circumstances and he in mine?', a question brought home to the wealthy in *A Plea for the Poor*:

He who toils one year after another to furnish others with wealth and superfluities – who labours and thinks, and thinks and labours, until by overmuch labour he is wearied and oppressed – such an one understands the meaning of that language, 'Ye know the HEART of a stranger, seeing ye were strangers in the land of Egypt.'

As many at this day, who know not the heart of a stranger, indulge themselves in ways of life which occasion more labour in the world than infinite goodness intends for man, and yet are compassionate toward such in distress who come directly under their observation; were these to change circumstances awhile with some who labour for them; were they to pass regularly through the means of knowing the heart of a stranger, and come to a feeling knowledge of the straits and hardships which many poor innocent people pass through in a hidden obscure life; were these, who now fare sumptuously every day, to act the other part of the scene, till seven times had passed over them, and return again to their former estate; I believe many of them would embrace a way of life less expensive and lighten the heavy burdens of some who now labour out of their sight to support them, and pass through straits with which they are but little acquainted.

In *On loving our Neighbours as Ourselves*, Woolman recalled the words of Job, 'if your soul were in my soul's stead'.

It is a simple and direct approach [wrote Reg], which could be applied with advantage today wherever idleness is rewarded with wealth or toil with poverty, and wherever a ruling race claims dominion over those whose inferiority consists in their past inability to defend themselves against conquest. The complicated jargon of Marxism leaves this great moral issue untouched, just as the no less complicated procedure of 'socialist' administration has done nothing to assert the principle in

169

practice. But Woolman went straight to the heart of the matter, and his repeated query is still the one that matters most. Until humanity answers it, politics are futile.

☆   ☆   ☆

During the war, at the invitation of George Orwell, Reg broadcast a few talks – on prison literature and on the first Russian voyage to Alaska – for Indian listeners to the BBC.

> Orwell was a difficult and unlikeable – even dislikeable – man [wrote Ethel to the present writer]. Reg did try with him, and wanted to like him, but it was no go. I only met him once – when he was down with t.b. and Reg and I went to see him together. I think Orwell piled it on a bit, you know. I mean, granted he went to lodge in a slum street but he didn't have to make it a room over a *tripe* shop!

Orwell suggested that he and Reg collaborate on a two-volume anthology, *British Pamphleteers* (Allan Wingate, 1948 and 1950), Reg to select and edit the pamphlets, write historical notes and explanations, find cartoons and deal with proofs, Orwell to compose a long introduction to each volume. He finished the introduction to volume one, which covered the period from the time of Queen Elizabeth to the French Revolution, but died before he was ready to tackle the second. That job was taken on by the historian A. J. P. Taylor, and Reg detested it so much that he refused to give copies of the book to anyone, even to Ethel.

In volume one, Reg studied 25 pamphlets, many of them republished for the first time since their original appearance in the 16th or 17th century, their authors ranging from Milton, Halifax, Swift and Knox to Winstanley, Defoe and Paine. 'The great function of the pamphlet', wrote Orwell, 'is to act as a sort of footnote or marginal comment on official history. It not only keeps unpopular viewpoints alive, but supplies documentation on events that the authorities of the day have reason to falsify.'

The second volume (French Revolution to the 1930s) included among the pamphleteers Burke, Hazlitt, Morris, R. L. Stevenson and Sanders Lewis. The disagreement between the views expressed by A. J. P. Taylor in his introduction and Reg in his notes to the individual pamphlets was complete. For instance, *Occasional Discourse on the Nigger Question* by Thomas Carlyle, expressed for Reg 'the essence of the Nazi racial policy and of the racial policy still pursued in South Africa' while to Taylor, 'the pamphlet here stands like an oasis of profundity among the sands of the Quaker Pease and the muscular curate Kingsley'.

*Labour, Nationality and Religion* by James Connolly was, said Reg,

a startling exposure of the way in which the high dignitaries of the Church and the Catholic gentry so often betrayed the interests of Catholic Ireland. It is a story little known even now, in Ireland, where the Church has benefited very fully from the revolution it did so much to discourage, whilst the social cause for which Connolly lived and died has so far reaped no results – a strange paradox indeed. In Britain the story is equally unfamiliar, Protestant prejudice having been unwilling to admit how much British imperialism in Ireland owed to unpatriotic Catholics, who worked with us almost to the very end to keep down their own countrymen. When Connolly was executed, after the failure of the insurrection in 1916, not only did Ireland lose her greatest son, but the world lost one of its most profound thinkers in the realm of social philosophy.

Regarding *Useful Work Versus Useless Toil* by William Morris,

it is important to realise that there is as much difference between the Socialism of the nineteenth century and what is called Socialism today as there is between the Tolpuddle Martyrs and the modern Trade Union Chief (whose objective is the House of Lords; or at the very least, a knighthood). The Socialists of William Morris's days would be distinctly perplexed by the sight of a Labour Government which had swallowed imperialism, monarchy and capitalism – even bolstering up a predatory economic system by introducing forced labour for private profit. 'Nationalised industries' run by boards as remote as any limited company, where the workers were still in perpetual conflict with their employers, would without doubt have horrified William Morris. On the other hand, he could deplore, as every socialist did, the exploitation of labour to produce rent, interest and dividends, and the 'useless toil' that created nothing – such as the stupid waste of human lives in competitive salesmanship, competitive advertisement, and the hundred other ways in which men are employed to snatch each other's bread or merely to add up the profits of other people in large ledgers.

He knew, long before the great slumps of the twentieth century, that a society was mad which made a blessing of mere 'employment' (as though the total amount of consumer goods could be increased by a rich man employing a large staff of household servants, whom the employer was supposed in some mysterious way to 'support', and as though a wealthy man did literally 'make' his own money and other people could eat it). [He did something else that was rare even among

171

Socialists] : He replaced the stupid conception of 'employment' as the thing to be aimed at by a creative conception of work as a pleasure in itself. The Socialist Society which Morris desired (and the dream which he left to haunt a world that drifts ever further from it) was therefore a world in which nobody sought 'employment'. Work was to be useful, its motive was to be service to the community, and its incentive was to lie in its social usefulness combined with the joy of the craftsman in the exercise of his skill and in the creation of things useful and beautiful. Hence Morris's Socialist League pamphlet, in 1885, was a challenge not only to capitalist values but also to the dreary conception of work which Socialists had inherited from the Capitalist system.

☆    ☆    ☆

30th January, 1948. Reg was on a bus when he saw the placards. Gandhi was dead. 'My first words when I had grasped the fact and read the blurred print of a newspaper were the same, I found, as those of many others: Thank God it was a Hindu. Had the assassin been a Moslem, the results would have been too frightful to contemplate.' What struck him in the days ahead was that men and women – factory workers, chars, housewives, and especially the poor – had spoken of Bapu's tragedy as something they had felt personally.

At the end of the following year, armed with a copy of John Cowper Powys's biography of Rabelais, he was one of a gathering of some 60 pacifists from many countries, and 25 of Gandhi's close associates, who attended the World Pacifist Conference at Santiniketan in West Bengal. He visited Sabarmati again, now a self-supporting colony teaching 'outcastes' useful trades and establishing them in Indian society. He was sad to learn that, elsewhere in India, attempts were already being made to 'explain away' much of Gandhi's philosophy – 'Gandhi did make some statements which I should not hesitate to describe as foolish. I think, for example, that his description of the Polish resistance to Germany in 1939 as "almost non-violent" was about as foolish as anything that a wise man ever said. Yet it is upon such isolated sayings that the revisionists rely in their attempts to modify the lesson of Gandhi's life, which was his real message to the world'. Uplifting news soon hit the headlines: at Lake Success, Michael Scott had appealed with passion on behalf of the tribesmen of South-West Africa.

Here I was in India, [Reg responded], the country for which I had fought, in my way and in my time. But here the struggle had reached a new phase – it was to be henceforward, as I had always maintained it ought to be, an internal struggle, a matter in which Indians alone must decide the destiny of their country. Those of us in Europe who really cared about freedom and justice should be looking now towards Africa. About the same time I read of the police firing on Trade Union demonstrations in Nigeria, which emphasised the same point. As I read the bland explanations of the Labour Government I recalled how the same people had done the same things and made the same excuses twenty years before, in India.

On 26th January 1950, the Republic was declared. Streets and houses displayed the national flag, the emblem that, in 1930, was penalised so severely that to carry it was punishable with 10 years' imprisonment. 'I ought to be glad that the long struggle has ended so triumphantly', thought Reg, but the events of Republic Day left him feeling flat.

All that really mattered, I knew very well, was political freedom, which had already been achieved, and social emancipation, which had yet to come. The Republic meant absolutely nothing – it was not even, properly speaking, a Republic at all. In fact Republic Day was something of a comedy. On the front page of the *Bombay Chronicle* there was headlined the message of H.M. King George VI, congratulating the Indian Government on 'the foundation of the Indian Republic within the Commonwealth'. The statesmen of Britain and India have been much congratulated on the 'formula' which they evolved; though what it all means I have yet to discover. What really made me smile was the wording used in this message. One naturally asks *what* commonwealth? 'The British Commonwealth of Nations' may be (and certainly is, so far as I am concerned) a euphemism for an Empire, which is not a commonwealth at all. It is, if you like, a thumping lie, since it implies that the tribesmen of Kenya, the British 'owners' of the land stolen from them and – say – Mr Herbert Morrison enjoy common rights and share common interests, their 'weal' or welfare being a matter of common concern.

He remembered a story about Gandhi's visit to London in 1931 when he went to see an old friend who had been devoted to the cause of freedom. Gandhi found him living in affluence and he said to his friend, quite simply, 'So you have got on'. This was what Reg now felt was all he had to say to the rulers of the new India, but then he recalled all the men and women he had met in the 'constructive centres', the nameless ones, like those who had made Indian independence possible, for without them even Gandhi would have been powerless.

Independence was a beginning and not an end, and it was a credit to the Indian intelligentsia that after two years they were impatient with their government.

By that I do not mean that independence is valueless unless it produces vast social reforms immediately – I value independence for its own sake and for the social changes which can only be achieved in a politically free country, however slowly they may come about. But the old catchword 'gradualism', which made slowness almost an end in itself was at best a perversion of the truth, and in our own time it has been exploded by the speed at which events move. If those who want peace are going to move 'gradually', they will find that the forces making for war will not obligingly wait until the gradualists have martialled their cohorts. [Speed did not necessarily mean taking short cuts], and I have for some time felt that the idealist in politics is always inclined to make this mistake. All corruption, graft, exploitation and oppression, in India or anywhere else, rests ultimately upon lust for power – by no means confined to the few who wield it – and the ignorance of the masses. In the case of the masses I am thinking of their lack of education (particularly) in methods of cooperation, in the best use of their existing resources and personal capabilities, and the lack of a common *faith* through which alone passive resistance to oppression can be carried out. On such a common faith personal self-discipline can be built up and developed into corporate self-discipline – the very essence of Gandhi's *satyagraha* and (incidentally) of a non-governmental society. Any attempt at 'speed' which does not begin at this point may succeed in overthrowing a bad regime, but is unlikely to create a better.

What could Westerners now contribute to the needs of India? Of all unlikely things, pondered Reg, it was simplicity, the simplicity of educated people who were not ashamed to work. (The educated classes in Britain were not as decadent as those in India). Cowper's lines came back to him:

> With oriental vices stuffed thy mind,
> But left their virtues and thine own behind.

'Perhaps, after all, many of the things which I have most condemned in my own countrymen, as I have studied their ways in India during two centuries, were not really "Western" traits at all.' He wondered if some of the worst crimes of Englishmen had been committed through the acceptance by the English of those 'oriental vices' and the neglect of the virtues of both countries. 'It was no accident that most of the worst social institutions of India were so carefully preserved under British rule – landlordism (though that system we created ourselves), the feudal principalities and (in the police and armed forces) even the ban on "untouchables". British rule was an imitation of all that was worst in India interwoven with some of our own worst institutions. The Viceroy affected the pomp of the Moghuls; but the best thing that India had produced, the village system with its *panchayats*, was systematically destroyed.'

It was a fallacy to assume that Gandhi had worked on peculiarly favourable soil. 'The conditions in which he worked were anything but favourable. The shallow nature of the supposedly ancient and traditional roots of *ahimsa* in India was demonstrated before he died; for the miracle is that he controlled that volcano of violence for so long. And again, the appeal which Gandhi made to the educated people to leave their pampered lives in order to serve the poorest people in the land was quite foreign to the natural tradition.'

He saw for himself the lasting effects of Gandhi's work in the Indian villages. The object of *Nai Talim* (Basic Education) was to educate people to face their personal and social problems. The schools, economically self-supporting so far as this was possible, offered no competitive inducements; the satisfaction was in cooperative service, in the dignity of manual labour. They were a microcosm of the de-centralised society and the West could learn a lesson from them. A simpler way of living would mean that instead of unnecessary furniture or superfluous clothes, we would have fewer possessions of better quality and of a more individual design. 'We might have to work longer hours', cautioned Reg, 'a very heretical suggestion these days. But, speaking as one who works very long hours at a job he enjoys, I should say that my work gives me a great deal more pleasure than I could obtain from shorter hours at unpleasant work.' So long as he could 'make do' at all, '*any* man who really enjoys his job would refuse to exchange it for something uncongenial merely for the sake of shorter hours and money for things which can never compensate him.' The happiest form of work was 'that which gives a creative outlet together with some sense of service to a community – even if one is only a writer and the most one can hope for is to provide a little entertainment'.

Independence was implicit in the relationship between staff and scholars at the Basic Schools; the teachers shared in the cleaning and cooking. In school self-government one could discover the value of cooperation, but it could only be fully developed when cooperation was applied to the economy of the community. 'When I was at school, I used to hear a great deal about the "team spirit", but it meant little to me because it was only applied to games, and the basis of games is competitive. You

175

cannot really develop a sense of cooperation in community service by learning to play team games. If that were so the schools which have made the biggest fetish of games would have turned out hosts of socialists, syndicalists and communists (with a small "c"). This is not noticeably the case; and the reason is that this "team spirit" is not applied at the level of production or for any real service to any community.'

If life had taught him anything at all, it was the futility of trying to calculate the results of a course of action, 'or even to judge by what we *call* "results" after the event – because results are never complete. People think they are working for one object and find that they have achieved something quite different; or if they fancy they have done what they set out to do, a later generation may find reason to take a very different view'. We never knew the end to which we were moving:

> All we know is the means which we are using. I have come to the belief that if we take care of the means the ends can take care of themselves; and *Nai Talim* is for me an outstanding example of the right means.

> I know no more than that. It may or may not be possible to achieve world peace and a society from which money and power have been eliminated – the kind of society I want to see. Meanwhile all I know is that, if I want peace and that kind of society, the place to start is here; the time, now; the people, my immediate associates; and the means are the direct application to the present situation of the principles I wish to establish in the future.

Of the scores of articles Reg wrote about Gandhi, one on the Mahatma and Christian Pacifism, in *The Visva-Bharati Quarterly*, stressed that 'scriptural warrant' had often obscured the free operation of the Holy Spirit in man and the Holy Spirit in man was still the ultimate guide. How recognise what was good except by its appeal to that which was good in ourselves, 'and even those Christians who claim infallibility for the Pope or the Bible are assuming an infallible judgement in themselves, to recognise infallibility when they see it!' Only a minority of Christian pacifists, influenced by Tolstoy who had also influenced Gandhi, had claimed that real peace, social justice and human freedom were inseparable. Gandhi had worried Christian pacifists because he failed to fit into any existing groove in Christian thought, and civil disobedience was 'un-Christian' and 'unpacifist', a strange verdict from people who were indirect beneficiaries of imperialism.

To orthodox Christians, the State was sacred, but States were of many kinds. Having considered it wrong to oppose a government, the moment it was overthrown by force and a new government set up by the rebels, the orthodox must show the same subservience towards them that they had to their predecessors. 'St Paul, in fact, was distinctly muddled when he said that those who resisted authority would be damned. That, surely, would only apply if they resisted unsuccessfully! If they succeeded and overthrew "the powers that be", which he claimed to be "ordained of God", they, in their turn, would become "the powers that be" and could claim the same divine sanction. And Christian pacifists would then have to make a holy duty of obeying the very men whose rebellion they had condemned the previous day.'

Gandhi had done much to rescue us from this ethical fog.

> I write as one who began as a Christian pacifist, spent some fifteen years in the wilderness of secular politics (as barren a field as ever a man ploughed) and returned to active work in the Society of Friends after the war. The change, as I saw it then, returning like a spiritual Rip van Winkle to the familiar scene, was already starting before the final martyrdom of the Mahatma roused the whole world to a new appraisement of the man it had laughed at and slighted. [The Christian world had at last begun to realise] the significance of Gandhiji as an exponent of Christian principles with regard to specific problems which Jesus, in his general ethical teaching, did not apparently discuss – though, of course, we must always remember that the recorded sayings of Jesus can only be a small fragment of all he actually said, even in the brief period of his ministry that is covered by the Gospels.

There were passages in the Bible (especially in the Old Testament) which condoned slavery.

> Yet the Christian conscience was slowly awoken on this subject, and (texts or no texts) Christians became aware in the nineteenth century that slavery was utterly contrary to the *Spirit of Christ*. The slave owners and their friends thumped their Bibles and thundered their texts about 'hewers of wood and drawers of water' and the like. But somehow it was the Spirit which lived and the letter which perished. And slavery perished with it. In much the same way, in spite of all the isolated and mutually contradictory texts that have been used to obscure it, the picture of the true Christ has been once more manifest to us in the quiet, unarmed resistance of the soul to armed force. We saw it last in Mahatma Gandhi, the man who loved us and fought us, the man who fitted none of our ready-made patterns, the Hindu who was a better Christian than any of us.

# CHAPTER XII

# Beards, Beds and – Beware of Africans

*Ballade of the Cheeses of Yore*

> The Cheddar cheese upon my plate
> Knew not the gorge that reared its sire,
> Dorset Blue Vinney's out of date,
> And Petit Suisse a vain desire;
> In some remote Norwegian byre
> The brown goat-cheese they still prepare,
> And yet unanswered I inquire:
> Où sont les fromages de mon père?

> Let no defeatist underrate
> The cheeses of our great Empire,
> Canadian cows I'll celebrate
> And toast their cheese before the fire
> If but Bel Paese bless my lyre,
> Rich Pommel and renowned Gruyère,
> And Fontainebleau my Muse inspire –
> Où sont les fromages de mon père?

> Stilton! When peril threats the State
> England hath need of thee. We tire
> Of lesser cheeses that of late
> Usurp the grocer's scales and wire;
> Rise Rochefort, terrible in ire!
> Up Gorgonzola, Camembert!
> God and St Ivel, knight and squire –
> Où sont les fromages de mon père?

## ENVOI

Fuhrer! Caerphilly shall conspire,
Brie, Wensleydale shall hear our prayer,
The Dutch have joined the Angel Choir –
*A nous, les fromages de mon père!*

(from *Og and Other Ogres*)

*Noble Savages*

The last 300 Boers, descendants of those who set out for Angola from the Transvaal in 1874, have been returning via South-West Africa. A repatriation committee has been trying to raise £30,000, and farmers are considering jobs for them as foremen, supervising African labour. Most of them are reported to be illiterate and unskilled.

For these poor savages a kindly nation
Offers free travel, rehabilitation . . .
A sum of thirty thousand pounds is named
(They cannot dig – to beg they are ashamed)
And Afrikaners wrack their brains, devising
Schemes to employ their talents supervising.

Thus the Japhetic oaf, devoid of skill,
Is still a voting citizen and still
Employable, because the ethnic schism
Enforces pigmentary nepotism:
Poor devils – why, they cannot read or write,
But, after all, at least their skins are white.

And soon, as foremen on extensive farms,
Their racial virtues and their ethnic charms
Will be among the bastions which protect
Those things for which the Boers have often trekked:
*Baaskap* and Calvinistic blood and thunder
And chattel slavery and the right to plunder.

And culture of a pure Caucasian kind
(Proprietary to the Racial Mind),
Civilization, higher education
For the Elect, by careful segregation –
The *Sjambok* now is the Good Shepherd's rod,
The epidermis is the road to God.

(from *New Statesman*)

179

Reg's regular haunt in the late 1940s and early 1950s was a Cypriot-run café in the King's Road, Chelsea, called the Bar-B-Q. Here, he would drink coffee, eat eggs-on-toast, write letters and chat with his bohemian friends – a girl known as Lizzie Lemon, the spectacular Quentin Crisp and the glamorous Joan Rhodes, later a famous Variety star.

To Joan, he wrote 'Odes to Miss Rhodes'. An abandoned child, she came to London at the age of 14, played draughts for money, worked as a busker, an art model and an assistant stage manager, kept company with Dylan Thomas, Lucian Freud and Henry Moore, and perfected a 'strong woman' act for the music halls, tearing telephone directories in half and throwing men over her shoulder. She set the fashion in leotards. She appeared on bills with Marlene Dietrich and Bob Hope and performed for royalty. She also entertained in a prison and had the warders trying to bend six-inch nails, which she afterwards broke in her hands. She told Reg that her autobiography would be entitled *Men I Have Picked Up – and Dropped*. Today, Joan Rhodes remembers Reg as 'a quiet presence' and as 'a night person'.

Quentin Crisp, author of *The Naked Civil Servant*, and an international success with his high-camp one man show, would not claim to have known Reg or, indeed, anybody well, 'but I sat around with him, in what his brother called "your tatty teashop" and occasionally visited him in Jubilee Place. He spent most of his time in various libraries making notes for his strange books. Although he found me (rightly) frivolous in the extreme, he was kind to me, persuaded his publishers to employ me as an illustrator and introduced me to his brother for whom I designed many book covers'.

Crisp drew caricatures of Bevan, Attlee, Stalin and Churchill for Reg's political pantomime, *Attleedin and His Wonderful Gamp* in the magazine, *Cavalcade* (1946). The show, we read, was produced by Crassus Q. Sesterces. Whitehall loose boxes and Westminster fauteuils free. Ten bob in the Pound or Family Circle. Gallery – pay as you go. Molotov cocktails served during the intervals. The cast were Attleedin (or Puss-in-Jackboots), The Widow Herbacious (His Aunt), Chu Chin Church (The Wicked Uncle), Gall Stones (a Financial Wizard), Fishanchips (an Austerity Fairy God-Mother), Stray-Chee (a Twit Nit), Bin and Ban (Clowns), Dubb-Dubb and the Jo of Muscovy (Lookers On), The Djin (a Powerful Spirit), and a chorus of Carpet-Baggers and Bureaucratic Blondes.

Scene Two took place inside or outside the Wailing Wall, Jerusalem. The chorus were disguised as Arabs and Jews.

1st SEMI CHORUS:
And did those Influential Men
   Walk in the Zionist processions?
And was the Holy River then
   Part of the Ratenberg concessions?
And did the Mandatories dice
   For mandates at the League of Nations?
And was Jerusalem promised twice
   By those conflicting declarations?

2nd SEMI CHORUS:
Bring us whatever gold can buy,
   Bring us our seats on the Committee,
Bring camels to the Needle's Eye,
   Bring Weissman to the Holy City;
We will not cease to immigrate
   Nor shall the cash rest in our tills
Until we've built a Jewish State
   With lots of dark – – –

(At this moment the carpet-bag lands and Pekinese crawl out)

THE WIDOW HERBACIOUS: It's no good blaming *me* for the tight
squeeze – it was your Portfolios, not my Ego. (The Wailing Wall wails)
What was that? Waterloo Bridge never did that sort of thing! Has that wall
lips as well as ears? Teeth, perhaps?

BAN: O, just an old wall – our modern pre-fabs
Are cast in a mould and tested in labs;
Just knock down the wall and erect a Partition
To suit the New World and its Social Condition.

BIN: Will you mind your own business?
Look there at the Banks,
They hold up the wall to fill somebody's Tanks,
And you can't pull it down without plenty of Yanks –
But somebody here has been playing some pranks!

(Slavonic sneezing off-stage. The wall trembles. General jitters as Attleedin
puts up his Gamp).

☆    ☆    ☆

After the disappointing sales of *The Wisdom of John Woolman* and the
first volume of *British Pamphleteers*, Reg was elated when his American

publishers, Doubleday and Co., suggested that he write another 'preposterous book on an improbable subject', such as *Cleanliness and Godliness*, 'with the same lighthearted treatment of scholars and scholarship'. Hence *Beards, Their Social Standing, Religious Involvements, Decorative Possibilities and Value in Offence and Defence Through the Ages*, published in Britain in 1950 by Allen and Unwin, and republished by Harcourt Brace Jovanovich in 1976.

He began his 300-paged treatise by saying that he suffered from an incurable disease: he was a Serendipitist. Serendipity was 'the profession claimed by Autolycus and attributed to Mercury – that of a snapper-up of unconsidered trifles. The word itself was derived by Horace Walpole from the adventures of those princes of Serendip who, said he, were always making discoveries by accidents and sagacities of things they were not in quest of'. Another definition of Serendipity was 'looking for a needle in a haystack and finding the farmer's daughter'.

Had Angels beards? Had Adam? Did St Peter shave? Some held the beard to be a sign of sexual conquest, some saw in it the results of over-eating or the symbol of sinfulness. To others, lack of beard was proof of a lewd disposition, then again excess of hair was evidence of lust. Ancient Egyptian priests shaved their whole bodies three times a week, such was their loathing of hair. The Greeks refused to have communion with the shaven. The heroes of Homer entwined their beards with gold ribbon. Early Roman senators expressed their grief by cutting off their beards or by tearing them out in handfuls. Beards were a protection against flies. They were banned in Venice, penalised at Lincoln's Inn. A Huguenot admiral used his as a sort of pin-cushion in which to lodge his toothpicks. Among the Bantu, beardlessness was regarded as a distinguishing mark between a man and a monkey. In the beardless 18th century, actors were alone in wearing moustaches and then only when impersonating murderers or highwaymen.

Mothers of Huns ironed the faces of their infants to prevent the hairs from growing. Shaving among the laity was effeminate, proclaimed the medieval church. Ryons, King of North Wales, sent a message to King Arthur announcing that he had overcome 11 kings and they had all done him homage by flaying their beards clean off; Ryons was fond of purfling (bordering) his mantle with the beards of kings and needed one more to complete the job. At Hardenberg, the burgomasters were chosen for the size of their beards and their feet; one of these beards measured eight feet nine inches and the owner tripped over it, falling down a flight of stairs and breaking his neck.

Emperor Constantine Copronymus set fire to the beards of hostile monks; the Count of Edessa pawned his. The Novgorodian Code laid down that the fine for plucking a single hair from a Russian beard was four times that for cutting off a finger. In the 19th century, Methodists pleaded for the beard – 'the fact that the Creator planted a beard upon the face of the human male indicates, in a mode not to be misunderstood, that the distinctive appendage was bestowed for the purpose of being worn'.

Pierre l'Eguillard wrote a book, published at Caen in 1580, in praise of red beards. A barber-surgeon at Leipzig in 1878 not only practised barbery, but bone-setting, blood letting, dentistry and chiropody, *and* he kept bees for stinging rheumatic patients into life. False beards were worn by the women of Argos on their nuptial beds. The Indian Pygmaei 'had hair and beards so long as to serve for vesture'. In 1947, the *Evening Standard* devoted its leading article to an appeal for the return of beards worthy of the descendants of Drake and Raleigh, 'the outlet which every man needs for his individualism in times of austerity and control'.

'Some time back Mr Reynolds added to the salty learning and gaiety of life by his study of *Cleanliness and Godliness*. He's done it again in *Beards*, and the masculine population, bearded and clean-shaven, solemn owls and merry wits, will lap it up,' beamed the *New York Herald Tribune Weekly Book Review*, and the *New York Times*: 'Mr Reynolds roars genially down the corridors of time shouting "Beaver!" Without splitting a hair, he writes of a tangled subject lucidly. He takes history on the chin and tells us all we shall ever need to know about beards.' Another American reviewer, showing great enthusiasm, said that 'Mr Reynolds must have amassed in his files the greatest collection of useless information ever compiled by mortal man'.

The English edition of the book was launched with a Christina Foyle Literary Luncheon at the Dorchester Hotel. Over 50 bearded celebrities were present including Dr Josiah Oldfield, Laurence Housman, Michael Bentine, Angus McBean, Clifford Bax, Hugh Williams and Arnold Haskell. Actor Bobby Howes pulled a bare-faced hoax on the lunchers by turning up in a stage beard. Sir Compton Mackenzie raised the greatest laughter with his speech beginning, 'I rise from this hedge – – –'. A beardless Reg made what he considered to be a poor speech probably because he had worked on it too meticulously. The chairperson was actress Hermione Gingold who told of a bearded benefactor of her childhood days whose eccentricity was such that he always arrived by way of the chimney. The whole event had extensive coverage in the *Daily Graphic, Daily Mirror* and *News Chronicle*.

Writing his works of historical serendipity involved an enormous amount of research, principally in the Chelsea Library – where, on a rainy morning, a bearded intellectual used to take off his socks and hang them on the radiator to dry – or the British Museum Reading Room. The speciality of Brown, a regular habitué here, was pornography, 'Cupboard' books. Each time he requested such a book, he was called upon to explain his motive, and then, duly delivered to him sizzling from 'The Cupboard', it would be closely surveyed by a member of staff. Brown was embarrassingly friendly:

> He would come up and ask what I was working on, breathing asthmatically and whispering with a slight stammer, until other readers turned baleful eyes on us and my own nerves were as much irritated by the sibilant whispering as they were agitated by murderous looks from nuns, parsons, blue-stocking economists, fascists, communists and smelly old men reading Sanscrit texts. We would move to a place where we could more easily talk. Brown always wanted to help.

☆     ☆     ☆

Still grieving for her father, Ethel travelled 7,000 miles through India and Pakistan, accompanied by Jean. Reg had encouraged them to join him at the end of the World Pacifist Conference – 'It would mean a book for you, Jean could take the photographs and we'd be doing a long overdue Adventurous Thing together!' – but the conference had been postponed for a time and they were obliged to go without him. Jean had fixed leave of absence from her job and Ethel's publishers were keen to bring out her account of the adventure, *Jungle Journey*, Reg to provide his usual counsel and criticism.

In the United Provinces, the two women, equipped with just a rucksack and a roll of bedding apiece, were the guests of M. D. Chaturvedi (Chats), the Chief Conservator of Forests, and Reg's old friend. They toured with him the dense jungles and vast forests, encountering tigers, panthers and bears from the back of a trained *shikar* elephant. Before reaching India, Ethel had been pestered with questions, and 'if anyone else asks why I am going to India, or what my work is – which a missionary asked me point-blank – I shall reply that I am going out to do anti-missionary propaganda, and that normally I am a lavatory attendant'. There was also a joke that from the jungles Jean would send home a cable: 'Ethel eaten by tiger. Writing.' But when they were actually in the jungles, and Reg had written referring to the promised cable, and a tiger, without warning, prowled towards them, somehow the joke lost its savour. However, they began to feel that there was no excitement in the world like tiger-hunting:

When we were out on the elephant and frightened we always vow 'never again', but once we are safely back at the bungalow, courage returns, and the next time, in full remembrance of how frightened we were the time before, we nevertheless go out again. [One of the things Chats taught them was] that it is not the paradox it seems to love the tiger and yet shoot it. That this man loves what he himself calls 'that great splendid beast' there can be no doubting, and he never loves it so intensely as when it lies dead at his feet. It is not so inexplicable. It is not merely that 'all men kill the thing they love'; it can also be explained in terms of male possessiveness, the desire to conquer, the power instinct. The tiger's beauty and strength can represent a challenge to a man no less than a woman's beauty and weakness.

When they saw the blood running out of the hole in the side of the limp dead body of the young tigress,

we could feel only the futility of that act of destruction. It is futile; but, if it comes to that, so is the act of love. A man spends his strength and power upon the body of the desired woman, and for the time being destroys himself and her in *le petit mort*, and is no nearer to possessing her essential essence. He returns, again and again to the pursuit of the same woman or another; each time it is the same but different, just as the story of one tiger is the story of all, yet every tiger is its own story. Behind all our grieving when something beautiful and innocent was killed there was this knowledge, this understanding – and infinite regret.

Much of 1950 Ethel spent in Connemara writing the novel, *At Sundown The Tiger*, taking for her text a quotation from Anatole France – 'The fascination of danger is at the bottom of all great passions. There is no fullness of pleasure unless the precipice is nigh. It is the mingling of terror with delight that intoxicates'. And the supreme mingling of terror with delight was to be found in the pursuit of the tiger.

She spoke, with Reg, on London pacifist platforms in the summer of the Korean war, and wrote *The Fields At Evening*, a novel of English farming life based, like an earlier novel, *Linda Shawn*, on memories of her maternal grandfather's farm. She re-told some Irish legends in *The Wild Swans*, and was persuaded to go to Morocco to learn about Arab nationalist aspirations (*Moroccan Mosaic*). Her companion on this journey was the journalist Irene Beeson, one of Reg's Chelsea friends. They travelled from Tangier to Tetuan, the capital of the Spanish zone, and then to the principal cities of the French zone. Miss Beeson also accompanied her to Egypt more than a decade later but by this time their relationship had deteriorated, not helped by the fact that they were both taken ill. (Ethel was left in the desert while Miss Beeson returned to Cairo.)

For the *Encyclopedia Americana*, Reg wrote articles on baths, beards, barbers, beds and banquets, and was commissioned by a firm making sanitary ware to contribute a long introduction on the history of sanitation for a commercial brochure. In 1952, he was appointed Field Secretary to the Friends Peace Committee, for which he lectured at schools and to undergraduates, and participated in Quaker work camps. Work camps served to recall people to a deeper and more elemental conception of what work could be. Self-governing groups of international volunteers lived and worked together, giving help to rural areas, old people's homes, schools for backward children, youth clubs and community centres in new industrial suburbs. It was a practical way in which Friends' concern for peace and understanding between people of different nationalities and backgrounds could be expressed.

*Opportunity at Eighteen* was a pamphlet by Reg, offering hints to those who were facing Tribunals:

> Other young men – those who go into the Forces – may have occasion to show their courage; but few of them will stand alone, as you will stand when you answer for your beliefs. They will march in companies, relying upon orders. The orders upon which you will rely come from within you.

He told the story of a pacifist in the first world war who was asked a hypothetical question about an imaginary threat to his own home and family. The chairman of the Tribunal was a Colonel,

> and the pacifist, before replying, said unexpectedly: 'Before I answer that, would it be in order if I first asked *you* a question?' The Colonel was a reasonable man – you cannot, or course, count on that; but on the whole civility and reasonableness will generally evoke some respect from a Tribunal and in this case it certainly did. 'Yes', said the Colonel. 'Suppose that I have joined the Army. Suppose I am fighting near my own home. And suppose that I am given a very important dispatch to deliver. Just as I am about to set out I am told that my family is in some terrible danger such as you have described. They are very near and it is not too late to go to their help. But this means disobeying orders. Will you tell me what I should do?' The Colonel thought awhile. 'It is a very difficult question, young man. But I think it is clear that you should obey your superior officer's orders.' 'Thank you very much,' replied the pacifist. 'Then my answer is that I already have my dispatch and *I shall obey my Superior Officer.*'

186

The community you should seek to serve, advised Reg, was not that of one nation or class in conflict with another – it was nothing less than humanity as a whole.

It is true that in practice you can only serve, at one time, a small group of people or perhaps one individual who needs your help. That makes no difference. The point is that you do not discriminate according to nationality or colour or class or creed. Your field of action may be a small village, but you can still live and think as a world citizen. That will give you a community sense far higher than that of the nation state, which is too large to be a community of individuals and too small to be the expression of universal unity – in fact it is a danger to both conceptions. [Summarising, he suggested]: Think always of the source of your faith. Remember that the Tribunal is only a milestone – your peace witness must be a matter of life-long dedication. And remember that no decision of the Tribunal can prevent you from doing the Will of God. You are there as a Witness for Truth – not to plead for yourself.

☆　　☆　　☆

On the literary front, Reg followed *Beards* with *Beds, with many noteworthy instances of lying on, under or about them*, published in America, and in England by Andre Deutsch (1952).

One of the most amusing books of the year, [said the *Chicago Tribune*, and the *New York Post*]: A long, scholarly, droll essay, filled with odd bits of information, and the author's peculiarly English wit, polished and mildly whimsical. Reginald Reynolds says he wrote *Beds* mainly in bed, surrounded by his sources. He must have been barricaded, for his references range from the Bible to Groucho Marx, [and the *Richmond Times Dispatch*]: Any information derived from *Beds* is guaranteed entirely useless. It is also warranted to be entirely fascinating. [To *The Friend* reviewer], the book, the result of research into folklore, mythology and ancient customs in many parts of the world, is a rare mixture of recondite learning, miscellaneous information, good fun.

One could stay awake by subtracting sheep (Groucho Marx). In 1726, at Godalming, it was firmly believed that Mary Toft had given birth to rabbits. Dr Graham, a public benefactor of the 18th century, was obsessed with the procreation of a generation to replace the 'present puny, feeble, and nonsensical race of probationary immortals, which crawl, and fret, and politely play at cutting one another's throats for nothing at all, on most parts

187

of this terraqueous globe'. For this purpose, a special bed was designed, on view for a mere half-crown. The doctor lectured three times a week, demonstrating the true nature and effects of electricity, air, music and magnetism when applied to the human body. One of his devices to enhance beauty and increase health and fertility, was the hymeneal couch; for £50 sterling, a childless couple could be sure of an heir by using this Celestial Magnetico-Electric Bed which rested on six massive and transparent columns; and, as a bonus, the bedclothes were perfumed with the costly essences of Arabia.

There was a Yorkshire practice whereby the mother of an illegitimate child was bound by a code of honour not to reveal the name of the father; but the girl's mother would search for him and the first man she found in bed would be the culprit. On the birth of a child, a Boro woman in South America would go out digging, while the father stayed for a month in his hammock. Among the Utes of North America, mothers, after giving birth, would 'rest' for 30 days on a bed of hot ashes.

Another most unpleasant bed was one made of ice, on which an aged Russian dwarf of the 18th century was compelled by the Empress Anne to spend a bridal night with a dwarf woman; it was the duty of the bride to tickle the soles of the feet of the Empress as she dropped off to sleep. Early in the 20th century, Bolivians, as a pastime, would lie in bed and spit at the walls and ceiling; and a sage of the 8th century gave directions to monks on how they should spit when singing psalms – he enjoined them to spit backwards, over the shoulder, and then to cross themselves quickly for fear of spitting on an angel.

In 1947, at Knoxville, a jury awarded a man the cost of boarding and lodging the defendant, a woman who had come to his house for dinner and who had remained in one of his beds, against his will, for five months because of her arthritis. The average modern American housewife walked four miles each year making and remaking one bed. The cartoonist Rube Goldberg slept with a pillow under his feet instead of under his head. In Newfoundland, Reg's friend, the Reverend James Whittle, found an odd bundle in his bed; it was a baby, kindly placed there by his hostess to act as a hot water bottle. In Abyssinia, it was customary for a husband and wife to share the same night-shirt, each having one sleeve. A London radiologist lay in bed with two grape vines growing over him.

A housewife in New York retired to bed for 10 years in response to a spirit message. A man from Alabama built a circular home, with a circular bed, modelled on the temple of the Vestal Virgins; his servants were known as Romulus, Remus and Cassius. Howard Hughes, the film producer, slept in a bed operated by 30 electric motors, with a dashboard covered with push-buttons by means of which he could tour his room and turn on hot and cold water. At New York's Sleep Shop, there were double mattresses for double beds. Held together by zip fasteners, these mattresses could be separated by a movement of the arm, indicating a preference for solitude; if the other occupant snored, a small mechanism made a noise and emitted air so that the offending party was awoken.

In South Africa, a hot-dog merchant discovered that on the mesh of a single bed he could grill 30 pounds of sausages at a time. Modigliani cultivated a spider as his companion and, so as not to disturb it or its web, refused to make his bed. The wealthy Jains of India, whose religion forbade them the destruction of any form of life, had hit on a method of preserving the sacred existence of the bug: they paid able-bodied men, who could spare some blood, to sleep in their bug-ridden cots, and when the bugs had supped, the employee would be dismissed and the owner of the bed take his place. A Victorian doctor claimed that women who loved their husbands generally lay on the right side of the bed. The reason? Read the Song of Solomon, chapter ii,6 and chapter viii,3.

☆    ☆    ☆

In January 1953, Ethel researched the lives of two Munster men, Gerald Griffin, all lyricism and drama, and the Reverend Francis Mahony ('Father Prout'), all wit and scholarship, for her book *Two Studies in Integrity*. In February, Reg set forth, rucksack on back, on a mammoth trek from Cairo to Cape Town with the aim of getting an overall picture of Africa resurgent.

He went first to Gaza where two thirds of the inhabitants were refugees, living on the borders of what was once their home.

> Tell the English and the Americans [said a Palestinian administrator], that if the refugees all become Communists the responsibility will be theirs. We never wanted the Mandate. It was forced upon us and we fought against it, but they had their way. This is the result. We know who betrayed us, and mere 'relief' doesn't solve anything. The camp schools are staffed by refugee teachers. Who can blame them if they reflect the same attitude in their teaching? Their hearts are hungry. [Reg added:] For their hunger – can one sufficiently emphasize it? – is not material. The exiled peasant hungers for the land that is so near – so near that Arabs will cross the frontier by night and risk the Israeli patrols to pick a few oranges in the groves which were once their own. Sometimes there is a shot – and an Arab may lie died or wounded in his own grave.

189

His host in Cairo was the fiery Arab patriot, George Mansour. George was happy to relate that when he tried to save himself from bankruptcy, among the few who stood by him were two Jewish creditors. Reg presented to the old exiled Moroccan leader, the Emir Abd el Karim, an advance copy of Ethel's book, *Moroccan Mosaic*; she had inscribed it for him, expressing her homage. In Upper Egypt, he met George's brother-in-law, Father Ayrout, the driving force behind 125 schools:

Members of the Coptic Orthodox Church, Moslems and Jews all spoke with deep respect of this man. By ability, by devotion and integrity and by a complete absence of bigotry he had enlisted their support. His impact on the well-to-do can best be compared with that of Gandhi in India or of St Francis in medieval Italy. He was not only getting at their pockets through their consciences – he was obtaining their active help.

Reg left Egypt with a feeling that the government was almost as much overshadowed by American interests as previous Egyptian governments had been overshadowed by indigenous feudalism. He travelled on through Sudan and Uganda, studying social developments, and then into Kenya where the land problem faced hundreds of thousands:

How can one expect them to look calmly at the vast alienated estates or to hear with equanimity of further schemes to introduce yet more settlers from Britain, each of whom will occupy enough land to maintain hundreds of families from the over-populated areas? I have heard and read many sophistries invented to justify this state of affairs. Perhaps the silliest was the solemn assurance I was given that no African would even *wish* to live in the 'White Highlands'. It was too cold, and so on. Yet thousands of Africans *do* live there, as servants and employees of Europeans. Driven by hunger, they even live there as 'squatters', allowed to cultivate a small patch of their native land in return for an agreement which binds them to work for the European 'owner'. If God indeed made the earth he must be puzzled about this. And after the Kikuyu eviction and exodus from the European farms, these local tribesmen, too, were being recruited (with the help of semi-starvation) for work in the 'White Highlands' – the land which they 'did not want' and in which 'no African wished to live'.

You must speak for us [said a Chief to Reg in Mbale]. There is nobody to speak for us now. Jomo Kenyatta is in jail. All our leaders are in jail. We cannot speak or we are arrested. [Mau Mau atrocities continued to take the headlines], but in small paragraphs of the East African papers, [observed Reg], or even between the lines, there were other unpleasant things to be noticed. Not content with having closed

190

down the Kikuyu Independent Schools (built up at great sacrifice by the people, with so much faith and hope, because of their almost pathetic belief in the importance of education), the Government had now announced the dissolution of the African Association of Farmers and Traders (Co-operative). It seemed that no vital institution whereby Africans could achieve anything for themselves was to be allowed to remain in existence. Education and cooperation were the most dangerous things, it seemed, if they were allowed to develop independently and to foster an independent spirit. Having killed African initiative, Europeans would be able to say once more that the African had none and was uncreative, incapable of doing or making anything except under European orders. But did nobody see that the closing of all such channels must inevitably drive more Africans to secret societies and terrorism? Had Africans, in fact (I asked myself) any other way left? There was Gandhi's way, of course; but that needed time and spiritual training.

Bombing from the air had been authorised and the military had been given power to shoot African 'suspects' at sight, without challenging them. Some months earlier, Colonel Grogan had said in the Legislative Council that the Government should 'take a hundred rascals, hang some of them in front of the others, and send the survivors home to their villages'. It was an open declaration of a counter-terror policy.

And the evidence was piling up that Grogan's policy was being unofficially implemented, especially by the Kenya Police Reserve. European settlers and settlers' sons, with arms and a very free hand to use them, they were the cause of more terror than the Mau Mau itself. They were called the White Mau Mau by many Africans.

Under the shadow of this double terror it was hard to get at the truth about anything in the Kikuyu country.

I was frequently warned of the danger I could bring to Kikuyu by meeting them openly. When, through the help of friends, I eventually *did* meet them, I heard innumerable stories of police brutality. If only one tenth of the allegations were true, the case against the Government would have been a heavy one – and from my reading of the affidavits I knew there was more fire than *that* in the smoke.

Not long before he had arrived in Kenya, an English barrister practising in Nairobi claimed to have unearthed several cases of murder. He offered the evidence of one case to the Governor of Kenya, asking for a full enquiry. (Reg saw a copy of the evidence and it seemed to him about as damning as any evidence could be.) Within 24 hours the barrister was ordered out of

191

Kenya. His office was broken into and his mail interfered with. Reg caught up with him in Tanganyika and was now regarded as his 'emissary' and therefore as a marked man. While they were lunching together, the Superintendent of Police interrupted them and told the barrister that his deportation order was to take effect as soon as a berth could be obtained for him. It all showed what a man had to cope with if he tried to expose the truth in Kenya.

From Nairobi, Reg's route was southwards, a journey of some 1,500 miles by road to the Copper Belt in Northern Rhodesia. He witnessed well-organised demonstrations against the colour bar and, outside Broken Hill, a road sign which read 'Beware of Africans'; this he chose as the title for the English edition of his book on the African pilgrimage. In Southern Rhodesia, he met Mrs Coleman who ran an inter-racial theatre group in Bulawayo:

> She had many stories which delighted me. I think the most revealing of them concerned a meeting at which an African chairman had to introduce her to an African audience. The chairman said, 'Mrs Coleman is the only European I know on whose lips the word *welfare* has never been heard'. With all my respect for the workers I met in Africa, I still think that a very high compliment. It was not, I hope, a denial of the value of such work, but an assertion that here was a European whose love of Africans never carried with it any hint of patronage.

It was at Lusaka that Reg first heard of Alick Nkhata, a local radio singer and collector of tribal music from all parts of Central Africa. One morning Alick, who was with an English friend of Reg's, wanted to buy a gift from a European shop:

> Africans are supposed to queue up at a small hatchway and not to enter the shop itself. But in some small-town stores this is not practicable and it was at such a store that my friend waited and presently Alick came out of the shop. He glowed with happiness and could only say: 'It's happened. It's really happened. I was waiting to be served when a European came in behind me. The shop assistant looked over my shoulder and asked what he wanted. And do you know, that man actually said, "Excuse me, but I think this gentleman was in front of me".'

A car journey to Umtali and a two-day bus journey to Beitbridge and Reg was on the borders of the Union (the bus had three compartments – 'Europeans', then 'Parcels', and, in the rear, 'Non-Europeans'). He talked with 'banned' leaders in South Africa, and with Father Trevor Huddleston:

At the moment he was taking a leading part in the opposition to an iniquitous plan whereby some 70,000 non-Europeans would be moved from their homes in the 'Western Areas' of Johannesburg – the latest *apartheid* drive, under the Group Areas Act. For many Indians, who were occupied in trade or professional men, it meant plain ruin. For the Africans it meant great distances to travel by utterly inadequate bus services. And now, with thousands already living in shanty towns, fresh hordes were to be moved 10 miles or more from the city. [The courage of Father Huddleston] was something almost tangible. The thing he feared was fear itself – the cowardice of his fellow-countrymen who knew the truth but might fail to speak out. And he feared the apathy of those who feel only their own wrongs and are indifferent to those of others. [The Afrikaner nationalists, Reg found, dismissed African opinion], but they equally resented what they called 'foreign interference' – although, but for 'foreign interference', they would not themselves be in Africa at all. Could they have it both ways – rule out the 'native' and the 'outsider' alike and set up as a law to themselves? So long as the vast majority were deprived of elementary human rights it was no domestic matter – it was the world's business.

He visited workers trying to build up centres of inter-racial cooperation, played with malnourished children, and passed that frequent sign on South African roads – 'Beware of Natives'. After staying with the Indian community of Durban, he spent time with 'a saint', the Quaker teacher Olive Warner who believed that to do any good in South Africa, one had to be very patient with Europeans, a patience which was cultivated only by people who cared passionately. He debated deep into the night with African teaching and medical staff, with, for instance, Jean Jolobe,

> the perfect prototype of emergent Africa. She was a woman of about 40, with the poise of her age; but she had the energy as well as the beauty of youth. She represented so much more than the African educated class; she was the educated woman, which is rarer – the married woman in a skilled profession, too, for she was a Sister at Lovedale Hospital. This face, which was at the same time mature and young, sensitive and courageous, symbolised so much for which I had no words. It was the new Africa which was coming into being – a thing of beauty, strength and wisdom and of latent moral force that must prove irresistible.

To Port Elizabeth – to New Brighton – That a society in such places gravitated towards something indistinguishable in substance from chattel slavery had long been clear to him.

There is not much difference, in practice, between the slave trade, which took Africans from Africa, and the more civilised process whereby so much of Africa was later taken from under the feet of Africans. [Chased from the soil, hounded by taxation into European industry], the African still required jails and floggings to make him sufficiently subservient. And further means were already being devised to drag him yet lower. [It was] the abyss of evil. [He believed that South Africa was fundamentally rotten but that human nature was always redeemable.] Formal religion may or may not play a hand – though most of the theologians will back the Devil. (Historically they always have.) But the human appeal of a human need will always sweep in all genuine saints; and who cares about the theologians, anyway?

The miracle was that any genuine radicalism existed at all among the white natives of South Africa: 'Once a European asked me some questions about non-European circles in Port Elizabeth. "What", I said, "do you expect me to tell you about your own town?" His reply was a variant of what I heard quite often: "You needn't be so modest. You know damn' well you get opportunities no ordinary European resident gets in a lifetime". I knew what he meant. It's one half of the truth. The other is what you can only get by long experience. But the impact on the outsider is still of value, so long as he realises his limitations. In self-defence, once, after hearing altogether too much of the opposite view, I wrote a parable. It was surprising how many Europeans, instead of taking offence at it, entirely approved of its content':

A certain man, coming into a room where a number of people had been sitting for some hours, remarked that the room was stuffy. The people sitting there were very annoyed at this remark. 'How can you presume to judge', asked one man, 'when you have only this minute come in?' Another said: 'It is always these people from outside who make this ill-formed criticism. Only those who have sat here for hours can possibly know whether the air is fresh or foul'. 'It is just to keep out ignorant critics like you,' said a third, 'that we keep all the doors and windows shut.' So they threw the intruder out and bolted the door.

The present rulers of South Africa were too essentially feudal to be fascist.

The racialism of the fascist is rarely compatible with a 'paternal' attitude to 'inferior races'. Nazis did not say that Jews were all right 'in their proper place'. Nancy Greshoff, the sharpest and shrewdest European critic of European ways whom I met in Cape Town confirmed what I had so often heard – that these Boer feudalists were often kind and good in their dealings with Africans as servants and retainers. I was continually reminded of the fact that, in spite of the powerful emotional appeal of *Uncle Tom's Cabin*, the case against slavery had *not* rested on the authenticity of Simon Legree as the typical slave owner. A bad system gives opportunities to cruel and ruthless people. But it remains a bad system quite apart from that. It is bad if the human relationships involved are morally unhealthy. I should call feudalism morally unhealthy because it is based upon the arrogance of the few and depends upon the subservience of the many – both objectionable, but often co-existing with fine qualities of character.

A young European girl from Pretoria wrote to Reg as she was keen to work with and for Africans, and he, who had only been months in the country,

sat and told her the people she should meet in Cape Town. She had no idea then how many Europeans shared the same attitude. So ended my pilgrimage in search of hope by sharing, even in South Africa, some of the hope I found there. [Four words sufficed: *Alles sal reg Kom* – all will come right.] I don't know what Jan Brand meant when he said it, but I know it expresses my own faith. For the future is not with temporal power but with the power that makes for righteousness.

Returning from his 8,000 mile journey, he called for more men and women to blend their skills and commitment with that of the Africans. He kept up a massive correspondence with the friends he had made; encouraged youngster after youngster to take an interest in African affairs; put people in touch with each other; and inspired many of the readers of his articles to give practical help to Africans in their struggle against poverty, illiteracy, racial discrimination and political frustration.

*Beware of Africans* (Jarrolds, 1955) was, largely, Reg's celebration of heroic souls, the pioneers of the New Africa.

Shrewd and hopeful commentary on Africa's future prospects by a keen observer, [said *The Star*]. It is not the author's fault that one closes the book with a feeling of powerless anger, [said the *New Statesman*]. He has tried very hard to be fair to everyone, and to avoid the usual trap of writing about Africa in terms, so to speak, of black and white. [One American reviewer accused him of believing that] everything the Europeans have done in Africa is bad and everything the natives have tried to do is good. [On the other hand, the *Cape Argus* of South Africa spoke of his] temperate outlook. Reynolds is not sentimental about the Africans he met. He is not blinded to their faults. [Another American reviewer found the book] unmarred by the bitterness that one might

195

expect from a man full of feeling about the essential rights of mankind. [And *The Friend* of Bloemfontein had no doubt of] Mr Jennings's sincerity.

'Mr Jennings' meant Reg: 'the reviewer got me right in line two but called me Mr Jennings from then on. He considered me careless and slipshod.'

### Meddlers From Abroad

Lord Malvern (formerly Sir Godfrey Huggins) has spoken of 'certain woolly-headed gentry – particularly meddlers from abroad – who want to hand the Government over to an African population'. He asked: 'Do they really think they can pronounce upon the eternal verities by counting noses?'

> There are some caves across the veld
>  Full of the Illustrated Gnus;
> But meddlers from the sluggish Scheldt
>  With guns and Calvinistic views
> And tally-ho and syphilisation
> Performed some swift extermination . . .
>
> The Bushman and the Hottentot
>  Knew nothing of religious creeds;
> Of land they had an awful lot
>  Without the proper title deeds;
> Meddlers with Bibles as their warrants
> Regarded this with some abhorrence.
>
> The English came to meddle next
>  (Converted slavers, bent on wrecking);
> The Dutch, considerably vexed,
>  Decided on a spot of trekking;
> But first they swelled the population
> By meddling in miscegenation.
>
> The British, not to be outdone,
>  Though suave and naturally urban,
> By further meddling had begun
>  To build a little place called Durban,
> Where some of their indentured meddlers
> Became quite prosperous as peddlars.
>
> And Cecil Rhodes, who thought it wrong
>  The Bantu shouldn't share their mealie

Went round about and up – along
　　To meddle with the Matabele
Who, in some fit of strange amnesia,
Were sold along with South Rhodesia.

With so much meddling it is queer
　　That some should now resent the entry
Of further meddlers who appear
　　As 'certain woolly-headed gentry',
Now treated with extreme revulsion
Or – like Miss Ainslie – with expulsion.

This meddling (it has been agreed
　　By those who've made a tidy packet)
Ought now to end – because, indeed,
　　Those who once owned the land now lack it;
To meddle with the Upper Crust meant
Uncomfortable re-adjustment.

And Huggins (who is now a Lord)
　　Wangler-in-Chief of Federation,
Deplores all meddlers from abroad
　　Lest Blacks should lose their Proper Station.
The Whites are (in their own opinion)
Ripe for another White Dominion,

In which Eternal Verities,
　　As Godfrey Huggins now discloses,
Will not – as in democracies –
　　Be voted on by counting noses:
Well . . . not exactly . . . just the *right* ones –
Sir Roy and Co will count the *white* ones.

(from *New Statesman*)

197

# CHAPTER XIII

# Those Darling Americans

ETHEL HAD WRITTEN A CAT STORY, *So Tiberius*, addressed not to those who sentimentalised the animal but to those who could appreciate its subtleties. In January 1954, she went to Burma which provided her with material for two books, aroused her interest in Theravada Buddhism and turned her against meat-eating, though she continued to eat fish and chicken on the principle that she would consume anything she was prepared to kill herself.

Both she and Reg debunked a then much-publicised figure, Dr Albert Schweitzer, 'the old humbug', as Reg called him, with his high-flown, pseudo-philosophising about Reverence for Life.

Schweitzer supported vivisection and wasn't a vegetarian [wrote Ethel to the present writer]. Also, at Lambarane, he practiced apartheid – the white and black staffs didn't eat together, and he never raised up a single black man or woman to be so much as a nurse, let alone a doctor. His attitude to the natives was precisely that – 'the natives', tempered by the disguised imperialism of paternalism.

Bertrand Russell, Augustus John, Ethel and Reg were among the signatories of a letter sent to Michael Blundell, Minister without Portfolio in the Kenya Government, expressing concern at the number of Africans who were being executed. The letter recalled that the Colonial Secretary had told the House of Commons that since October 1952, 756 Africans had been executed and that no fewer than 508 had been charged with offences less than murder; 290 had been condemned for 'unlawful possession of arms and ammunition'.

Reg's article in the *American Scholar* – 'Just a Few Bricks in the English Glasshouse' – caused a literary controversy. His bricks were hurled mainly at English critics of contemporary American literature of which he thought highly. To his astonishment, the *Times Literary Supplement* (26th November

1954) devoted a critical but courteous leader to the article. Then it was attacked by John Lehmann in the *London Magazine* (February 1955):

Mr Lehmann was, of course, annoyed because I had taken some prize examples of fatuous criticism from a review in the *London Magazine*. Even in his rage he was just wise enough not to quote the actual passages I'd condemned; for they would have needed no comment to provoke laughter. Instead he exhausted a limited vocabulary of abuse. My article was 'scurrilous', 'ludicrously muddled', 'disgruntled, scandalous and ill-informed'. It contained a 'typically cheap innuendo' and constituted a 'virulent display of bad manners'. My 'embittered imagination' had produced a 'baseless concoction of nonsense'. The *TLS* had conceded that I'd made 'one admirable point' by contending that much English writing was deplorably limp. At all costs Mr Lehmann was determined at least not to be limp. Unfortunately his corybantic display included only two statements of fact which could be either verified or refuted. They occurred in one sentence, in which I was accused of 'attacking the English for speaking their minds on one page and deriding them for being too soft and obsequious to speak their minds in the next, mixing up P. Wyndham Lewis with D. B. Wyndham Lewis, and so on'.

What was meant by 'and so on' can best be gauged by the value of what preceded it. The contradiction existed only in Mr Lehmann's mind. My contention was – and still is – that I can always appreciate any critic who *has* a mind, knows his subject and can speak frankly, without either patronage or sham humility.

But I am really grateful to Mr Lehmann for the Wyndham Lewis jibe. I'd referred to D. B. Wyndham Lewis; and no intelligent well-informed English reader could have even suspected a misprint (let alone a 'confusion') because 'DB' was bracketed with Monsignor Ronald Knox in a context which made it clear that I had in mind a lively Catholic group, the spiritual descendants of the 'Chester-Belloc' – with which the other Wyndham Lewis never had the remotest connection. Having long admired 'DB' as one of our really brilliant satirists, but never having known him personally, I wrote to him apropos of the *brouhaha* in the *London Magazine* and received two delightful letters from him.

I'd been inclined to indignation by Lehmann's implied conclusion that anyone describing D. B. Wyndham Lewis as a social satirist must be 'mixing' him with the other fellow. 'DB' said it was kind of me 'to engage these types on my behalf. I never see their funny little magazines and things nowadays'. I'd suggested that my meaning might have been clearer had I added Johnny Morton's name when speaking of Knox and D. B. Wyndham Lewis, but that (on an after-thought) it had occurred to me that an hysterical editor might easily think I was confusing Johnny Morton with H. V. (*In the Steps of the Master*) Morton, or even with that old Tudor rascal who invented Morton's Fork. (Imbecility unlike reason knows no boundaries.) The possibilities of further confusion on these lines offered the perfect playground for 'Timothy Shy'. In dealing with Lehmann he thought I should also distinguish Johnny Morton from Orton, the Tichborne Claimant, Dr Horton, 'the late non-Conformist', Mrs Norton, the poetess and a place called Gorton. But it would be even more important to distinguish Mr Lehmann himself from his possible great-aunt Lisa, whose gifts as a composer might 'have become sublimated in exquisite advanced prose'. Incidentally, it was an English reviewer – John Davenport – who was the first to tell me of his disgust with Lehmann over the *London Magazine* attack.

For Benjamin Pollock Ltd., the toy theatre firm, Reg wrote two short plays, *The Silver Palace* and *The Flying Saucerers*. *The Silver Palace* was adapted from Green's characters and scenes in the play of the same name:

> Aha, Miss Lu-Lu, kiss your uncle –
> But not, you fool, on my carbuncle;
> The reason, girl, is very simple:
> It is a very painful pimple.

The characters in *The Flying Saucerers* were either Martians or Earthians. The curtain rose to disclose a Martian landscape with Flying Saucers flanked by Martian Wings. The voice of a Radio Announcer was heard:

> You who have read your comic strips
> Know all about the rocket ships
> In which, I'm sure, you've often seen us
> Leave for the Moon, or Mars, or Venus.
> Today our story starts on Mars,
> The happy home of chocolate bars,
> And people who, you will agree,
> Are very much like you and me,
> Except that they are hatched from eggs,
> And have six arms, or maybe legs.
> Their language, as is widely known,
> Is fortunately like our own –
> They learnt it when they first began

To read the strips on Superman
Who was, of course, American.
So now you'll see the curtain rise
On Martie, who has won a prize
(You'll soon hear what the prize is worth)
For the best essay on the Earth
By little Martians under 10;
The subject: 'Are there really Men?'

'Now look', (said a policeman to Martie on earth),
   'you've got two legs too many.
That's not illegal, bad or vicious
But what we calls acting suspicious'.

'Oh, please, release him!' (pleaded Arthur Mann,
   a boy Earthian), 'I've a thought:
Look, with six arms a person ought
To be a wizard at the wicket –
*Dad, we could teach this Martian cricket!*
He'd play for us against Australia
Where we have often met with failure'.

*Announcer:*

Soon little Martie played for Kent
Then to Australia he went
Engaged to play the English ticket
And show Australia some cricket.
There, when our Martian hero landed,
*He beat them* – though not single handed,
Because, of course, he played with six,
Which put the Aussies in a fix.
To England when he then returned
He said that Arthur Mann had earned
A trip to Mars – and so he did,
That plucky little English kid.
A grateful country gave a party
For Arthur and the clever Martie
Supplying space-suits for the trip
And other things, which we can skip.
But Mrs Mann said it was wrong
(Because the journey was so long)
To pass the hours just idly sitting,
She gave them balls of wool for knitting

201

And placed on board the Flying Saucer
The works of Milton, Donne and Chaucer.
Now we shall see his parents learn
Of Martie's fortunate return.

☆    ☆    ☆

In July 1955, Ruth Ellis, the mother of two children, was hanged for the shooting of her lover. Ethel and Reg had been shocked and distressed by the refusal of the Home Secretary to grant a reprieve.

> I believe that capital punishment is indefensible in any circumstance whatsoever [said Ethel], that judicial murder is a barbarism out of which civilised people should have grown long ago – and in some 30 countries civilised people have, without any increase in the murder rate – not only because it precludes all possibility of righting a judicial error, but because it is degrading to those who carry out the sentence and who are required by law to witness the execution, and because of the inexpressible suffering caused to those close to the executed person – parents, husband or wife, brothers and sisters, children.

As her contribution to the campaign for the abolition of capital punishment, she wrote the novel *Pity the Innocent*, the story of a boy whose mother was hanged in circumstances similar to those of Ruth Ellis.

Ethel's first husband, Jean's father, died and she sped to Devon to the house where, in recent years, she had been a warmly received guest. She and John Porteous had become friends, and it was

> absolution for me for the wrong I had done him in my youth. Certainly we sat many a time in a pub in those Devon years – since 1945 – reminiscing about 'the old days', all bitterness between us long since spent. I was deeply grateful to him that he could put aside bitterness – but why oh why, I asked myself that Sunday rushing down to Devon to be with my daughter in her bereavement, did I not tell him so whilst he was there to be told? Why was I not more open with him, more truly a friend to him, instead of preserving as I did that nervous reserve? There was a certain psychological trickiness in the situation, to be sure, but I could have had more trust, more courage, made more effort. I had always been so grateful that we could talk over 'the old days' in that impersonal way, but we should not have been impersonal; we should have brought everything out into the open; it was for me to do it and I lacked the moral courage, and now that I faced the realisation it was too late. Others may absolve us for the wrong we do them; our problem is

to absolve ourselves. Life gives us the chance and we fail to take it and finally death sweeps it out of our reach, finally and forever. Once again the old searing infinite regret . . .

Reg gave six short talks for the BBC Home Service on John Woolman, and wrote the introduction to Christopher Lake's Peace News Pamphlet, *Freedom for Cyprus*. In a filing cabinet destroyed in the Blitz, he remembered saving articles which appeared in *The Times* in the mid 1930s, speaking of Cyprus as the 'Cinderella Colony', stating facts about poverty and administrative neglect, and warning of the opposition to British rule among Cypriots.

But it seems that, in colonial affairs, even the most respectable Jeremiah can make no headway until Colonial revolt forces governmental attention and that of the popular press. It is a fact curiously ignored by the enemies of democracy that people denied constitutional freedom and what we regard as its normal expressions will sooner or later find an alternative of their own.

[The British occupation of Cyprus began] with quite the most sordid piece of dark-stain bargaining in the history of Europe. When, in 1878, the Powers met at the Congress of Berlin, each national representative gave a solemn undertaking that his government was not bound by any secret agreement affecting the discussions. Every one of them was lying. The secret agreement made included many deals which were undoubtedly contributory causes of the first world war, and a plain betrayal of the persecuted minorities under Turkish rule. The diplomacy of Disraeli was a defeat for Russian liberalism from which it never recovered. France's share of the loot was to be confirmed in the occupation of Tunis, which is only today winning back its independence; and Britain was 'leased' Cyprus and its entire population, like so many chattel slaves, in return for her support of Turkey. That is what Disraeli called 'Peace with Honour'.

[He well remembered that in 1930, not long after his return from India], where the Labour Government of that time made a record in brutal repression unequalled even by the 'National' Government, two years later, I could still be shocked at the cynical way in which Labour's Colonial Secretary defended the banning of Socialist literature in Cyprus and repressive acts against the Cypriot Trade Unions. That Colonial Secretary was Lord Passfield (Sidney Webb), whose Fabian conscience evidently found nothing revolting in the procedure. Even the ILP, avowedly anti-imperialist, was never able to take such matters seriously enough to give them precedence over domestic issues. In a by-election they were forgotten altogether, as I was more than once reminded when I tried to voice colonial questions at what was considered an inopportune moment.

[Ignorance was no excuse]: Until our last colony is free, the people of this country have no right to indulge in ignorance. We are self-appointed trustees. Nobody forced upon us the responsibilities of empire: we grabbed them, and remain collectively responsible for all that is done in our name until decency and necessity induces us to quit. [What was rapidly becoming a necessity could be speeded] and even given a modicum of grace, if at the last moment the public conscience began to function in Britain. In that case we could still pull out without leaving the long legacy of bitterness which will otherwise be our parting gift to Cyprus.

*From a Scroll Found by Lake Windermere*

Jeffreys, thou shouldst be judging at this time:
   England hath need of thee – with whip and gun
   The Cypriot-hunting Season should be fun!
Thou hast not wallowed in so foul a slime,
For Britain's honour is not worth a dime:
   A Greek can hang for sheltering his son
   While thugs go free, whatever they have done,
If it should suit us to condone the crime.
Thy talents are in need – but not unique:
   In open market who would have employed
   Thy meagre gifts, if offered Lennox-Boyd
   Or any of his peers? For, in their eyes,
Freedom is but a menace to their Clique.
   Justice is felony at their Assize.

Great knaves have been among us; Titus Oates,
   Bottomley, Cecil Rhodes and many more –
   Gamblers in lies, gold, diamonds and gore,
But reckless racketeers, who burned their boats.
   Today's Synthetic Villains, changing coats,
   Play saint or martyr, blackguard, pimp or whore,
   Prating of Peace when whipped for making War
And buoyed for either course by slavish votes.
Courageously, with Olive Branch in hand,
   They clout their weaker neighbours on the head;
   But, when they meet a stronger one, instead,

Like curs they growl, but come (like curs) to heel.
Can such lick-spittle grovellers understand
How Cypriots and honest patriots feel?

(from *New Statesman*)

☆      ☆      ☆

He completed his autobiography, *My Life and Crimes*, and sailed for
New York on a four-months' lecture tour of the United States at the
invitation of the American Friends Service Committee. In his absence,
Ethel and Gilbert Turner, a librarian friend, proof-read the book, made an
index and coped with the complications of the publisher's libel queries.

In the summer of 1956, on a train from Chicago to Boston, he was
jubilant:

> Here I am, charging crazily about this vast country from East to West
> and North to South. This is a 21-hour journey, and when I get to
> Boston it's by no means over. But I'm having a great time. Have just
> finished an article (my second on this trip) for *Peace News*. First one
> described my arrival in New York and how I met Eleanor Roosevelt
> and other notables the first evening, also TROD ON TALLULAH
> BANKHEAD'S TOE. This constitutes a record for English Friends
> visiting America. I am having a *tremendous time*, and have very little left
> for writing letters, let alone articles. I've even had to *refuse* to write
> verse for the *New Yorker* – my greatest literary ambition for years past,
> suddenly made realisable by a direct request; and (of course) I can't do
> anything for the *Statesman* from here. What do I care? This is worth 10
> deaths, and they would all be happy ones. I go from camp to camp –
> mostly students and teenagers. They are darlings. I love them all and
> they love me. I have adopted so many sons and daughters I have lost
> count. All I mind is the heartbreak of saying goodbye to each crowd in
> turn.
>
> I grow younger every week and have not been so fit for years. I swim
> a lot, talk a lot, sing a lot and lap up affection like a cat with a saucer of
> cream. I have also discovered that I am INDESTRUCTIBLE. I
> should be worn out, but I thrive on exhaustion, for I've never known
> such sleep as I have these days. I want to see the DEEP SOUTH and
> the struggle for Negro rights. I have met a lot of Coloured people –
> some at every camp or conference I've been to, so far. They are very
> high among my new friends. I think I may even die of *happiness*; but I
> will try not to do that, as there is still so much to do; also I want to

embrace the whole world and share this thing which is too much for me. Do I sound crazier than usual? I certainly *feel* it! Life is GOOD and there are so many WONDERFUL PEOPLE (especially my sons and daughters) that everything must come right in the end. I feel more like a young man in love than a staid old geyser of 50.

At a talk given to a Quaker gathering in Mount Holly, New Jersey, he showed how the wisdom of John Woolman was relevant to the problems of the 20th century. A recent incident had been on his mind:

> It concerns a happy afternoon at one of the many institutes I have been attending – a family institute in New England. I went down to a lake with a number of children, with the intention of swimming, and then suddenly thought it would be nice to take a boat out into a lake. I did not discover until I got down to the quay where the boats were moored that I was allowed to take only five including one adult. I had with me six children, and I knew that two of the children would have to be disappointed. I looked at them and wondered – and my eyes fell upon a brother and sister. The girl's age was 11 and the boy was only nine. I knew that I loved them more than the others. I deliberately said to them, 'I'm sorry, I won't be able to take you'. And I said that to them because I had confidence that the mutual affection that existed between me and those children was such that they, if any among those children, would be able to understand why I told them they were not coming. They made no complaint.
>
> Afterwards, when I told their mother, I think she was the proudest mother in that camp. I said to her: 'I treated them as though they were my own children. Had they been my own children I would have expected them to hold back and let the others go. I gave them the privilege of not going'. She said: 'You don't know what a privilege it was. You can only measure the privilege by the great desire that they had to go'. Those children had learned or were learning that the reward of goodness is not a material reward. The reward of being good is that you are set harder tasks and that people impose upon you and upon your goodness. The reward of goodness is that you are trusted to be even better than you are.

This experience illuminated one aspect of a parable that had often bothered him, the story of the Prodigal Son.

> I think I am not the first person who ever worried about that elder brother – the brother for whom nothing was done because he had remained at home and had been a good boy. And it suddenly occurred

to me, after that little incident, that it was the elder brother who really let the father down, very badly. The father had trusted that the elder brother would understand his attitude to the younger son. Instead of understanding he was only jealous. He didn't realise that his reward was to be unrewarded. That was the greatest trust and confidence that the father could show him.

Shortly before he had arrived at a workcamp in Ohio, the campers had gone on an expedition into the Kentucky mountains.

Before they made that expedition they had, so I heard, a discussion about whether they could use segregated facilities. They were an all-white group, so there was no difficulty about their using them; but it was pointed out by one of them – and, significantly, that one was a girl from North Carolina – it was pointed out by her that they were not an all-white group by choice, but by chance. Had there been one single Negro among them, they would not have been able to use segregated facilities. She felt that they should act as though there were coloured people with them, even though in fact and by chance there were not. Due to her insistence that group put up with considerable discomfort for the three or four day trip, refusing to use any segregated facilities.

On a later occasion I met a member of that camp who came to one of our teenage institutes, where, in one of the discussions, the word 'practical' kept turning up. People are always looking away from what is right to what they call 'practical'. That girl recalled the story of how, thanks to the firmness of another girl, a North Carolina lass, they had refused to use segregated facilities in Kentucky, and the comment that she made on what they had done showed to my mind amazing depth. The words that she used were something like this: 'We had to decide which was the practical thing, to spend four days in comfort or to live at peace with ourselves afterwards'. She had seen that it is not 'practical' to do a thing if, in fact, it leaves you with an uneasy conscience. Her words were similar to Woolman's when he objected to violating *his* conscience – 'I cannot write thy will without breaking my own peace'.

In our day, as in Woolman's day, there was always this problem of what is 'practical'.

If we look deeply into it, if we look at it (as Woolman would say) 'in the light of pure wisdom', it will resolve itself into a question of what can you do and still be at peace with yourself? [What also came back to his mind whenever he thought of the problem of segregation was the story told by a woman missionary.]

She had served for many years in South Africa and said that when she first went out, at the end of the very first day, she was overwhelmed by the atmosphere of racial intolerance and the horrible attitude of the white people towards the various non-European groups (not only Africans, but what they called 'coloured', or mixed blood, and the Indians as well). It was so horrible, with so much humiliation, so much degradation. . . . At the end of that first day she said to an old missionary who had lived out there for years: 'I can't bear it here. I can't stay. It hurts so'. And the old missionary said to her: 'You needn't worry while it hurts, my dear. *It is when it STOPS hurting that you can begin to worry'*.

That was a saying that he would never forget,

for it sums up what I know about the growth of insensitivity, where people live in evil conditions from which they can't escape. In a mere six months in Africa I noticed to my horror that things which had shocked me profoundly when I first saw them were ceasing to shock me as much. And I said to myself: 'What on earth would happen if I stayed here longer – would I become completely insensitive?' I don't believe I would. But I know that I would only retain my sensitivity if I continued to exercise my imagination and to put my soul in their soul's stead, regularly every day and many times each day. Woolman's formula is the only one whereby we can really have a live sense of any problem involving personal and human relationships. Intelligence and knowledge are desirable things, but for this purpose inadequate. In human relationships sensitivity is God's essential gift.

Perhaps one had most to learn from Woolman in the business of trying to feel with and for people who held repulsive ideas:

I was once in a tough spot during my travels here, at a seminar in the south. It was a desegregated, inter-racial group. People living around didn't like us. Among a number of ugly incidents was the burning of fiery crosses outside the place where we were meeting. I had to leave before that thing was over. It was a month's seminar and I had other appointments. So with great reluctance I had to go at the end of a difficult, tense week. Naturally I was very much concerned about that group and begged the director to write and tell me how things developed after I left. One of his letters to me, I think, got to the heart of it. He said something like this: 'These fiery crosses are a soul searing experience. How does one get at the mind which makes this appalling distortion of the symbol of the cross?' In our own way, we had followed the Woolman example, once the young people realised what they were really facing. We made no publicity about the thing. Even now you will notice that I haven't named the place. But what we could do to improve relations was limited to the people we knew about. We invited the students who were still in the college where we were holding our seminar. We knew that many of these students were hostile, so we invited the hostile, segregationalist students to come and meet us, to speak to us, to put the case for segregation and to discuss it – which I am sure was in the best Woolman tradition and certainly worked very well. But the question of the director still rings in my mind. How do we get at the mind that distorts the symbol of the cross? That was the problem that Woolman set out to answer, and I feel that only by seeking the same sources that Woolman sought can we hope to find the answer to it. [And that brought him to the source of Woolman's inspiration.]

Some time ago, again in one of our teenage institutes, where I had been talking, we began discussing a familiar subject, the need of a child for security, for *emotional* security – the fact that every child needs love. (And are we not all children in this respect?) But it occurred to me during that discussion that although this is true there comes a point in the lives of some men and women when they seem to be able to go on without that emotional security so far as their fellow human beings are concerned. But when I put it to that group of youngsters that there were people who were able to get beyond the need of human love, in the sense that, though completely alone, they could still go on loving others, the only reply I could get from one of them (the others had none) was that such people relied upon their own spiritual reserves. At that point I said – and it was the only reply possible – 'In that case I should be lost'.

But I think that every one of us knows what is the real answer. It is the answer that was given by James Nayler, lying at death's door, robbed, beaten, a lonely man, a failure in all that he had done – at least, an *apparent* failure. He says of the spirit that had sustained him, 'I found it alone, being forsaken. I had fellowship therein with them who dwelt in dens and desolate places of the earth, who through death attained this resurrection and eternal holy life'. And we find the same answer when we return to John Woolman and his well known words: 'And then I said, "I am crucified with Christ, nevertheless I live; yet not I, but Christ that liveth in me. And the life I now live in the flesh is by the faith in the Son of God, who loved me and gave himself for me"'.

☆     ☆     ☆

Ethel had pinned the Scrooge label on herself by issuing postcards to her friends asking them not to send her Christmas cards. 'Beautiful as many of them are', she wrote, 'I don't really like them, regarding them as a sad waste of money and a serious cluttering of the mails. I hope you will have whatever kind of Christmas you like best and will respect my Scrooge-like – if you like – desire to have it obtrude as little as possible on my consciousness.' Her wishes were mainly respected but a few of her friends were unable to resist posting to her the jolliest of robins-and-snow cards. She also received some anonymous insults when the matter got into the press.

Fresh from his American tour, Reg poured out articles on the Suez invasion, and Britain's 'Satanic Government': 'never have our rulers so deliberately violated their own consciences'; 'because we ever allowed such men to exercise authority, we have need of repentance'.

*Letter to Nasser*
'Visit the hospitable, historic UNITED ARAB REPUBLIC.'
(UAR Tourist Office advertisement in the *New Yorker*)

> Historic Sir,
>   Most hospitable Colonel
> I see you're advertising in a jolonel,
> Your pyramids and your engaging Sphinx.
> Is Dulles going? How is trade in Brinx?
>
> I always liked your pin-up, Cleopatra,
> With Roman lovers in a queue to flatra –
> Including *veni-vidi-vici* Caesar,
> That perfect military-pickled gaesar:
> I'll bet, in bed, he bored her with *De Bello*
> And said that Pompey was a pompous fello;
> However. . . . Like yourself, sir, and Montgomery
> He fancied methods short and sharp and somery.
>
> *My* trouble is, I do not like your Junta.
> Some Brass-hats might; why not invite a punta
> For stakes political? Perhaps de Gaulle
> Or little Franco (who is in a haulle)
> Or your new colleagues, like the blokes in Burma
> And Pakistan, whose seats are rather furma.
>
> But these have jobs; and – at your shop in Cairo –
> Ne Win would be a novice and a tairo.
> Leave Win to win and Pak to Ayub Khan –
> Monty's your man: just watch him storm the bhan!

When had the Turks a bashier bazouk?
His Gospel's not in Matthew, Mark or Louk
Or John – but in those portions of the Bible
Where the Divinity was strictly trible . . .
Colonel, there's just one snag: like Lou Quartorze
L'état, c'est lui.
    I am, sir, truly yorze,
      Reginald Reynolds.

(from New Statesman)

*My Life and Crimes*, dedicated to Ethel, was published by Jarrolds in 1956 to critical acclaim. Gratitude was expressed

> for the courage and uninhibited gaiety with which a life roughly covering the first half of this century has been recorded. [Reg displayed] a catholicity of understanding and a relentless power of seeing himself without illusion. [He pleaded guilty] to the biggest crime any man ever committed – that of thinking for himself and acting independently of Party, faction, group or organisation. Wherever men hoped and worked for peace and for the progress of the colonial peoples, there was Reginald Reynolds in the thick of it, sometimes getting into the hair of his friends as much as that of his opponents. But this book is more than a do-gooder's narrative. It ought to delight everyone with its uninhibited gusto, wit and humanity.

CHAPTER XIV

# Japan and Australia

*Good News*

'Premier's Words of Comfort. H-Bomb Patrols over Britain.'

*(Manchester Guardian* headline and sub-head)

God rest you merry, gentlemen,
　When you are all abed;
The friendly little 'Hydrogen'
　Is cruising overhead.
It's there to kill the Russians when
　The rest of us are dead –
　O, tidings of comfort and joy!

The wise men of the Occident,
　With Sputniks for a star,
Their Precious Gifts in panic spent –
　They have not travelled far;
And in this strange predicament
　They don't know where they are –
　O, tidings of comfort and joy!

The sight of their incompetence
　King Herod much enjoyed;
He said, when told that for Defence
　These antics were employed:
'They talk of babes and Innocence,
　But what of Selwyn Lloyd?
　O, tidings of comfort and joy!'

The story of the new Noel
　Is in a secret file:
No shepherds ever watched so well

Their large Atomic Pile
And Magi show the way to Hell
By way of Christmas Isle –
O, tidings of comfort and joy!

The shadow of the pendulum
Moves at an even pace
For them as sells the Vacu-um
And them that's selling Space –
We'll all be blown to Kingdom Come
To save Macmillan's face –
O, tidings of comfort and joy!

(from *New Statesman*)

*Hiroshima*

'The schoolmen teach that all this globe of
earth shall be consumed to ashes in a minute . . .
There might be hell or heaven.' Now hell has birth, with
all creation in it.

God-like – invincible death beneath his hand –
A child surveys a city. His the power
When executioner and prisoner stand
Waiting the dreaded hour.

Yet this is Ninevah, spared for love of men,
Spared for their foolishness. When they are dead
God wept in me for the gourd again; and then:
*They did not know*, he said.

(But man knew mercy once, in one who prayed
Ten worthy of salvation should suffice
To save doomed Sodom from the fire that made
Its final sacrifice.)

On all humanity the weapon fell,
On Pity the intolerable pain;
Man saw himself at last – the face of hell,
Seared with the brand of Cain.

(from a Japanese pacifist paper)

Reg showered affectionate letters on his friends in the United States
and, in Britain, he sang the praises of the American Friends Service
Committee's educational programmes. He felt that their use of non-Quaker

213

and even non-pacifist lecturers was a source of great strength. Every effort was made by the AFSC to produce real discussion in which different points of view could be aired. The organisers were willing to experiment with new methods and were

> aware of the danger attendant on a superficial and emotional 'conversion' to pacifism, which may lead to disillusionment and a rejection of what is true with what is false. It was to me a fascinating experience to watch the development of young minds through a process which often included the necessity of defending a newly discovered idea against heavy intellectual fire. [What the AFSC seemed to have re-discovered was that] the chief function of education is to liberate the mind and give the Holy Spirit a chance to take over.

He began writing *The Loadstone*, his long poem and the summing up of his Christian faith, at the end of the war and he worked at it on and off for years, regarding it as his *magnum opus*. Sadly, it failed to interest the publishers. He was sure that, in a world which acclaimed the work of T. S. Eliot as poetry, he, whose work was rooted in an older tradition, had no chance of recognition. He published a few extracts from it in obscure magazines but the poem was a complete entity and its fragmentation was merely a gesture of despair on its creator's part. As his *New Statesman* satirical verses brought him more and more popularity, his impatience increased, for it was as a serious poet that he wished to be remembered.

> From time to time [said Ethel], I would try to take up the matter of *The Loadstone* with him, urging that he renew his attempts to get it published, but he always brushed all such attempts to discuss the matter aside. He declared that the so-called poetry which got published nowadays was prose-chopped-up, and unintelligible prose at that. Nobody wanted anything that rhymed and was intelligible, certainly not if into the bargain it was 'religious'. More than once he concluded such re-openings of the subject with the remark, 'Perhaps when I'm dead you'll be able to do something with it'. The last time he said it was two months before he died. I told him that I hoped to have done something with it long before then. I had a publisher in mind for it, one who was adding poetry to his list. I am glad, now, that I did not get round to showing the work to this publisher before Reg's death, because when I did so, afterwards, he turned it down with the very words Reg had himself used when declaring that he could not hope to get it published – it belonged, the publisher said, to an older tradition.

> *The Loadstone* is not for me [wrote Ethel to the present writer]. I feel disloyal saying it, but Reg knew, I think. What he *didn't* know,

214

though, and which I could never have told him, is that though he was desperately anxious to be accepted as a 'serious' poet, and not just as a satirist – he called himself bitterly 'the *New Statesman's* funny man' – he was, in fact, as a serious poet, terribly *derivative*. He greatly admired Chesterton and Yeats – I think above all others, and above all Chesterton, and if you know your Chesterton you'll agree, I think, how derivative is much – *most* – of *The Loadstone*. Almost to the point of parody! He was a brilliant parodist. But it should all have begun and ended there, with parody and satire. When he was dead I tried to get it published by Jarrolds, who did *My Life and Crimes*, and was very upset when they told me frankly that it was all very old-fashioned. I in fact scrapped two of the later pieces before asking the Society of Friends if they would do it. There's that romantic Christianity in *The Loadstone* which also is sheer Chesterton, romantic-dramatic (and Francis Thompson's Hound of Heaven, and echoes of Gordon Bottomley and Elroy Flecker) – and not for me. In his heart and mind Reg was a poet – but not on paper.

[He had taken his title from William Law]: When, therefore, the first spark of a desire after God arises in thy soul, cherish it with all thy care, give all thy heart into it. It is nothing less than a touch of the divine Loadstone, that is to draw thee out of the vanity of Time into the riches of Eternity. [He added, to one copy of the poem, a quotation from the Quaker scientist Sir Arthur Eddington, which epitomised his attitude to the search for truth]: Reasoning is our great ally in the search for truth. But reasoning can only start from premises; and at the beginning of the argument we must always come back to innate convictions. There are such convictions at the base even of physical science. We are helpless unless we admit also (as perhaps the strongest conviction of all) that we have within us some power of self criticism to test the validity of our own convictions. The power is not infallible, that is to say it is not infallible when associated with human frailty; but neither is reasoning infallible when practised by our blundering intelligence. I think that this power can be nothing less than a ray proceeding from the absolute Mind. With this guidance we may embark on the adventure of spiritual life uncharted though it be. It is sufficient that we carry a compass.

*The Loadstone* was eventually published by Friends Home Service Committee in 1960 and, as Reg would have expected, sold very poorly. Still, in the words of Mabel King-Beer, 'he has left us with a precious legacy, the record of a personal and deeply experienced spiritual pilgrimage'.

Hell is their natural home whose fences stand
To guard a private claim on common land;
Hell is a speculative builder's plot –
Where heaven was, he builds: and heaven is not;
Hell is exclusive righteousness, that cods
With pampered piety its pocket gods;
Hell is the penal law that shuts us in
And fetters charity to punish sin;
Hell is the thirst whereby our souls confess
Their arid tyranny a wilderness.
Threatened by mercy, menaced by the light,
This is the fatherland for which we fight.

Myth is the core of Truth. Though youth take wings
And seek the sun beyond the upper air,
He but embodies in his time the prayer
Eternal in mankind's imaginings.
Pinioned on dreams we rise; ambition brings
The molten wax, the fall. For those who dare
Death waits in vain – their golden memories share
The truth of tales and insubstantial things.

I know not whence the race of man descends,
For what dim Eden of forbidden bliss
Our hearts still yearn, or where the pathway ends;
But there's an axis to our lives, and this
The soul's magnetic compass comprehends;
The rest is ancient night and the abyss.

(Extracts from *The Loadstone*)

The life of Gilles de Rais had been long in his thoughts as an allegory for our own time, a Pilgrim's Progress out of the Middle Ages.

He made notes for an historical novel with Gilles as its central character, and struggled with it intermittently for years without completing it. He visualised the subject as a film as well – should he contact Orson Welles, John Boulting? It was important to emphasize that Gilles was an actor and showman (Cecil B. de Rais). He intended to compare medieval black magic with modern finance, to demonstrate the universal duality of man, 'e.g., we have wars – we are selfish and narrow-minded and yet cannot conduct them without heroism, sacrifice, community sense'.

Gilles de Rais, who appeared like an embodiment of the legendary Knight Bluebeard, was one of the most remarkable and sinister figures in history. Born in 1404 of a famous family of Bretagne, he was a confidential friend of Jeanne d'Arc and at her side he so distinguished himself as an army leader that he was appointed Marshal of France at the age of 25. Later, he withdrew to his castles where he held court in great splendour. Financial difficulties drove him into the arms of alchemy, and this was accompanied by a darkening of his moral sense, so that the noble companion of Saint Joan degenerated into a sadistic libertine. His first victim – one of many – was a small boy whom he strangled. He then cut off the boy's hands, gouged out his eyes and offered them to the devil.

His hideous crimes exposed, he begged to be received into the Church from which he had been excommunicated. In impassioned words he declared that even *he* was redeemable. His feigned remorse moved many to tears. Peasants gathered on the road that led to the place of execution. Gilles asked them to pray for him. Some were determined on a three days' fast for his sake. Between the rows of peasants, weeping and praying, he went to his death. He was no longer proud even of his final success as an actor. Touched by the compassion of the ordinary folk, he walked like a man in a trance.

According to Reg's treatment, a strange vision came to him. He had commended his soul to St Michael and St James, and it was the voice of St Michael which he first heard, asking on what grounds he held himself to be redeemable. Gilles gave a faltering and conventional answer. The vision grew clearer and the weeping onlookers were almost forgotten. St James demanded to know what excuse he had for a great fraud perpetrated upon the simple faith of the people. Gilles said that the heart of man was good though his understanding was weak. He himself had been condemned more by human folly and credulity than by the malice of his enemies, but the heart could make amends for the head, and hadn't he helped the people to do this?

St Michael asked him what good could come of a false repentance. Gilles felt that he was well and truly condemned. Then he was once more aware of the people and whispered that he had sinned. For himself he had no hope. His prayer was now for those who had shown compassion. The prayers of the peasants could not alter the justice of Heaven, but prayers were the measure of man's own state of grace. These people were surely, he said, better men and women for having forgiven Gilles de Rais. He reached the place of execution. There was a hush and everybody fell to their knees. To Gilles, through his own compassion for the people, understanding had come at last. He knew now that hard hearts were worse than 'sin' and that redemption came, not through innocence, but through love. Even through 'sin' a man might be saved from lack of charity, and so death embraced a man redeemed indeed.

☆    ☆    ☆

Ethel was not in tune with the theatrical revival of the mid to late 1950s. She thought Samuel Beckett's *Waiting for Godot* pretentious nonsense and left at the end of the first act. She did likewise at a performance of John Osborne's *Look Back in Anger*, seeing no reason why she should sit through three acts of a play depicting an excessively rude young man ranting on, in a half-baked way, about Life, Society and Sex. It was all such old-hat, such a labouring of the obvious; she was amazed that the Beat Generation were no further on than that.

She sold the film rights of her Indian novel, *At Sundown The Tiger* (the film was never made), wrote *The Country of the Sea* about her travels through Brittany and, in 1957, sailed twice to Sweden, the result of a conversation with Reg on the subject of what she should write next. Reg's descriptions of lecturing at summer schools and work camps in America had stirred her imagination but why not, he suggested, set a novel in the Folk High Schools of Sweden? Her hero could go as a visiting lecturer to the Folkhögskolan and, in the satirical vein of *Comrade, O Comrade*, she could tilt at all the initials, beloved of cultural organisations, that infested the modern world. Christina Foyle reminded her of the Swedes' addiction to throwing themselves out of high windows to the danger of the public – 'Be sure to walk on the outside of the pavement', she cooed. Another old friend, Allen Lane of Penguin Books, warned her of their Teutonic formality and endemic unknowability, and Ethel herself had to admit that many of the Swedes she met lived up to their reputation as 'God's frozen people'.

Between the two Swedish trips, she attended Jean's wedding at a register office in Totnes, and took on responsibility for a disturbed young woman and her two small children who were living in squalid conditions. Ethel wrote numerous letters trying, and not succeeding, to get the woman fixed up with a domestic post. She also failed to find decent accommodation for the family, so had no alternative than to bring them to Oak Cottage where, during the Occupation, as her friends called it, she worked, against an unaccustomed background of noise, on the Swedish novel, *Fragrance of Hyacinths*. Reg flew to Tokyo at the invitation of Japanese pacifists. At the air terminus he had his usual attack of not wanting to go. 'I'd rather be you flying to Tokyo than me literally left with the baby!' said Ethel grimly. From her good dollar earnings the previous year, and a generous donation from Jean, she managed to buy and furnish a small house for the woman which she would inherit on Ethel's death.

During the 1950s, when Ethel was in Connemara and Reg was in Chelsea, a burglar broke into Oak Cottage, taking as his spoils Reg's winter overcoat, his one respectable suit and all his underwear. A girl from Dublin, lodging at the cottage, informed the police on her return late that night. She phoned Reg who, the next morning, was asked to identify the stolen goods found in the possession of a Mr Stanley.

Reg spoke in Mr Stanley's defence, duly reported in the press as 'Judge compliments Quaker who turned the other cheek'. At the age of 14, the court learned, Mr Stanley was banished to an Approved School for travelling in a train without a ticket, 'a thing, sir', the old reprobate told the Chairman, 'which you or anyone else might have done'. 'Yes, that's true', said the Chairman before sentencing him to seven years preventive detention. Reg was horrified, 'but', Mr Stanley reassured him, 'it would have been an even heavier sentence but for you turning up to speak for me'.

Ethel and Reg visited him in prison, Ethel telling him that Reg had been particularly fond of the handwoven Connemara tweed suit he had made off with, as it was a gift from her. Mr Stanley gave Reg the name and address of the friend he had passed the suit on to but the friend, Reg soon discovered, had disappeared. However, when Mr Stanley's mother died and he inherited a little money, he sent Ethel £10 with which to replace the suit. Ethel then wrote to Mr Stanley saying that she had faithfully carried out his commission and that Reg's new suit was a grand fit. She added that if he ever lapsed when he 'came out' – and lapse he did – Reg would be so grievously disappointed that he would no longer want to wear the suit of which he was at present so proud.

After Reg's death, Ethel kept in touch with Mr Stanley, sending him books and writing to him. On the expiration of his sentence, she helped him collect his belongings from Scotland Yard and served him tea and cakes at Oak Cottage. One of his favourite words was 'refrained'. From Brixton Prison, he had written to Reg apologising 'for all the trouble and expense I have caused you. Had I known I was encroaching on the preserves of a fellow author I would most certainly have refrained'. In 1938, Mr Stanley, a homosexual and an epileptic, had published *A Happy Fortnight*, an autobiographical book (with a preface by Sir John Squire), an account of a holiday spent with a young man.

Ethel entertained him on his release from Parkhurst Prison and, later, visited him in Wandsworth Prison and spoke for him at the Middlesex Assizes. He went to live in a hostel for discharged prisoners, worked as a road sweeper, a nightwatchman and a porter in a Fulham hospital. He moved to a one room furnished flat and invited her to tea, opening the bottom of a side-board and revealing tins upon tins of food, all stolen from the hospital. Ethel harangued him angrily and never saw him again, though he continued to write to her. In one of his last letters he wrote that he had a

*Reg and John S. Hoyland*
[COURTESY: TONY SKELTON]

*Reg in his 'burglar
Suit'*
[COURTESY: JEAN FAULKS]

*Reg – pacifist, anarchist, satirist – and historian of the water closet*
[WALDEN HAMMOND – COURTESY: JEAN FAULKS]

lump in his shoulder and please would she wish him luck. She did so but there was no reply. Mr Stanley, burglar and author, had died.

☆　　☆　　☆

In Connemara, Ethel drafted a novel about a young working-class rock'n roller, *The Blue-Eyed Boy*, then returned to Oak Cottage, nursing her sick mother night and day, and resumed work on the book, her study connected to the sickroom with a battery bell on a long flex.

Reg's Japanese experience included lecturing at the Third World Conference Against Atomic and Hydrogen Bombs and For Disarmament in Tokyo. The passionate voice of Japan, and the song of the children, was

> Gentle rain gathers poison from the sky
> And the fish carry death in the depths of the sea;
> Fishing boats are idle, their owners are blind –
> Deadly harvest of two atom bombs:
> Then landsmen and seamen, you must watch and take care
> That the third atom bomb never comes.

He received a long letter from two Japanese schoolgirls, one of many spontaneous efforts made by youngsters in Japan to speak, through him, to people in Britain. Again he found the theme of rain:

> Whenever it rains, we can no longer be merry, as we used to be. . . . Something dreadful, I cannot tell what, comes to one's mind when it rains; and a younger sister innocently says: 'dreadful rain, isn't it?'. . . . We speak of Harusame (spring rain), Shigure (late autumn rain), and so forth as poetic features of the respective seasons. Little children – nay, all the people of Japan – are they robbed of the pleasure they have sought in the rain?

With Japanese friends, he went on a camping expedition to Hikawa in the beautiful valley of Okutama. A girl of 15 presented him with 500 coloured paper cranes, fashioned from toffee wrappers, to distribute to children in England. The same year, two American teenagers had sent him an illustrated book for children, *The Little Prince*, with an inscription that warmed his heart: 'To Reg, because he loves children, because he loves beautiful books and because *we* love *him*.' There was great wisdom in *The Little Prince*: 'It is the time you wasted for your rose', said the fox to the Little Prince, 'that makes your rose so important'. 'Of course', wrote Reg in *The Friend*, 'that is the secret of so much. The time one "wastes" on children can make them more precious, and the value of the 500 cranes lies partly in the thought of all the time "wasted" in making them'.

222

What did we mean by the word 'wasted'?

The outpouring of a box of precious ointment? Nobody can say what is wasteful until he has a clear idea of the values involved. Time spent in the creation of something beautiful, without *commercial* 'value', is economic waste but spiritual investment. The Little Prince has helped me to see that my 500 cranes combine the gesture of the widow's mite with the extravagance of frankincense and myrrh: they are the present of the poor, but rich in a prodigal expenditure of time and skill. Antoine de Saint-Exupéry, the author of *The Little Prince*, speaks of 'the lights of the Christmas tree, the music of the Midnight Mass, the tenderness of smiling faces', as the ingredients of 'radiance' in his recollection of Christmas gifts in childhood. They were not merely *things*, any more than my birds are merely things. 'Good for the heart, like a present,' says my illuminating author. Good for the heart, like 500 paper cranes.

The best thing about the cranes was that they were not his at all; they were only resting in his box before a long flight into many homes.

The 'wingèd life' is, therefore, in no danger of destruction by me, and I dwell confidently in 'eternity's sun rise'. For the time I am wasting on my paper cranes is adding to their value in a very curious way; and when the last one has flown away I shall write to little Miss Miharu Kobu, who made them, to tell her that her wish has been carried out. I don't really know her but I am sure she will be very happy, so the thought of it provides the 'radiance' of which I read in *The Little Prince*. And into hundreds of homes a little of that radiance will fall, although you might think it was just a paper bird in the bright colours of a toffee-wrapper.

In Tokyo, he met Miss Nagata, a teenage victim of the Nagasaki atom bomb. She had a hole in her windpipe and was unable to speak unless she closed it with her hand. She had turned down a trip to Moscow, not wishing to be used again for propaganda purposes, even though Russian surgery offered her the prospect of being healed. He admired the fact that the fiercely independent young woman refused to be a pawn, refused to accept the symbolic role of Victim Nagata. She wanted just to be a person. He was disconcerted by the unconscious exploitation of human tragedy in the attitude to Hiroshima and Nagasaki, encouraged by sight-seeing visitors from abroad. He decided not to visit either city.

*Little Bomb*

> Little Bomb, who made thee?
> Dost thou know who made thee,

223

Not so DIRTY as the last,
With a CLEAN, effective blast,
Annihilating all, with just
The very minimum of dust?
Did he tell thee that he means
No mutations in the genes,
Minimising (so he hopes)
Radioactive isotopes?

Little Bomb, *I* made thee,
All of us have made thee.
When the World was old and sad
Power drove our rulers mad;
All their cruelty and fear
In thy lineaments appear.
These, with my own apathy,
Framed a fearful cemetery
Where the human form divine
Drivels to its last decline.

Little Bomb, who'll drop thee?
Lunacy will drop thee;
Lunacy, which generates
Hateful poisons, poisonous hates,
Lunacy, which offers Earth
Painful death and monstrous birth.
Thou a bomb and I a bloke,
We shall both go up in smoke;
But, if that is only bluff,
Strontium 90 is enough.

(from *New Statesman*)

☆      ☆      ☆

*Bulletin*

The population of 10,000,000 is composed of
approximately 800,000 Europeans, mainly French. The
local ones are Arabs, Berbers, Kabyles and Tuaregs.
(Account of Algeria in an information bulletin issued
to passengers on the M.V. *Fairsea*)

Ladies and gentlemen, this is Great Britain.
The population
(So far as I can remember) is, at a rough approximation,

Some 45,000,000, comprising
(Which you may find surprising)
One Eskimo, three Sea Dyaks, and a Hottentot,
Some Indians, Pakistanis, Chinese and a lot
Of chaps from Jamaica. The others are crude
and sottish
Natives – Welsh, Northern Irish, English and Scottish –
Of whom we will make some passing mention
In case they escape your attention . . .

Bits of this country are visible in favourable conditions
(Which are rare) on the starboard side. Its
exports are inhibitions,
Neuroses, social failures and members of the Upper Classes,
Refugees from the independence of the masses.
Addicted to delectable and servile islands,
They also invented, in Kenya, the White Highlands;
And – wherever cheap labour is available –
They will mine, make or grow anything saleable.

The British climate is bleak, hostile and treacherous,
The natives uncouth, acquisitive and either
puritanical or lecherous
(Or both). Their political life, under Paramount
Chief, MacFuddy-Duddy,
Is obscure, disingenuous, atavistic, primeval and
muddy,
Based on anachronistic obsession
With imperial aggression.

(from New Statesman)

Invited by Mullers the publishers to contribute to a series of children's books on foreign countries, Ethel suffered the loneliness of Sweden again to write about that land of 'God's Frozen People'. Reg had already produced for Mullers a child's life of Gandhi (*The True Book about Mahatma Gandhi*, published posthumously in 1959), and his advice to her on writing for the 12-14 age group was 'Just do it simply, that's all. It's very good for one – curbs any tendency one may have to high falute!'

Ethel took part in a television programme, *The Book Man* (May 1958), and in the summer she and Reg combined a visit to Mr Stanley in Parkhurst Prison, Isle of Wight, with a brief holiday in Brittany. Mr Stanley asked Reg to autograph a copy of *My Life and Crimes* and showed them both a photograph of its author that he had clipped from a book and put into a small frame. They could only spare a few days for Brittany as Reg needed to be back in London to study the newspapers and 'hatch' his weekly verse for the *New Statesman*; sometimes this took him a couple of days, sometimes a few hours.

> In Dinard [wrote Ethel], he became mildly neurotic over the endlessly repeated notices along the Promenade du Clair de Lune warning people that it was *interdit* to promenade there in bathing costume, riding a bicycle, or with a dog not on a leash. It had the effect of making him feel that he must at once get into bathing trunks, mount a bicycle and ride along with a dog at his heels. [When she suggested a trip to Mont St Michel, he baulked.] 'All those postcards and souvenirs? And didn't you say you can only go round the Abbey in a conducted party? I think I'd hate that.' [Reg had been twice in India , Ethel pointed out], without seeing the Taj Mahal, and all he had been able to find to say when, without in the least wanting to, he had made the trip from Cairo to the Pyramids, was that they were big.

His article for *Peace News*, 'The Map of Mrs Brown' – which brought him the biggest mail he had ever received – stimulated pacifists into reconsidering their position. He started out by saying,

> I do not remember any time in my life when I have felt so powerless or so intellectually isolated. [It was not that he was a defeatist] : The more sterile my own thinking becomes, the stronger is my conviction that the solution of our major problem – the abolition of war – is so obvious that I cannot see it.

As a Quaker, he sought peace by the ways of peace.

> But the world crisis is, for me, a personal crisis of utter frustration. One curious thing is that if the world crisis became a personal crisis for everyone it would cease to exist; for one aspect of the problem is that the state of society is critical just because most individuals are indifferent to it.

Many of his friends and colleagues had programmes, and he divided them into three groups. Group One was the Pacifist Old Guard,

> good old sloggers who cling bravely to the belief that the slogans and activities which have been proved and tested by decades of dismal failure deserve our allegiance and will at any moment lead on to victory.

Group Two were the Perfectionists who

> having proved that there can be no peace without a complete social, political, economic, psychological and spiritual revolution, they

nevertheless leave me with an awkward feeling that they are talking very good sense about town planning when the immediate and urgent necessity is a fire engine, which they reject as a palliative.

Group Three had a sense of urgency, believing that

> if people can be induced to take one step towards peace they may see the sense of taking a second and a third,

but their passion for action was not directed by any real understanding of what they were up against. That left him unhappy about all three groups but without constructive suggestions of his own. It also left 'the vast majority of mankind (quite uninterested in any of their would-be saviours) shambling like zombies to destruction'.

Gandhi had had the best qualities of Group Two and Group Three.

> He could, like an Old Testament Prophet, try to convert an individual ruler – such as Smuts or Irwin. But he also knew that Prime Ministers and Viceroys were not (like Old Testament Kings) free agents. While those whom they represented remained unconverted, rulers could be replaced as easily as the human tools they used for repression: the soldier, the policeman, the prison warder and the executioner. No campaign against capital punishment would make much progress if its main activity was to picket prisons and seek to convert the hangman. When a hanging takes place the whole of acquiescent society is the executioner; and, while society continues to approve, someone will always be found to do the work. I have seen it stated that it would be worthwhile to persuade even one single worker at Aldermaston to give up the work of death – the construction of nuclear weapons. That is true. It would be even better to persuade one single hangman to give up hanging. It would represent a very high percentage of the profession, which is very limited in numbers, and it would have a more spectacular effect – perhaps even a deeper one – on the mind of his employers: the public.

But such a success could only have, at best, a peripheral effect on the mind of Society, and Reg had a growing conviction

> that it is Society, rather than its employees in the work of death, which could – *if we knew how* – be enlightened, stirred up to emotional realism and convinced.

It was the mind of 'Mrs Brown', who voted for the MP who supported nuclear weapons in Parliament, which worried him. When she thought about war at all, she seemed to be incapable of imagining what it would mean to herself or to anybody else.

The shadow of the hangman once more provides a startling analogy. In the days when hundreds of men, women and children in Britain were still hanged every year for small thefts, under savage laws, that great penal reformer, Edward Gibbon Wakefield, asked himself how this was possible. Why did not the fear of such a frightful penalty deter people from petty theft?

[The answer Wakefield found was that] *the penalty was so great that it was beyond the average person's powers to imagine it.* Or, alternatively, that he shut his mind to it. He pointed to the fact that for hundreds of years people had believed in Hell Fire, but that this belief had made little difference to human behaviour, because an eternity of Hell Fire was impossible to imagine and easily 'shut out' from one's calculations. In exactly the same way the reality of nuclear war is too great to be imagined and easily excluded by unconscious mechanisms of the mind.

[This brought Reg to a conclusion which was unavoidable.] It is stupid to try to frighten Mrs Brown because her imagination refuses to comprehend your modern brand of Hell Fire. And it is foolish to argue with Mrs Brown because she is not really rational in her objections to your case. She is merely 'rationalising' what she wants to believe; and if you drive her out of one bogus line of defence, with tremendous effort, she will take refuge in another. [How to discover where the 'blockage' was and how to try to remove it?] If you and I were conducting a big business, producing an excellent commodity in which we had complete confidence, and if nobody would buy it, would we spend our time in forms of advertisement which had been proved to have no effect on our potential customers? [His programme for Mrs Brown – and Mr Brown and all their relatives – was to begin with a survey.] What we need is a few social psychologists, willing to give some time as instructors to a team of men and women who would set out under the instructions of the social psychologists on a fact-finding mission. The results of their field researches would then be studied by the psychologists, and out of their findings we might hope to discover the art of making Mrs Brown 'vulnerable'.

If a way could be found, it would be, most likely, through some form of emotional release enabling Mrs Brown to *feel* the truth of things which were at present only intellectual abstractions. Group Three was in a hurry and so was Reg. 'But I see no point in hurrying up another cul-de-sac. The quickest way to hurry in a country unknown to you is to consult the map first.' The map of Mrs Brown had yet to be made. There was no time to lose.

☆　　☆　　☆

228

One of his dearest friends, the Quaker and Gandhian, Jack Hoyland, had died in 1957. Jack, peace worker, lecturer and author, was a spiritual tornado with staggering energy and a gigantic laugh. Writing his biography (*John Somervell Hoyland*, Friends Home Service Committee, 1958) was a labour of love for Reg, especially as Jack and Gandhi were coupled together forever in his mind. The closest link between them was a sense of urgency,

> combined with that serenity which comes only to those whose confidence is in things eternal. Each of them grudged time wasted when so much was to be done – Gandhi contending to the last against hatred and fractricide among Hindus and Moslems, Jack pleading for the 'have-nots' and denouncing the abominations of war. [But in neither man was there any panic]: they could see beyond human wickedness and folly the power and the glory of God.

Jack and Reg shared a boundless enthusiasm for work camps which, at their best, were, they believed, pictures in miniature of what the whole world could and should be.

> Jack gave to that movement a new and more personal meaning which helped to inspire numerous off-shoots. Indeed, for my part, I do not think I shall ever again handle a saw or an axe or a pick or a shovel or drive a fork into the good earth, without remembering Jack and the sacraments he made so real to us, teaching us to find Christ in the raised stone and the cleft wood.

Ethel worked on her third volume of autobiography, *Brief Voices, A Writer's Story*, in Connemara and London and Reg sailed for Australia to lecture on war, peace and race relations under the auspices of Australian Quakers. She saw him off at Southampton on an emigrant, one-class Italian ship with almost 1,500 passengers aboard (see appendix). Children played hopscotch on the top deck, women were tearful and men drank from enamel mugs, one of them pouring tea from an old biscuit tin. Ethel and Reg stood together in the cold and darkening day with that dreaded feeling of desolation that invariably accompanied long goodbyes.

She walked back from the quayside to the town. She had never wanted him to undertake the Australian tour. He was in poor shape physically but was going to Australia, he said, because he was wanted there and ordinary working people had paid for his passage, which was why he was travelling the cheapest way possible, six-to-a-cabin, hoping to 'give those good people some change out of what they've put up for me'.

From Aden, he sent her a poem, written on board ship:

> The Pilgrim Poppa, grilling manly torso,
> Sprawls on the deck in Port-Said-purchased hat;

Here by this floating Serpentine (but more so)
The Pilgrim Momma chides her Pilgrim brat.

They talk of Wogs and Niggers, trash and treasure
And bargaining. The urgent wail of sex
From Tin Pan Alley stirs in strident measure
The unfulfilment of the lower decks.

They sense no lure in the Arabian magic
Vast, to the East, across the narrow sea,
Nor know the Western shore where, bright or tragic,
There swells a continental pregnancy.

The tales of Sinbad, scimitars and raiders
And of strong, silent Englishmen – each ghost
Is lost upon this Lido, like the traders
Who still hawk bodies from the evening coast.

Tonight the dance, the celluloid emotions,
Bingo and cards and couples in the dark,
Where burning limbs (smothered in soothing lotions),
On passion's frail, synthetic tide embark.

I am alone. No destiny indentures
My foot-loose fortune to the Southern Cross;
Unlike the true adventurer's adventures
Mine is some phantom ship or albatross,

Or world of ancient mariners, whose histories
Still haunt such seas from the abyss of Time,
And out of Africa the ancient mysteries,
Old hopes, old fears, and Nemesis of crime.

From here, where once the seas were rent asunder,
I hear the bondsmen moan and Pharaoh boast
*Before those cliffs of water fall in thunder*
*Upon the chariots of the mighty host.*

Reg arrived at Perth in fierce heat on 1st December, 1958.

Never have I been so lionised [he wrote to Ethel]. I seem to have made a
hit with almost every department of the University; and the University
Extension Organiser, who arranged two lectures for me, has written to
his colleagues in Melbourne and Sydney, urging them to use me to the
full.

He made a broadcast, gathered material on the plight of the Australian
Aborigine, and addressed the Perth Fabian Society on 'The Map of Mrs

Brown', dealing gently with the eggheads and highbrows who, living in their own rarefied atmosphere, were frequently out of touch.

> At the end of the lecture [wrote a member of his audience], he invited questions and someone asked a question so involved and rambling that I completely lost the thread of it. Reg listened patiently with his eyes closed – and all eyes turned on him, wondering what he'd make of it. Rising, and with the greatest courtesy and a slight inclination of the head, he said: 'Yes, exactly so, I couldn't agree more'. It was superb artistry.

Ethel received a letter from him, written on the train from Perth to Adelaide, on 16th December. The same day she also received a cable dictated by him from an Adelaide hospital. He said that he had 'apparently had a haemorrhage' in the train 'involving temporary loss of memory', but he was now much improved, she was not to be alarmed, and he would write in a few days. Then, at midday, she received another cable, from Adelaide Quakers, saying that he had died that evening. He was 53.

In fact, he did not have the haemorrhage – which was cerebral – on the train but in the house of his Adelaide hosts the day after his arrival. He had collapsed, falling unconscious to the floor, a half-written letter to Ethel on his work-table. He was taken by ambulance to the hospital, not regaining consciousness until the evening. The following day he felt far better and insisted that Ethel should not be worried by being cabled the news of his illness. The day after that he was able to dictate the cable to her and he seemed to be making good progress but the following afternoon he lapsed into a coma and two hours later he was dead.

Ethel had not been distressed by his cable. She was well used to his haemorrhages. The last had been during the previous summer in Tokyo where he had recuperated in the home of a Japanese family and where he was given a delicious drink called The Taste of First Love, and when he wanted to smoke and the doctor advised against it, one of the daughters of the household picked him a gardenia so that he might inhale its perfume instead of tobacco smoke. 'He came back in love with the Japanese and the gracefulness of their ways', said Ethel, 'but wherever he went he came back in love with the people.'

In the letter he left her with his Will, he begged her to see that the things in which they both believed and which he defined as 'love, and the struggle for justice, truth, beauty and all the non-material things' had a life and reality of their own, a spiritual origin and purpose which death would make utterly futile and meaningless 'unless they are part of eternal life, as I believe, as I *know*, they are'.

This is not argument or reasoning [he had written], but something deeper than reason. All the deepest convictions come from this source – love, the belief in goodness, in freedom, in justice, in beauty – these things cannot be 'proved' to have any validity. We just *know* them. Reason itself cannot be 'proved' because you could only 'prove' the validity of Reason by reasoning. And so everything in the end begins with faith – that kind of belief which is so rooted in one's consciousness that one can't escape it. That is why logic begins with 'postulates', because it has to *begin somewhere*. And where you begin is below logic, below reasoning, in the convictions you cannot escape. Faith as I understand it is not what I choose to believe, but what I *cannot* choose *but* believe.

'I wish', wrote Ethel, 'we had talked of these things, for I think that by different roads we would have reached the same conclusions.' When Reg wrote of 'all the striving and loving' not being a 'meaningless effervescence on the surface of a dead material world', but that 'something eternal moves in us, which we lay hold of in our moments of unselfish love, of purest integrity, of identification with all that is beautiful in life', Ethel found herself translating that 'something eternal' into terms of the Buddhistic conception of rebirth –

that idea to which something in me inclines but to which my reason has not yet given full assent. But certain it is that because Reg 'lived in mankind' all that was fine and courageous and of good example in his life will continue to live in mankind; all over the world there are men and women, of all ages, of all races, all *kinds* of people, brilliant people and humdrum people, highly educated people and people with no education, who have gathered strength to live and work from their contact with this gay, warm, vital personality, housed in a body so ill-equipped for all the strains imposed on it. His spirit will live on in them.

In the more personal sense in which he wrote of his spirit enduring after physical death – 'remember that whenever you think of me I shall be there' – our conceptions of life and death cease to run parallel. Would that I had such faith! Had I died first – as he hoped, that I might be spared this pain, he feeling himself better equipped to bear such a heavy weight – he would have felt my spirit as a living entity close to him for the rest of his life and drawn comfort from it, as he felt his parents' spirits close to him after their deaths. It would have been true for him. But such a conception of the human spirit is not true for me. I did not know when I walked back through the November twilight at

232

Southampton, the distance between us widening with every step, with every second, that it was the final parting. I know it now.

In *The Loadstone*, there was 'A Prayer for Light'. Ethel had not read it during Reg's lifetime – 'it waited till I should have need of it'.

> And thou, thou sister grace,
> The healer of the mind,
> Show me thy face,
> Ascetic Unbelief
> Whom men call blind;
> Lest in my hour of grief
> From wilful dreams I waken
> To find the Gods are dead
> And I, forsaken.
>
> And, when the pruning's done,
> Though you should leave but one
> Green bough of certainty
> And there should be
> A single bud of passion,
> Of these alone
> I will refashion
> Commandments, not of stone,
> But writ indelibly:
> 'This every doubt withstood,
> This overcame
> All chastening of the blood'.
> For that which feels your rod
> And still abides in me
> Shall be my God.

CHAPTER XV

# Ethel Alone

AMONG THE LETTERS, from all parts of the world, with which Ethel was deluged after Reg's death was one from India with the words,

And sometimes he felt that he was tired, many times he felt faint. His tenacity however bore him fruit; for his journey never ended. He always felt grateful for the endless pursuit; for he knew that to hope was better than to come to the dead end of the fulfilment of hope. [To Ethel, the words were inevitable, part of a pattern]: Part of the pattern, too, was the fact that in the Adelaide hospital his doctor was a Malayan Indian called Krishnan. In the end it all makes a pattern; according to the law of *karma*, of cause and effect, it cannot do otherwise.

If only, she grieved, they had been together more while they had the chance. Reg knew that she always tended to blame herself 'for everything real or imaginary' and, on her 58th birthday, he had written to her:

I wish to state, and hereby and hereinunder do solemnly state, assert, maintain, affirm and say that E. E. Mannin can and should and must acknowledge to herself that if I should fall from a tree or under a 'bus on this same said day she has no cause to reproach, torture or upbraid herself but only to say that she has been a most wonderful and most loyal friend, counsellor, helpmate and standby to me, R. R., giving me love, affection, understanding, sympathy, food, drink, and lots of good and beautiful clo', also mending my socks, washing my horrible garments, typing my positively frightful verses and bearing with my capacity to be the dupe of perfidious wimmin. That is my testimonial and you had better keep it in case you ever need to be reminded of my considered opinion of the said E. E. Mannin, given under my hand on this 9th day of October, etc.

When she first read it, she was touched and amused, little realising that just over two months later, she would be re-reading it blinded with tears, unconvinced of everything except her husband's sincerity.

234

In *Brief Voices*, dedicated to the memory of Reg, she recounted her writing life from 1938 to 1958; she had ready the carbon of the typescript which she was about to airmail to him for his criticism on the day of the news of his death. Before he sailed for Australia, he had selected 132 *New Statesman* verses which he hoped would be published in volume form and Vicky, the cartoonist, had agreed to illustrate the book for nothing, for love of Reg. But a publisher was never found; the verses were too topical and ephemeral to be a commercial proposition.

She went through his wardrobe, 'as cosmopolitan,' he had said, 'as that of Portia's English suitor' – sandals from India, shoes from Burma, a yukata (bathrobe) from Japan. . . . They had never made a major journey together and although they used to joke that one day they would meet at the traffic lights of Singapore or Colombo or Hong Kong, in their hearts they neither of them believed it.

> We were often asked [said Ethel], why we didn't travel long distances together, but it wouldn't have done, since we both had to get books out of a journey and if we weren't to duplicate each other in print, we needed separate sets of experiences. The issue was further complicated when we began sharing the same publisher. Moreover, since we didn't have secretaries it was very useful if one of us stayed behind to look after the other's affairs – not least the endless flow of mail.

She listened to Bach's *St Matthew Passion*, Reg's favourite music. She thought of Exeter where he had spent five days in prison and three and a half months in hospital. It was also the place where she sat every week by a stove in the cathedral reading the *News of the World* until it was time to visit his sick-bed –

> it was the *News of the World* because being intellectual but strenuously resisting the idea, Reg felt constrained to read what he called the 'trash press' in order to prove his non-intellectuality. He frequently assured me I missed a lot by not doing so.

She remembered the sinister significance Hospitality had for him. As he wrote in *My Life and Crimes*:

> It is usual, when one lectures or addresses meetings in the provinces, to be offered Hospitality. I frequently avoid this, as I have so many friends up and down the country that I can often escape the unknown quantity which this dreaded word implies. The thing I really fear is the earnest, humourless host who can only imagine one in the context of one subject and brings his friends in to continue the meeting far into the night. Or – even worse – there was the elderly gentleman who planted me in a chair, sat down behind a table as though he'd been

about to interview me for a job, and began with 'You and I have got to find points of contact'. All possible 'points of contact' fled from my mind. I could only concentrate, fascinated, on the wobbling of his dewlaps as he waffled on and showed me, one by one, all the books he'd bought at bargain prices.

She read the obituaries and the reminiscences. Peace activist Stanley Keeble recalled Reg's swift answer when he was accused of 'straining at a gnat and swallowing a camel' – 'I am a vegetarian'; and when he was attacked for being too destructive of the social system – 'you have to demolish a ruin before you can erect a new building on the site'. *The Times* said that he was a passionate supporter of liberty and equality for all peoples and races, and that he was among the small group of people in this country who offered to go out to the Pacific in protest against the British nuclear tests.

No one was ever less interested in fame or money or a career. He was a rare human being, a 17th-century Quaker saint living out of his time today – or perhaps, as I sometimes think, living as more people must live, if individuality and a knowledge of things that make for happiness are to survive in an Admass age. (*New Statesman*)

Few people in the Western World could have been so deeply affected by the searing flash of the first Atomic Bomb as he was. Stunned by this new horror of immense man-made human suffering, it was surely the Grace of God which prompted Reg quite suddenly to pick up a copy of Woolman's Journal. Gradually a whole philosophy of life and conduct unfolded, which was in itself the answer to many queries that had been in his mind. Behind that philosophy there was the clearest evidence of a soul illuminated by no earthly wisdom [from a text signed by the Clerk of Kingston Monthly Meeting, Religious Society of Friends].

*Africa South* had an especial regard and affection for him, as they had now an especial grief:

A regular contributor to this magazine, he was also a friend, always ready with suggestions for articles and plans that would advance the cause of African democracy, sending us postcards with help and advice scribbled in every corner. He was an intensely passionate person, with deep convictions and the determination to act upon them. An intense feeling for humanity, its struggles and sufferings, moulded his politics, just as a perfect genius for friendship, for direct and immediate contact with those he met, characterised his personal life. His judgements were severe, and he could allow himself the severity because he thought of himself as no different from the general human run, no 'Quaker saint', as he has been described by some since his death. Human entirely, and a great deal more constructive than saintly forbearance was the anger and bitterness of his attacks on the oppressors of this world – imperialists in India, racialists in Africa, the makers of war everywhere.

It was not possible to listen to Reg with complacency, said Kenneth Barnes.

Like the Christ he served, he brought not peace but a sword to our hearts, and into the outward quiet of Friends' Meetings he continued to throw disquieting thoughts, searching out our reservations, our unexamined assumptions, our self-deception. In every generation we need a William Blake or a Reginald Reynolds to attack our false piety, to turn our thoughts inside out, to ask us what we really believe, to make us think whether we are any better than those self-righteous humbugs whom Jesus lashed with his tongue.

Reg was a man of vision, said *The Friend*, an eccentric Englishman and a prophet and visionary,

a restless spirit devouring thoughts and ideas and expressing himself in a thousand ways. He opened many doors, and often had to pass through them alone into the unknown, alone apart from his faith in God. There is still time for us to follow some of the paths he trod, before those doors are shut and the weeds of complacency and conformity cover up his burning footprints.

Reg Reynolds dead! It was the hardest thing for *Peace News* writers to believe,

for he always was there, however pressed with work, friendly and ready to greet admirers, scroungers, hangers-on, anarchists and Conservatives, atheists and Christians. By his side there was the inevitable briefcase bulging with notes, papers, work waiting to be done, work half done, work ready for the publishers, work to be looked at again because he was not satisfied with it. And at some point in every conversation he would dip into the bag and bring out a card, or find one in his pocket, with notes all over it so that you wondered whether he could ever find the note he needed; but all he wanted was to add another note about something you had asked him, or something he wanted to remember, or some reference he wanted to check. . . . Reginald Reynolds has left a notable contribution to literature in a number of different fields. His indifferent health over many years handicapped him here. There has always seemed to me to be much evidence in his writing of the kind of brilliance which, given a more

237

robust constitution and a longer life, could have made of him one of Britain's outstanding literary figures. . . . No words can portray Reginald Reynolds – as I write this, they are singing the Hallelujah Chorus on the radio; it seems appropriate.

The memorial meeting held at Friends House in London was an unforgettable experience for those who attended it, and it was Ethel who mainly made it so.

> There was a lot of pious solemn wuffle from Friend after Friend [she told the present writer], and never for a moment a glimpse of the real Reg – until I got up and said that having listened to the tributes from Friends, I, as a non-Friend, but the person closest to him, wanted to bring him alive into the room with all his wit and Rabelaisian humour and huge sense of fun, a man who wore bright clothes and liked his pint and his pipe, and there were those present who were grateful to me, including Jean – who told me afterwards that listening to all that solemn pious stuff 'that wasn't a bit Reg', she wondered, 'Isn't Mum *ever* going to speak?' But I waited till the others had had their say, and then I had mine and there were those who could scarce forbear to cheer – and the ghost of Reg amongst them, then Jean and I and some others went across the road to a pub and drank to the memory of 'ole Reg', as he liked to call himself.

His Gandhi cap, his khaddar shorts, which he wore when he took Gandhi's ultimatum to the British Raj, and a pillowslip Gandhi had given him as a Christmas present Ethel sent to the Gandhi Foundation in New Delhi. Miscellaneous 'Regiana' was eventually lodged in the archives of the Friends School, Saffron Walden and in the Library of Friends House, London. A large collection of letters from Laurence Housman was presented to the Bromsgrove Public Library; they chiefly concerned Laurence's religious and political views but were enlivened by bawdy material which Laurence had begged Reg to destroy.

Tributes continued to stream through Ethel's postbox, from old lags, young students, and friends and colleagues from all the peace organisations with which Reg had been connected – the War Resisters International, Friends Work Camps Committee, the Pacifist Research Bureau, the Friends of India. . . . It was clear that he had passed on his love of life like light or warmth. The smallest spiritual unit, he had said, was the human soul which was as dynamic and explosive as the atom, 'and I believe, what is more, that it can have chain reactions. I don't only believe that, I know it'. 'In his socialism', wrote one friend, 'there was a vision, a spirituality, that reached beyond all parties and politics.' Reg had remarked on his socialism thus:

By what moral right did one man or a group of men impose laws on others, when their title was merely that they were stronger, luckier, or more cunning (or that their ancestors had been so) than other mortals? By what right did one nation judge itself fit to rule over other nations and judge some other peoples unfit to be free? What was the origin of big landed estates? Was any man born with a title-deed to land round his neck? If so, why not to the air we breathed? It was no sillier. For me there had only been one answer to each of these questions. I had seen that wealth came from the soil and the sea and from man's labour and ingenuity – yet it was clear that neither hard work nor brains were sure passports to wealth, which could be enjoyed by people who did nothing and whose only claim was based on 'ownership'. So far as this meant God's gift and the products of human labour I could accept wholeheartedly the definition of Proudhon that Property is Theft.

It seemed to me insufficient to redistribute wealth: a means must be devised to maintain the new equilibrium. For that end Socialism was my own answer before I was given a name for it. It was the proper way to treat any common heritage; and the more I had seen and heard and read about the economic mad-house in which I was living the more urgent it had seemed. It was not merely that the greedy rivalries of nations in this uncoordinated world led almost inevitably to war – they also made cloud-cuckooland of the world in time of peace. When people talked about 'making work' for the unemployed I always asked why anybody should *wish* to make work. Did we eat potatoes in order to grow them? In a properly organised society nobody would wilfully make work.

If, I would say, the world can feed, clothe and house a man who is doing something useless or destructive, you can equally well keep him in idleness. Why find work for him to do? But it is better still to share out the work by which his needs are already supplied, letting him help, which is reasonable. Capitalism can't do that. It's against its nature even to try. When a new machine is invented, which saves labour, does your capitalist continue with the same number of men, working shorter hours? No, he either tries, by costly competitive advertisement, to extend his sales or he sacks some of his men. Only a socialist society can afford to look at a human problem from a human angle. There is only one sense in which any man *wants* work, and that is the psychological sense – he wants it because he enjoys making or doing something. But that has nothing to do with the economic problem, except that the greater the leisure we can offer people, the greater opportunity they will have for pleasure, if that is their idea of happiness. [*My Life and Crimes.*]

☆    ☆    ☆

In Reg's files, Ethel found a scrap of paper on which he had written, 'Religion to me is a ready-made language used to clothe a growing experience. It only fits at some points'. She herself was aware that the Quakers represented what she was always clamouring for – Christianity liberated from the Church and priesthood – but, despite a deep respect for them, their 'too solid worthiness' was too offputting.

Similarly, she steered clear of political groupings, so, in anarchism

I find myself unable to go all the way with Bakunin because of his belief in the use of revolutionary violence as a means to an end; nor all the way with Tolstoy, whose anarchism was pacifist, because he was a Christian, and I am not. Nor all the way with that other aristocratic anarchist, Kropotkin, because I am not convinced that his theory of mutual aid as a basic law of life, as against the Darwinian theory of the survival of the fittest, is valid. In the Independent Labour Party I was found insufficiently Marxist and too essentially pacifist; but in pacifist circles I am not at home, being too essentially revolutionary, with an inordinate inability to love my fellow-man. Collectively the human race is loathsome everywhere, stupid, brutish, anti-social. Very often I feel like the man leaning up against the bar in the *New Yorker* drawing and declaring that he hates everyone, without regard to race, colour or creed. It is hyperbole, of course, for I like and feel affection for a number of people, and a few I admire.

She discovered *The Desire and Pursuit of the Whole*, Frederick William Rolfe's ('Baron Corvo') autobiographical novel, 'the most wonderful novel ever written, bar none!' She expounded Reg's ideas as outlined in 'The Map of Mrs Brown': 'If the "hidden persuaders", the social psychologists and publicity experts, who work so powerfully to sell a certain kind of detergent, a particular brand of cereal, or anything else that has to be marketed, could be engaged to work as powerfully to sell the idea of peace to that same public we might get somewhere. Research is continually being carried out on juvenile delinquency, race riots, homosexuality, prostitution, but never on the leanings to mass suicide by people not individually suicidal'.

She confessed to having been in love a number of times over the last 20 years but, when writing of sexual emotions, she had always spared the lush

240

details, unlike Emma Goldman whose chapter headings in her massive two-volume autobiography caused her endless amusement – 'Sasha Makes Love to Me', 'I Refuse to Bear Children', 'Ed Wants Me to Bear Him a Child', 'I Leave Ed', 'I Call Ed Back to Me', 'I Leave Ed and Go on Tour', 'Sasha's Calvary Sears my Soul', 'Ben Pleads for Understanding'. Her own *Confessions and Impressions* read, she reckoned, like 'a Sunday school prize by comparison with these erotic outpourings'.

She tore apart the 'National Insurance racket':

What private company would dare to impose the terms the government imposes on this *compulsory* extortion? What private company would dare to say when the time came to pay out the pension for which over a long period of time you had been paying in – 'We will only pay the pension due to you provided you don't earn more than £3 a week. The pension for which, if you are self-employed and have been paying in £31.4s a year (if you are a man), is £2.10s a week, so you will have to live on not more than £5.10s a week – or forfeit your pension!' Of any private company who dared to say such a thing we should say they were the most impudent barefaced robbers who ever walked the face of the earth. But it is what the government says to its National Insurance victims – and not one person in a hundred protests, so far as can be observed; most people grumble and pay out; others try to persuade themselves and others that it is a good thing. When you are over 70 you can earn what you like and keep your pension. Ha-ha-*ha!* It is so easy, we all know, to get a job when you are 70! And what of the people who have no earthly chance of reaching even 65, when the pension is payable, let alone 70, when they can earn what they like? What of them? They are still required to pay in for what they haven't the remotest chance of drawing out. Dishonest? Or just barefaced robbery?

Reg had been exasperated by the system:

In the summer of 1958 he was in hospital with his old trouble, hypertension, and in what he himself called 'a desperate throw' to recover some of the money he had been paying in year after year he put in for sickness 'benefit'. He received a form-letter telling him nothing was due to him. He wrote asking why and received another form-letter telling him that he had paid no contributions during the preceding year. With his blood pressure soaring to danger point he wrote again, pointing out that he had sent in his card fully stamped the previous year and foreseeing some such trouble as this had taken the precaution of registering it – and fortunately still had the receipt. He threatened that if another form-letter were sent instead of a proper answer he would arrive in person as soon as he was out of hospital – which would endanger only his own health, he said, though they might prefer to avoid the embarrassment of an outraged citizen having a cerebral haemorrhage on their premises.

In answer to this threat of *hari-kiri* the Ministry sent a sad little man round to see him when he was out of hospital. At the sight of this drab fellow-human the lust for battle expired in the outraged citizen. 'I just feel sorry for him and myself and almost everybody', he said. The little man laboriously filled in a form about lost contribution cards though it was not Reg who had lost the card, and Reg signed it. After a long delay he received another form-letter, with a postal draft for £2.14s. or some such sum. He wrote back that this was inadequate; he also pointed out that he had still received no explanation for the whole exasperating business. As a result of this letter the 'benefit' was increased to £3.13s but still with no explanation as to why the period of illness shown by the certificates had been reduced by one third in allocating the 'benefit' – a term he found bitterly ironical.

After he had threatened to write to his MP, to the Minister of National Insurance, and to the press, it was explained that the original error was due to the fact that although his card had been received the contributions had not been 'posted' to his 'account'. This explanation came three months after his claim was first made. That £3.13s Reg considered the hardest he ever earned, 'if wear and tear and frayed nerves and heightened blood-pressure are taken into account'. He had fallen into such despair after leaving the hospital that he foolishly refused further certificates from his doctor, on the grounds that the bureaucracy were determined to swindle him so that it was a waste of time signing the things. He pointed this out later to the Ministry, after its climb-down and admission of error, adding that their form-letters and inefficiency had caused him financial loss as well as anxiety and ill-health, but there was no comment; leaving him to assume, perhaps unfairly, that driving sick people to despair was part of the normal routine.

That £3.13s is all Reg ever had out of the National Insurance since it started, and he did not live long enough to draw the pension for which he had year after year paid in from his meagre and erratic earnings.

☆    ☆    ☆

Since Reg had been so happy there, Ethel felt a longing to visit Japan. (*The Flowery Sword*, Travels in Japan, 1960.) Travelling third class and

242

alone, she covered the country from end to end, from Hokkaido in the far north to Nagasaki in the far west. In Tokyo she stayed with Reg's beloved Inoue family. At Hiroshima, she talked to bomb-affected patients and, with two Buddhist monks, led the 1959 Tokyo-Hiroshima Peace March on its first day.

Before the march, she addressed the mass meeting of 10,000 delegates in the forum of Hibiya Park. She was determined to say that it was not enough to be against nuclear weapons – war itself must be outlawed. The outlawing of war had been written into the constitution of Japan, and she hoped with all her heart that neither of their own will nor as a result of any pressure from outside would this be contravened. She went on to tell the crowd that she had been entrusted with a letter from the patients in the A-Bomb Victims' Hospital in Hiroshima, expressing their good wishes for the march as they could not leave their beds to be present in person. Her speech received an ovation.

A 13-year-old Japanese girl gave her an essay to read. It was called 'Memories of dear Regi':

> . . . he seemed young, though he was tall and thin like a grasshopper and his back was bent and he didn't care about his clothes and always wore sandals. When he was swimming, though he seemed young, in the end his years went against him and he was clinging to the side of the boat.

Ethel reflected that Reg had often tried to be younger than he was and that this had not deceived the young people he so liked to be around.

*Sabishisa* (1961), the Japanese word for loneliness, was the title of her novel with a Japanese background.

> Glad you liked it [she wrote to the present writer], as it's a novel I stand by. I wanted to write about *love* (as opposed to sex) and *death*. The character of 'Jonathan' is an amalgam of Reg and me. In fact it was Reg who had the romance in Japan; and of course it was Reg who died. I wanted to show that *marriage* isn't just a matter of the bed, but something very deep, of the mind and spirit, of something hard to put into words – a *sense* of something. In that sense Reg and I were utterly *married*, whatever either of us did outside of that relationship. We *belonged*. It's none of it very original or profound, I suppose, but it was something I wanted to say. [In the novel, 'Jonathan' explained]: I mean by being married much more than any legal or religious arrangement. Many people are married without being married in the sense I mean. Perhaps more than not. I mean something mental and emotional – something which goes so deep that nothing can touch it

243

*Reg shortly before his death. 'Certain it is', wrote Ethel, 'that because Reg "lived in mankind" all that was fine and courageous and of good example in his life will continue to live in mankind.'* (Brief Voices, *1959*)

*Ethel in her sixties, at Oak Cottage, and a revolutionary to the end – 'Throughout my career I've tried to expose the many wounds of Christ-crucified – in terms of the brutality, cruelty, injustice of our times, from Spain to Vietnam. Haven't we all a moral duty to record our protest and our anguish? I'm more than ever convinced of the need for social revolution – world revolution, revolution in all countries! Massive Gandhian campaigns of non-cooperation and civil disobedience! Sorry to sound so primitive, so elementary, but what else?? But the British – the British have as little aptitude for revolution as they have for making love!'* (from letters to the author, 1976)

[PAUL TANQUERAY – COURTESY: JEAN FAULKS]

from outside. So that the two people concerned become part of each other. There are such marriages. Sometimes they last 50 or 60 years. If Vanessa had lived and we both had become old that it is how it would have been with us. It had to be like that. Till one of us died.

✩    ✩    ✩

Reg always said that one day he would go to the Middle East and write a book stating the Palestinian case. It was because he did not live to do it that in 1962 Ethel accepted an invitation from General Kassim's government to tour Iraq and then other Middle Eastern countries, out of which came the book, *A Lance for the Arabs* (1963),

> and as a result of my first visit to Gaza at that time the idea for the novel designed as a 'reply' to the lying Zionist novel, *Exodus*, and which I called *The Road to Beersheba* (1963). I invented very little in this, indeed I could have told more, such as those small black 'Israeli' planes coming over and *machine-gunning* the wretched Palestinians. But I feared to be accused of 'piling it on', though I was so accused anyway. The novel *The Night and Its Homing* (1966) is in a sense a sequel to *The Road to Beersheba* inasmuch as it speaks for the Resistance as *Beersheba* spoke for the so-called refugees – so-called because they are in fact an entire nation displaced and dispossessed.

Overriding hate-mail and abuse, the Palestinian cause preoccupied her for the rest of her life. In *The Arab Need for a Gandhi* (Indian Institute of Advanced Study, Simla, 1969) she wrote that, to the militant Palestinians, a massive movement of civil disobedience and non-violent resistance would no doubt seem very tame compared with the excitement and daring, the splendid heroism of guerilla warfare,

> but, as Gandhi said, the physical possession of arms is the least necessity of the brave; *satyagraha* takes tremendous courage – and an equally tremendous faith. The Palestinians have the one, abundantly, and given the spiritual leadership they might in time develop the other. I do not believe that they can regain their lost land and national sovereignty by force of arms or acts of sabotage, because they are opposed by an enemy of vastly superior technique, organisation and discipline, whereas the Arab dream of unity endlessly eludes realisation, and this failure is their undoing. It was not of the Arabs that the American-Irish poet, Shaemus O Sheel, wrote early in this tragic century:

246

They went forth to battle, but they always fell . . .
Nobly they fought and bravely, but not well,
And sank heart – wounded by a subtle spell.

It was, I think, of his own people, the Irish, that he wrote those
sorrowful words, but it could have been written of the Arabs in their
struggle against those who have usurped their ancestral lands and
scattered them, displaced and dispossessed, into the wilderness, to rot
in refugee camps or live out their lives in exile in the West. Is it too
much to hope that the Arabs, with their high courage and impassioned
love of their ancient land of Palestine, which they have continuously
inhabited for thousands of years, might come in time to realise that the
way of violence is the way of death and destruction, and as Gandhi, the
greatest apostle of non-violence since Jesus, has said, in his profound
wisdom, that *satyagraha* is the surest victory. May the spirit of Gandhi
come to them, for their need is great.

She also broke a lance for the Palestinian Arabs by writing countless
letters of support to her friends in the camps and by responding to press
reports and radio and TV coverage. This, in 1972, to a broadcaster who had
interviewed Said Hammami of the London PLO office:

It was quite preposterous of you to suggest to him, a Palestinian, that
'half a loaf is better than no bread'. As he so rightly pointed out to you,
the Palestinians have never been offered even half a loaf! In 1947 (do I
need to remind you?) their country, Palestine, was carved up and *two-
thirds* (and that the most fertile areas) given to one-third of the
population, Zionist Jews, foreigners from all over the world, of all
nationalities, with nothing in common but their religion. A million
Palestinians, *the indigenous people*, were displaced and dispossessed,
many of them at machine-gun point and at a moment's notice, in only
the clothes they stood up in (as at Lydda, in the summer of 1948, as I
showed in my novel, *The Road to Beersheba*, the facts for which were
given to me by Palestinians from Lydda, forced out into the burning
wilderness on that terrible trek to Ramallah, of which Glubb, in his
book, *A Soldier with the Arabs*, wrote that 'we shall never know how
many children died') and as Said Hammami told you last night, that
million is now, since 1967, a million and a half. How would *you* like it if
foreigners from all over the world took over England and forced the
indigenous people, the English, into one corner of it – say the Home
Counties – herding them into camps, to survive for 25 years and more
on starvation rations supplied by some form of international charity –
how would *you* like it if some smarmy broadcaster from outside
suggested that half a loaf was better than no bread – especially if you

247

were one of those who far from having half a loaf had only a very thin slice, dry and stale at that – a crust? Said Hammami is one of those who grew up in a camp, a so called 'refugee', but in fact one of the million Palestinians robbed of their national identity, of their country, of their homes and lands and capital, of the very *name* of their country. . . .

In her book *Aspects of Egypt* (1964), she described her second visit to the Beersheba road in Gaza and reported that her novel *The Road to Beersheba* had been totally boycotted by the national press. The *Glasgow Times*, however, had reviewed it favourably, 'the reviewer declaring that he was determined to recommend it even though it got the paper banned in Cairo and Alexandria. He praised it in the belief that it was about *Jewish* refugees. It was impossible not to have a fantasy of distraught Cairenes and Alexandrians angrily demanding at street-corner kiosks where was their *Glasgow Times*'. Her book on Jordan, *The Lovely Land*, appeared in 1965, followed by more novels with a Middle Eastern setting, among them *The Midnight Street* (1967), the story of a coup and a counter-coup in an Islamic city, and *Free Pass to Nowhere* (1970), the story of an ex-minister of transport and a Christian in an Islamic country who was detained for two years in a desert prison when the government in which he had served was overthrown.

☆     ☆     ☆

She sold her Connemara cottage, for £1,300, in 1962. She was exhausted by the long journeys to and from Ireland and weary at the sight of her immaculate garden being turned, in her absences, into an overgrown, weed-choked mess. Besides, in 1961, she had become a grandmother, an experience out of keeping with isolating herself in the wilds. A couple from Dublin bought the property and they intended, they said to Ethel's delight, to live there all the time but within a year a Galway newspaper carried the advertisement – Connemara cottage for sale. Previously the residence of a well-known writer. Price £2,000. Her sailing-dinghy *Kathleen*, which she was going to give to her neighbour, had, she was told, rotted away on the beach. The brass name-plate was sent to her as a momento of happy days with Reg. She would look at it, and remember, and be sad.

In the early 1970s, she visited Chelsea for the first time since Reg died, when she had gone to deal with his 'effects'. Now, seeking copy for one of her travel books about England, she passed the Six Bells where he would sit in the garden drinking draught cider and sometimes she would sit with him, but not often, 'for he knew too many people and there was no peace'. She came to Jubilee Place, finding the whole terrace boarded up, waiting for demolition and redevelopment. She peered down into the fusty basement room he had loved, where he had worked deep in dust, hemmed in by his filing cabinets and shabby old books. Near the end of his life he had moved to another room at the back of the building, with a tiny annexe of bathroom and kitchen and looking on to the garden in which she had planted geraniums and marguerite daisies for him.

The Bar-B-Q in the King's Road was still a restaurant but trading under a different name and patronised by hippies jerking to loud rock music. The shops Reg knew – fruit and veg, bread and milk – had vanished, replaced by boutiques. When, she mused, he returned from Italy in the mid 1950s with a pale blue suede suit, even his Chelsea friends announced that Reg had really gone too far this time, 'and it certainly was sensational, that forget-me-not suit on the tall thin Reg with his striking hawk-like face and straight blond hair, and faintly I disapproved, though, I supposed, vaguely, that it was all right in Chelsea'. How times had changed! That suit today would not be worth a second glance. And what would Reg have made of SW3 in the 1970s? He would surely have been most indignant that his adored 'Chelsea village' had merged, in 1967, with the Royal Borough of Kensington.

She took one last lingering look at the place where Reg and so many of his friends 'lived and had their being in a rabbit warren of decaying rooms. They were the true Bohemians; perhaps the last of them'.

As a member of the select band of long-established authors who earned their living from writing books – and she averaged two a year for more than 50 years, and was translated into French, German, Dutch, Spanish, Italian, Arabic and the Scandinavian languages – Ethel had a devoted if diminishing following, and was constantly being asked to reminisce about her time as one of Britain's most famous literary women. Although she much preferred to discuss what was happening *now*, and to imagine what *Reg* might have felt regarding a particular issue, she was happy to give her guests the floor, to draw them out, to eagerly hear their opinions and to patiently, and lightly, deal with their questions – what was Nasser like, and King Hussein? How did you and Reg rescue Jews from Nazi Germany? Tell us about your meeting with Somerset Maugham. . . . In her seventies, she still retained her slim and shapely figure, and her warm soft voice was unmistakably that of a Londoner. She had never been impressed by 'celebrities'. In spite of her achievements, she could think of herself as nothing more than just ordinary. She could be savagely self-critical. Some of her early novels, written in a kind of creative auto-intoxication with flashiness and lyric ecstasy rampant, she would summarily dismiss. Like Reg, she delighted in telling stories against herself.

Oh Ethel, Ethel, Ethyl, *dearest!* [Douglas Goldring had reprimanded her in the 1920s], Alas and Alack! How *could* you? And will you ever speak to me again if I confess how your article (on Beauty) tortured me? Shades of Plotinus! Oh help, oh help! One can justifiably expose one's life and loves to the public gaze, exhibit one's person, turn the limelight on one's father or mother or husband or wife; but surely the artist must have *some* reserves and reticences? 'Oh, I du like bew-tee! S'ever ser nice. Yew know . . . Shakespeare and Christ and Michael Valentino and what all. Makes yer feel so goopy-like insides, dearie. Wow, oh, super-wow!' Ethel, *what* cheque could they have paid you sufficiently colossal to induce you to put the name of the author of *Pilgrims* and *Hunger of the Sea* to such bilge?

She remembered being threatened with expulsion from school for refusing to salute the flag on Empire Day; being told by the actor Godfrey Tearle of the American producer of a Biblical play who inquired about the 12 characters grouped together on the stage and when informed that they were the 12 Apostles, said, 'Aw, let's make it 40'; and another American producer who, keen to make a film of *The Well of Loneliness* was advised against it as it was all about Lesbians, to which he replied, 'All right, let's make 'em Austrians'. She remembered being complimented by Bertrand Russell – 'Talking to you is more exciting than making love to almost anyone else'; dancing with Arnold Bennett; accepting a valentine from the Russian ballerina, Thamar Karsavina; being earnestly assured by a Pakistani that *Confessions and Impressions* had influenced a whole generation; and at the Chelsea Arts Ball, roaring with laughter at a young actress who, as the New Year approached, exclaimed, 'O God, another year of sleeping alone!'

She was disappointed that some of her more recent books – on loneliness, and the practitioners of love, and *Curfew at Dawn*, a novel about a blind-deaf young man – received scant attention, but then again, that was only right, she supposed; she was such an Old Hand and there were so many new writers coming up. *The Burning Bush* (1965), a novel with which she was well-pleased, was a study of the relationship between two men in Egyptian Nubia. *Bitter Babylon* (1968), a novel set in San Francisco, showed the effects of the Vietnam war on two generations. One of her characters lamented the moral corruption of politicians, the total inadequacy of organised religion, the decline into fatuity and decadence. Only violence seemed to make any impact – the political assassination, the military coup, the napalm bombing of civilians in the name of just wars. Protest was the answer:

in every struggle for justice and freedom people have to die, whatever the tactics. But the struggle has to be waged, the protest has to be

250

made, effective or ineffective. And thank God for the minority everywhere that protests, speaks out, demonstrates. [To belong to the minority was to be different], and to be different is to be indecent, and to run the risk of elimination. This is the day of the masses, and the mass is the average man.

She revealed, in *Stories From My Life* (1973) that she had always been an *isolato*, that except at weekends she was almost always alone and that was the way she liked it. She had a great respect for family life, it was a good design for living, but to make a success of it called for a kind of grace which she had never been given: 'I wanted always to be free; the cat that walked alone. For some of us to be lived-with would be claustrophobic, suffocating'. Friends it was pleasant to meet occasionally but it was not essential; it *was* essential, however, to have regular contact with the intimate, nearest-and-dearest circle. She was more than ever convinced of the need for social revolution. She admired the courage and dedication of guerillas, like Che Guavara, while regretting their tactics. Her hope for her cause of causes – Palestine – was remote. It was unlikely that she would live to see 'Palestine as *Palestine* again, with the indigenous people, the Palestinian Arabs, in control, a nation again, Moslem and Christian, co-existing with a Jewish minority'.

In her last book, *Sunset Over Dartmoor* (1977), a final chapter of autobiography, she devoutly wished that there would be no life hereafter: 'One life is *quite* enough. I shall be extremely put out if after my death I wake up in Eternity and find I have to go on, in some form or other, all over again'. She had never been a feminist because 'as a revolutionary socialist I have always seen the struggle of women for social equality as part of the general egalitarian struggle'. She could not understand 'why when even in this "permissive" society there is an attempt to save people from physical self-destruction by clamping down on the purveyors of hard drugs' that it should be considered repressive and anti-democratic 'similarly to clamp down on the purveyors of hard porn, in an attempt to save people from spiritual self-destruction'. She was glad that in the late 20th century, Western society was 'splendidly free' in the sense that people demanded their rights, undeterred by fear of the establishment: 'A spirit of militancy moves among the masses when confronted with social injustice, and this I find entirely admirable'.

☆　　☆　　☆

She began to feel that Oak Cottage had served its purpose. She hankered after· somewhere smaller and warmer with a more manageable garden, somewhere, perhaps, near her daughter, and Jean it was who urged her to view a house, close to hers, overlooking the Teign estuary at Shaldon in Devon. Oak Cottage, her home for 45 years, was sold and 'Overhill' bought. She had no pangs at leaving Wimbledon, 'none at all. I was doing what I wanted to do, and all went smoothly, thanks to the remarkable efficiency of Pickfords (very nice) men. And this place is unique, too. No ordinary suburban bungalow! Like OC it was designed and built by a man for himself – and so is different'. But Oak Cottage was where she had done the bulk of her work, in the book-filled study overlooking the lily-pond. The tiles on the roof had been specially baked and hand-made. The dining room opened out onto a loggia with a grassy slope leading up to a belt of tall elms. In May, a piece of woodland became a mass of bluebells. There were over 50 varieties of roses and over a 100 bushes.

Even in old age, she continued to write up to 50 letters a week and Reg was mentioned in many of those sent to friends and acquaintances. His royalties went to especially needy families in the Gaza camps:

He had so little money and always longed to help what he called 'those poor Arabs' and it grieved him that he could do so little. [What he thought about 'God'], I don't really know for the only time I attempted to find out he proved Quakerishly evasive and referred to 'that of God in every man' without defining what he meant by 'God'. I was irritated and didn't pursue the discussion, just telling him that the Quakers were the Jesuits of religious nonconformism! Which in their evasiveness and get-outs I think they are. I am a flat-out atheist, wanting a scientific explanation for everything and not feeling any Supreme Being of Life-Force-you-could-call-God behind the universe. . . . For two people so close mentally and emotionally, Reg and I lived remarkably separate lives. For 'mentally' close I think I should really say *politically*, for there was a sense in which we *weren't* mentally close – Reg's innate Quakerism precluded it; it didn't come between us, but I was as outside of it as Reg was outside of my 'Neillism' and my spell of Catholic gropings. [When she re-read *The Wisdom of John Woolman*, she was brought up short]: it *wasn't* the 'development of a conscience amongst the slave owners' that brought about the emancipation of the Negro slaves; it was *the sheer weight of the Abolitionist movement*, led by people such as Woolman, and *Reg bloody well knew it*, except when he was having a bout of Quakery piety.

In the 1970s, 'a scurrilous novel' depicting Ethel and Reg was published, Ethel as 'Edna Malone' of 'Elm Cottage'. The author had been a comrade of theirs in the 1930s,

and he had nothing but kindness and friendship from Reg and me. It's true he makes 'Edna' a nice person, but he had no hesitation in falsely representing her sex life and her marriage, and exploiting her in a pornographic novel. The suggestion that when married, I yet kept a room for the occasional resident lover is abominable. It's outrageous, too, writing of the 30s, he speaks of my marriage subsiding into a Platonic relationship; at the time he was coming to Oak Cottage my relationship with Reg was at its height.

She was enheartened by the excellent reviews of her own novel, *The Curious Adventure of Major Fosdick* (1972), a gentle dig at high-falutin' dogoodery, set mainly in a region she knew well, the Pathan country of West Pakistan. About a highly praised novel by a fashionable woman writer, she wrote:

It's all a lot of bullshit, the great tragedy of the girl of 21 widowed after a year of happy marriage; it's when people have been married for the best part of a lifetime and are widowed or widowered that it's tragic. Young sorrow is as soon over as young love, the way a child's grief is shortlived. It's *old* love bereaved that is tragic. [And on a collection of short stories]:I hate that *dense* kind of writing – which I regard as very feminine. Pas pour moi! But no female writers seem to be for me, except Colette, who understood the human heart, and dear old Dorothy Parker, whose *astringency* speaks very much to my condition.

[On Jane Austen, 'that dreary spinster']: When I addressed the students at Damascus University in 1966 (they had a banner stretched across the entrance arch, Welcome, Ethel!) I delighted them by telling them that reading the works of Jane Austen was a waste of time if they wanted to know about contemporary English life, or, for that matter, even about the real life of the period. I also found Jane tedious, I said. I said all this because so many of them had complained to me about how boring and difficult they found the required reading of Miss Austen. To me she is for the *aunties* of both sexes. [On Joseph Conrad]: *Victory* will always be, for me, his finest novel. I admire him tremendously, and he's the only author I can and do re-read again and again. What I find so compelling about his books is the quality of conflict – psychological – emotional – and especially the conflict of loyalties, which always fascinates me. [On Charlie Chaplin]: Yes, I know *Limelight* was quite excruciatingly sentimental, yet I saw it twice and loved it, though admitted that it brought out the worst in me. [On Daphne du Maurier]: I was attracted by her in the thirties, but never took her seriously as a writer – but of course she romped past me and left me nowhere in sight! She used to call me Charlotte, insisting that I bore some resemblance to Charlotte Bronte. [On Barbara Cartland]: 70 million copies . . . and 150 virgins! Jean says she does no harm, but I don't agree – I think this kind of muck and falsity is quite as harmful as pornography – and for the same reason: a debasing of sex.

[On herself]: I as a writer fall between two stools – not literary enough for the highbrows and not popular enough for bestsellerdom. Not 'popular' in the sense of being able to write romance-fiction or thrillers, I mean. [Occasionally, she would rashly promise a correspondent something which she would later, thinking better of it, withdraw, and then would come the letter of apology]: Oh lor. Mea culpa. Dotty old Ethel. I am abased and abashed. I bite the dust! I grovel! [It gratified her that she received more letters about *Sunset Over Dartmoor* than for any other book, but after that, she wrote nothing, nor had any desire to] – I always thought I'd write to the grave's edge, but I was wrong. So that on this last lap I have a feeling of emptiness and uselessness. Don't aim to be old – it's a weary-dreary business. I keep very well, glory be [she wrote in 1982], but physical energy in short supply, and has to be rationed. I'm whacked after only an hour's gardening these days!

Following a fall at home and the fracture of her pelvis, she was four and a half months in the local hospital and although at first she seemed to make progress, she suddenly started to deteriorate. She died in 1984, aged 84. Said Jean: 'It was pitiful to have to watch her get worse week by week. I feel her loss acutely'. She was 'quite overwhelmed by the number of letters I received from all sorts of people. It's comforting to know so many people enjoyed and appreciated her friendship'.

*The Times* gave her a long obituary notice, crediting her with honesty and sincerity, with championing the underdog, and with generosity in giving money to the causes she believed in.

Francis King, in the *Sunday Telegraph*, also mentioned her contributions of money and voiced the opinion that

although sometimes illogical in the passions of her views and sometimes careless in the haste of her writing, she was a woman whose genuine hatred of poverty and injustice gave a glow to even the less successful of her publications. All her long life can be seen as a process of growing and improvement. Ironically, therefore, she was at her best both as a person and as a writer when she had become least known to the public at large. [In the 1930s, he said, she was] as well known as Beverley Nichols or Godfrey Winn – with both of whom she had much in common. [Ethel would have been amused at this – 'Bev Knickers and old Godfers! *Do* me a favour, mate! Oh God, O Montreal!'] For all the emotional romanticism that haloed her writing [continued King], she presented a somewhat metallic front to the world. Subsequently, she learnt to be less exacting in the demands she made on life, on herself and on others.

For 26 years Ethel had lived without 'ole Reg', her lover, her husband, her best friend, her alter-ego. For 26 years she had kept safe a lock of his hair which was to be cremated with her. In their devotion to each other, in their passion, their fearlessness, their tenderness, their selflessness, their humour, their scorching honesty and innumerable kindnesses, they had been as one. It was something to have done as they had done. Theirs was a time too brief.

*The Constellations of Eternity*　　　　　　　　　by Reginald Reynolds

> The constellations of eternity
> Shall hold these things: the Spring, the hawthorn tree,
> The sudden stillness over Evesham Vale,
> Silence melodious as the nightingale.
>
> Promiscuous buttercups whose shameless heads
> Greeted the morning from their bridal beds,
> Moments fortuitous that left no trace
> In other firmaments have lasting place.
>
> Through dim Millenia I'll still recall
> Ephemeral ecstasies, remembering all
> A sprig of honeysuckle meant, a word
> Murmured in sleep that heart alone had heard.
>
> Time was too brief and space too small to fashion
> Infinite paradise in mortal passion,
> Yet our true selves are elements that move
> To changeless measures of undying love.

# Appendix

From a letter written by Reg Reynolds to Kathleen and Tony Skelton.

On the High Seas
November, 1958

My dear Kath and Tony,

Writing letters (or anything else) is not easy on this ship: it's a floating nursery-cum-night club-cum lido. By day it's hard to find a square foot of deck space to sit on and, if you do sit down, children trip over you or are sick down your neck. By night its lounges become cinemas and gambling-dens or dance-halls of the Montmartre pattern – or should I say Smokey Joe's?

In a word it is an *Emigrant* ship, Italian owned and chartered by the Australian Government for 10 years; and the passengers are mostly very young couples with very small children and babes. At the boat drill we had it made clear that a fire or collision would cause the most macabre thing of its kind since the Titanic went down – what with nearly 1,000 adults and some 500 children crowded into so small a space. The officers and crew addressed them in fluent pigeon English, being as they are all Italians. . . . Basil Burton sent me a very nice farewell letter – I figure that such an official farewell from the President (of the Saffron Walden Old Scholars Association) is roughly the equivalent of a Twelve Gun Salute!

# Index